7ɔ

Virgin Coconut Oil

How it has changed people's lives,
and how it can change yours!

Brian and Marianita Jader Shilhavy

D0179404

Tropical Traditions, Inc.
West Bend, Wisconsin
USA

Virgin Coconut Oil
How it has changed people's lives, and how it can change yours!
by Brian and Marianita Jader Shilhavy
Copyright © 2004-2005 Brian and Marianita Shilhavy.

Third Printing June 2005
All rights reserved. Printed in the United States of America
No part of this book may be used or reproduced in any manner whatsoever without written permission from the publisher.

Tropical Traditions, Inc.
PMB 219
823 S. Main St.
West Bend, WI 53095
USA
www.tropicaltraditions.com
ISBN 0-9760578-0-8

Editor - Jonathan Lindvall

Cover design by Jonathan Chong

Contents

Introduction

When Abraham Lincoln served as president of the United States in 1862, 48 percent of the people living in the U.S. were farmers. Today, that figure is less than 2%. Along with the age of industrialization and technology we have, by and large, lost many of our community family farms and, with that loss, also the loss of many traditional farming skills. Few would argue that our food sources here in the U.S. have suffered as a result, as a consumer-driven economy seeks to support its lifestyle of ease and comfort with cheap foods produced by fewer people providing the labor back on the farms.

But there are new market trends and demands from consumers who are now placing greater value on traditional skills, and healthier food produced "the old fashioned way." The 21st century sees a whole generation of "baby boomers" heading into their senior years, with complex health problems that did not plague their parents' and grandparents' generations, in spite of all the "medical advances" the 21st century brings us. Traditional ways of producing food are coming back into the spotlight, as some are questioning whether those responsible for filling the shelves of our grocery stores and supermarkets truly have our best interest in mind, or represent our core values.

In the Philippines, by contrast, about 50% of the population is still small-scale family farmers. Some would see this as a negative thing but others, like Marianita and me, see that this is actually a strength in the 21st century. My years in the Philippines showed me a way of life where people are still connected to their communities and sources of food. While mass-produced foods are undoubtedly choices available to the majority of Filipinos in the 21st century, in most places the community market still operates where one can find "native" or locally-produced foods, much the same as it has been for hundreds of years.

The alarming trend, however, in the Philippines as well as in most developing nations, is the desire to prosper as the U.S. has, and follow the way of industrialization and technology. I am certainly not anti-technology. But I do believe there is great value in traditional ways of producing food. As more people wake up to the fact that there are just certain things in nature that cannot be improved upon by man, because they follow the laws of nature set forth by the Creator, traditional ways will also reap economic value by providing a quality product to the consumer that technology cannot provide.

When Marianita revived the traditional way of making coconut oil, as you will read about in Chapter 1, only a few left in her home community from her parents' generation still knew how to produce this quality coconut oil that we named "Virgin Coconut Oil." A massive training program had to be instituted to teach the younger generation how to produce this quality product. We were within only one generation of losing this traditional skill. A few years later now, we have shown the world what a traditional skill, producing a quality product that cannot be mass-produced, can do economically for the Philippine economy and what it can do for people's health, as is evidenced by the more than 100 testimonies recorded in this book.

This book is the result of four years of research and feedback from thousands of people who have begun to incorporate Virgin Coconut Oil into their diet. We started an internet discussion group called Coconut-info four years ago that grew to over 7000 people, and is now the Coconut Diet Forums on www.coconutdiet.com. All the archives from past years, which include many of the testimonies which you will read in this book, are stored on www.coconutdiet.com. You can search tens of thousands of messages for yourself to see what people are reporting about the effects of Virgin Coconut Oil in their lives.

Brian Shilhavy

Note: Many of the chapters in this book have been previously published as separate articles and are "self-contained" units. Hence, some of the research is repeated in different chapters. One does not need to read through the chapters chronologically.

Chapter 1

The Virgin Coconut Oil Story

The road leading up to Mt. Banahaw.

Marianita's Story

I grew up in the Philippines during the 1960s and 1970s. My family lived in a small rural community of about 100 families. We lived on the side of a mountain, and everybody in our community earned their living from agriculture—primarily coconuts.

My father was a farmer, and his main crop was coconuts. He had some rice plantations and grew some other crops, and he was also the principal of our local government elementary school. But his main source of income in the 1960s and early 1970s was from coconuts.

He made more money from the sale of his coconuts than he did as a school principal, for example. In the Philippines, the government only provides education through 6th grade in many places. High school and college are usually privately run and beyond the cost of most of the poor. My father sent all eight of his children to high school and college through the profits of the coconut industry, graduating 3 school teachers, 1 nurse, 1 medical doctor, and myself, a nutritionist/dietician.

The people in our farming community while I was growing up primarily ate food that they had grown or raised themselves. Our diet consisted mainly of rice, coconuts, vegetables/root crops, herbs (especially garlic and ginger), and some meat that was raised locally. Trips to the market were made once a week to buy primarily fresh fish caught in the ports nearby. My parents' generation would have ground their own rice by hand, leaving intact most of the bran and nutrients. After World War II, during my time, however, rice mills started popping up making it easier to mill rice. The first mills used in my day were "crude," and did not polish the rice, so we basically still ate healthy grains. Later, the mills became more sophisticated and began to polish the rice making it bright white. All of our food back then would have been considered "organic" by today's standards, as we had no access to chemical fertilizers or pesticides. Living in a tropical climate, our animals, such as chickens, cows, goats, etc., all grazed on natural green vegetation.

Coconut and coconut oil was used daily. My parents' generation made coconut oil by hand, using either the boiling or fermentation method (see Chapter 2). After World War II, desiccated coconut plants and coconut oil mills were established for the booming baking industry in the U.S. Refined coconut oil started to make its way into the local economy as well, but at that time even the refined coconut oil made from copra (dried coconut meat) was done through a mechanical pressing that did not use solvent extracts. While some people still made coconut oil by hand the traditional way, many began buying the cheaper, odorless coconut oil in the markets. Our natural diet was definitely a high-fat diet—a diet that was high in the saturated fat of coconut oil.

So what was the health of the people like in our community, where everyone ate a diet high in the saturated fat of coconut oil? Our community was part of a larger community of some 50,000 people that was served by a single government doctor in those days. While pharmaceuticals began to be manufactured in the Philippines after World War II, people in communities like ours could not afford them. We had our own traditions of dealing with simple sicknesses using local herbs and coconut oil. When people did go to town to visit the local government doctor, it was usually not for the kind of ailments that westerners go to the doctor today, such as diabetes, cancer, heart disease, thyroid problems, etc. These illnesses were virtually unknown in my younger days. People went to see the doctor to treat wounds, or from sicknesses common in the tropics, such as malaria, diarrhea, dengue (a sickness spread by mosquitoes), etc. My father was well into his 60s before he made his first visit to the doctor, and that was for a head wound. He died in the late 1980s in a car accident in the U.S. He was in his 70s and in perfect health. Three of his older sisters still survive him to this day and are in great health. One is in her 90s. Another one of his sisters, my aunt, is in her late 80s and still lives in the remote area of the Philippines where I grew up, eating a traditional diet. She taught us how her generation made coconut oil by hand, which is the basis for the Tropical Traditions Virgin Coconut Oil. She still shuns modern conveniences (such as electricity) and eats mostly food that she herself has grown on her farm, and she has excellent health. Her first visit to a doctor was when she was in her early 80s. I myself have no memory of being sick growing up. I suffered my first "cold" when I was in my 30s, after I married my American husband and spent a year in the U.S. eating typical U.S. food found in grocery stores.

This picture of life in the rural Philippines is typical of those who grew up in my generation or my parents' generation, eating traditional foods with an abundance of saturated fat found in coconut oil. Sadly, it is no longer true today. Since the mid-1970s demand for coconut oil fell so low that coconut farmers could no longer afford to support their family on the income of coconut harvests. Many people left the farms and went to the cities to find better employment, and soon adopted new dietary trends similar to western diets. Cheaper mass-produced industrial foods, particularly meats, now replace most of the local traditional foods we used to grow or raise ourselves. Snack foods and other fast foods are now often made with hydrogenated coconut oil to keep it solid at the high air temperatures experienced in our tropical climate. The rice is now polished and grown with chemical fertilizers, and soft drinks loaded with refined sugars are found on every street corner, replacing the natural "buko juice", the water from the inside of the coconuts, that my generation grew up drinking. Even the coconut water drinks still sold are usually loaded with refined sugars. Our traditional, high-fat low-carb diet has been replaced with many refined high-carb substitutes. Growing up it was very rare to see anyone considered overweight, and almost never considered "obese", but even that is changing now as the diet has changed also.

After graduating from Centro Escolar University in Manila with a degree in nutrition, I went on to become a certified Nutritionist/ Dietician. I worked for over eight years as a hospital dietician and nutritional counselor in the Philippines, using my knowledge of Filipino/tropical foods to help people recover from illness. I later married Brian and left the Philippines for several years.

In 1998 Brian and I returned to the Philippines with our three children and renovated the old family farmhouse where I grew up on Mt. Banahaw. By this time the coconut industry was severely depressed due to the negative U.S. campaigns against tropical oils in the 1980s and 1990s. Coconut farmers could no longer support their families on the income generated from harvesting coconuts.

Brian's Story

When we first moved to Marianita's home area where she grew up in the Philippines, I was struck by the simplicity of life and how the rural Filipino in a farming community lived in the 21st century. They still used water buffalo as their draft animal for plowing, for example. They were hard-working people with a rich history and culture. I felt privileged to be able to live there as a foreigner, and to allow my children to grow up in their mother's culture and learn their mother's language.

Having been issued a free visa by the Philippine government for our first year in the Philippines under the "Balik Bayan" program instituted by former President Ramos, we began to apply for permanent residency in the Philippines for our second year there. One of the things I had to do to meet this requirement was pass a simple physical exam. I was in relatively good health, other than the fact that I had taken antibiotics (tetracycline) off and on for many years for a chronic acne problem

I had. While I had some concerns about long-term use of antibiotics in the back of my mind, every time I addressed those concerns with various doctors I was told that many people used tetracycline for long periods of time to deal with acne problems. So when the time came for my physical exam, I was "on" a prescription of antibiotics. But my blood test revealed an infection in my body, a urinary tract infection. I was stunned, as it seemed the antibiotics were losing their effectiveness on me. I decided then and there that it was time to take responsibility for my health, and to stop relying on drugs and doctors. I went on a fresh juice fast and the infection left.

Meanwhile, I was astounded by the health of the older generation that lived in this rural farming community. There was one old man who was over 100 years old and still walked down the mountain to town and back once a week on market day. My wife's aunt was in her 80s and in excellent health. Many other older people that you would normally see in nursing homes in the U.S. at their age were living full and active lives in this community. So I started studying their dietary habits and their herbal traditions as well. We began making changes to our own dietary habits, and using some of the herbs that grew wild on the mountain. We started making our own herbal products and marketing them locally.

During my research I decided to see what I could find out about coconut oil, the main dietary fat that everyone in this community consumed. I had always been taught that this was a "bad" fat, but here was a community of older people that did not seem to be dying from all the supposed bad effects of coconut oil I had always heard about. My research astounded me—especially the writings of Dr. Mary Enig.

When I first read about the health benefits of coconut oil, I asked Marianita if there was a more natural way to extract the oil from the coconut, so that we didn't have to buy the refined coconut oils found in all the stores in the Philippines. She said there was a method the older generation used to extract the oil by grating the fresh coconut, extracting the coconut milk, and then letting the coconut milk stand in a covered bucket for about 24 hours. After 24-36 hours, the oil naturally separates from the water producing a crystal clear oil that retains the full scent and taste of coconuts. So we started making our coconut oil that way and using it for our cooking needs with our three children. We called it "Virgin Coconut Oil," because it was so different from the refined products we could buy in the stores. We couldn't believe how great it tasted, and how healthy we felt. We had been living on Mt. Banahaw for almost two years by that time, and in the year 2000 telephone service was provided to our rural farming community, allowing me to put up a website about our Philippine Herbs. I also put up a website highlighting the research and truth about how healthy coconut oil really was. I decided to put our Virgin Coconut Oil up on the website, not really expecting people to order it because it was a bit expensive since we had to hire people to make the oil, and shipping to the U.S. cost quite a bit because of the weight. There was also all that negative propaganda against coconut oil that was accepted as fact in the U.S. We were so surprised when people started ordering, and then re-ordering it because they felt so great after using it! They told us there was no other coconut oil like it on the market.

> Dear Tropical Traditions, I wanted to drop you a quick note to tell you how great your Virgin Coconut Oil is! I have been on your product now for about 6 months and consume approximately 3 tablespoons per day. In just a short amount of time I noticed a higher level of energy, and I have lost weight! I also apply it to my skin and hair and people have commented on how beautiful my hair and skin look! I also get these open cuts in the winter along the cracks of my finger and fingernails and they bleed and are very painful, but when I apply your coconut oil the night before to these open wounds it dries them up and heals them overnight! Your product is definitely a miracle food and I highly recommend it to others. I have tried a lot of other brands prior to using yours and have not gotten the same results that I have using your Virgin Coconut Oil, so it's definitely the best coconut oil I have found on the market! Thank you and keep up the good work! Best regards. **Roger** - Phoenix, AZ

Before long we had businesses contacting us asking how to order our Virgin Coconut Oil in bulk. There were very few places in the U.S. even carrying any kind of coconut oil, and the few that did exist were only marketing it primarily for cosmetic purposes. It was almost impossible to find a good quality edible coconut oil, and none that were what we called "Virgin." So we discussed how we could mass produce this kind of oil and almost abandoned the product because we didn't want to lose the traditional way of making it. In the end, we decided to just keep making it the same way, by having other coconut farming families in our community also make the oil the traditional way.

So we set out to revive the old traditions of Marianita's parents' generation by once again making a natural, chemical-free coconut oil. Marianita developed a system that trained families in traditional coconut oil production according to strict organic standards. This gave them an opportunity to produce this natural oil to meet new demands for this product in the U.S. and around the world. Today there are hundreds of families in the Philippines once again earning enough money from coconuts to support their families. They are independent business owners, and not laborers. When you buy Tropical Traditions Virgin Coconut Oil, you are supporting these families in the Philippines.

Leaving the Philippines

We loved living in the Philippines in our small rural community. Often when we went into churches and other places, people would ask us when we were going back to the U.S. We would simply reply that the Philippines was our home, and that we had no plans to move at that time. This would invariably cause very confused looks from people, because no one could imagine that anyone who had the chance to live in the U.S. would choose to stay in the Philippines. Everyone they knew who had the opportunity to leave would stay in the U.S. and just visit the Philippines from time to time. It was just understood that life was better in the U.S. We tried to explain to people that the rural lifestyle in the Philippines had great value, and that life in the U.S. had many negatives as well. We would point out how our own health had changed since moving to the Philippines, and how our children were much better off in a small rural community. We tried to convince them that there was great wealth right there in the countryside, a kind of "wealth" that is difficult to find in more industrialized countries. But no one took us seriously. They thought we were just very unusual.

But as the Virgin Coconut Oil business continued to grow, and we continued to teach more families how to make it and pay them good money for it, people started listening a little more. No one believed us at first when we explained that people in America will pay money for a good organic product. They just couldn't imagine that the "lowly" coconut oil, made the way their parents and grandparents made it, was something that would produce income as an export. When we first went to the Philippine Coconut Authority (PCA) to apply for our export license, they asked us which class of coconut oil we were exporting. There were various classes of refined and crude coconut oil, but we told them it was "Virgin Coconut Oil." They didn't understand, and decided that what we wanted to export was "crude" coconut oil. On a later trip we met with someone who quizzed us a bit more extensively as to what we were having the families produce, and he stated that what we were making was "white coconut oil," which was something they had found a few years earlier when extracting the remaining oil from coconut that had been used to make coconut milk. They had found that it was crystal clear oil, but that there was no market for such a product in the Philippines at that time, since the average Filipino would just buy coconut oil for a cheaper price at the stores. So they finally issued us an export license for "Virgin Coconut Oil," the first one ever issued by the PCA, and it was numbered 001.

In late 2002 our stay in the Philippines came to an abrupt end. By now we had quite an operation going and several managers in place overseeing all the producers. One night one of our managers who lives in the area told us that she had seen some strange men walking around the day before. Being in a small community where virtually everyone knows everyone else, they stuck out. So she sent her children home right after school that day, before it got dark, instead of letting them stick around to play with our children. I glanced at my wife when she told me this, and she looked knowingly back at me. We recognized the risks of an American living in a rural mountain community in Quezon Province, in the known path of the NPA (New People's Army) communist insurgency group. Once before there had been some unknown men in the area, and we had taken no chances. We left our home on the mountain immediately, only to find out later that the men were police cadet graduates carrying out exercises in the jungles of the mountains. Could this be a similar situation?

I asked my Marianita, "Should we leave?" We were planning on taking a vacation later that week anyway, but we had not packed yet, and it was almost dark. I hesitated for a minute, but then decided not to take any chances, and I told her that we would go to the nearby capital city and spend the night in a hotel and come back the next day to pack our things and start our vacation. She agreed, and we left. A couple months earlier someone had broken into our warehouse where we collected the oil, and had stolen some of our equipment we used to dry herbs. So we had a security guard now that stayed at the warehouse in the evenings. As we left and he reported for work that night, we told him about the "strange men" that had been seen and asked him to investigate it.

We came back early the next morning to find our telephone and electricity disconnected, and our security guard visibly upset. He reported to us how fortunate we were to have not been around that night. At about 2 a.m. in a pouring rain storm, several men armed with assault rifles had come around looking for us. Threatening to blow up our warehouse, they forced our security guard to the ground with a gun to his head, and told him that they were the NPA and that we had failed to pay our "revolutionary taxes," and that they would return at any time to collect it.

He advised us to gather our belongings and leave as soon as possible. We looked at our beautiful mountain home with tears in our eyes. Our time in the Philippines had come to an end. The business had become too successful, and a foreigner could not live there safely anymore. I was stunned. We always knew that there were groups like this around us, but we had lived there peacefully for four years. We were respected in the community for improving people's lives. But now in some people's eyes I had become the rich foreigner: a target for kidnap for ransom. We left our home immediately, and then left the Philippines a couple of weeks later. We just praise God that we had our management team established to carry on the business after we left, as they continue to do today.

We learned later that the actions of these men were not quite consistent with how the NPA operates, and that they were probably just a kidnap-for-ransom gang posing as the NPA. We continue to pray for the Philippines. We believe that the way to help the poor is to help provide an atmosphere in the Philippines that encourages economic development and new businesses. The Philippines is a very rich nation, and has much to offer the world.

> We are traveling healers. We work mainly in California and the western United States. Our work is a synthesis of techniques from around the world. We first used coconut oil in Manaoag when we were studying with Marcos Orbito. Once we returned to the United States, we could not find a wonderful coconut oil like the one we used in the Philippines. When we discovered Tropical Traditions it was like a gift from God. The oil is so pure and smells so wonderful. Although we bought it for our healing work, it soon became a staple in our diets and in our bathroom. Now our clients are using it to eliminate Candida from their systems, restore health to their hair and vibrancy to their skin. We

are continuing to learn about the many benefits of this wonderful oil. We can't imagine not having it in our pantry and on the road with us. Not only is this the only oil we use for our work, it is the primary oil we use in our kitchen. Thank you Tropical Traditions. You have been a life saver. **Morningstar and Michael**

Chapter 2

What is Virgin Coconut Oil?

In tropical countries like the Philippines, coconut oil is still the main dietary oil. Tankers transporting refined coconut oil like this are a common sight.

Refined Coconut Oil

Most commercial grade coconut oils are made from copra. Copra is basically the dried kernel (meat) of the coconut. It can be made by smoke drying, sun drying, or kiln drying, or derivatives or a combination of these three. If standard copra is used as a starting material, the unrefined coconut oil extracted from copra is not suitable for consumption and must be purified—that is, refined. This is because the way most copra is dried is not sanitary. The standard end product made from copra is RBD coconut oil. RBD stands for refined, bleached, and deodorized. High heat is used to deodorize the oil, and the oil is typically filtered through (bleaching) clays to remove impurities. Sodium hydroxide is generally used to remove free fatty acids and prolong shelf life. This is the most common way to mass-produce coconut oil. More modern methods also use chemical solvents to extract all the oil from the copra for higher yields.

RBD oil is also sometimes hydrogenated or partially hydrogenated. This happens mostly in tropical climates, since the natural melting point of coconut oil is about 76 degrees F, and already naturally a solid in most colder climates. Since coconut oil is mostly saturated, there is little unsaturated oil left to hydrogenate. Hydrogenated oils contain trans fatty acids. (See Chapter 3 for more information on the dangers of trans fatty acids.)

Virgin Coconut Oil Production

Virgin Coconut Oil can only be achieved by using fresh coconut meat or what is called non-copra. Chemicals and high heating are not used in further refining, since the natural, pure coconut oil is very stable with a shelf life of several years. There are currently two main processes of manufacturing Virgin Coconut Oil:

1. Quick drying of fresh coconut meat which is then used to press out the oil. Using this method, minimal heat is used to quick-dry the coconut meat, and the oil is then pressed out via mechanical means.

2. Wet-milling. With this method the oil is extracted from fresh coconut meat without drying first. "Coconut milk" is expressed first by pressing. The oil is then further separated from the water. Methods which can be used to separate the oil from the water include boiling, fermentation, refrigeration, enzymes and mechanical centrifuge.

The method we chose to use in the Philippines is the traditional fermentation method. The coconut milk expressed from the freshly harvested coconuts is fermented for 24-36 hours. During this time, the water separates from the oil. The oil is then slightly heated for a short time to remove moisture, and then lightly filtered. The result is a clear coconut oil that retains the distinct scent and taste of coconuts. This is a traditional method of coconut oil extraction that has been used in the Philippines for hundreds of years. Laboratory tests show that this is a very high quality coconut oil, with the lauric acid content being 50 to 57%. This oil is not mass-produced by machines, but made by hand just as it has been done for hundreds (if not thousands) of years. Since our family members live in the community where the coconuts grow, we personally guarantee that the best organic coconuts available are used in producing this Virgin Coconut Oil, and that no chemicals whatsoever are used in the growing or processing of the coconuts. Our coconuts are also certified organic according to strict USDA standards. In addition, all of our coconuts are hand-sorted within 24 hours of harvest. Only those nuts that produce the highest quality coconut oil are chosen, while the rest of the crop is sold to copra dealers. Because of our extremely selective procedure for selecting the coconuts, we pay a higher price to the farmer. Almost all other "virgin" coconut oils on the market are mass-produced and do not pay this kind of attention to detail, that begins with choosing the right nuts.

> I love Tropical Traditions Virgin Coconut Oil. It is the best I have tried, and I will continue to use this oil forever. **Kelly** - Lander, WY

> I am thankful to God that I found your website! In April 2003 I started using Tropical Traditions coconut oil in desperation. As a middle-aged woman fighting thyroid disease, my weight had increased significantly and I was having difficulty regulating my thyroid function. Needless to say, my weight gain and deteriorating thyroid were creating a sense of urgency in me to find an alternative method of feeling better. I was absolutely amazed at the fast results after using 2 tablespoons of the coconut oil on a daily basis. I lost 15 pounds within three months of starting the coconut oil and have shed 2 dress sizes! In addition, I have been able to reach my ideal weight (and maintain it!) this past year with my daily intake of coconut oil. While I am still on thyroid medication for my severe thyroid disease, the dosage is minimal and I am convinced that my daily intake of coconut oil helps to keep me on the lower dosage of medication. I challenge everyone who is now utilizing another oil to start using Tropical Traditions' coconut oil. In an age of fast food and obesity, there are many who could benefit greatly by utilizing this coconut oil in their products rather than the [trans] fats currently being used. I will not use any other brand of coconut oil! I implicitly trust Tropical Traditions' method of processing and their quality product. I am convinced that Tropical Traditions is genuinely concerned for the health and well-being of the general public and I highly recommend them! **Joyce** - Wichita, Kansas

One of the main differences between Virgin Coconut Oil and refined coconut oils is the scent and taste. All Virgin Coconut Oils retain the fresh scent and taste of coconuts, whereas the copra-based refined coconut oils have a bland taste due to the refining process. Some grades of refined copra-based oils are also now sold that have a coconut flavor, but are usually bitter and have a burnt taste to it. They are a form of "crude coconut oil" that has not undergone all of the deodorizing process, and they have a shorter shelf-life.

A recent study done in India[1] comparing refined coconut oil (CO) with Virgin Coconut Oil (VCNO) found that VCNO obtained by wet process has a beneficial effect in lowering lipid components compared to CO. It reduced total cholesterol, triglycerides, phospholipids, LDL, and VLDL cholesterol levels and increased HDL cholesterol in serum and tissues. The results demonstrated the potential beneficiary effect of Virgin Coconut oil in lowering lipid levels in serum and tissues and LDL oxidation by physiological oxidants. This property of VCNO may be attributed to the biologically active polyphenol components present in the oil. There are probably many other as yet untested benefits of VCNO over regular refined coconut oil.

> I am really enjoying your coconut oil. I tried a different brand of coconut oil several years ago when I heard about the health benefits of coconut oil, but it was so bland and tasteless that I couldn't even eat it. Yours is so delicious I eat it by the spoonful!! **Donna** (Coconut Diet Forums)

What is "Extra Virgin Coconut Oil?"

Some retailers and manufacturers of Virgin Coconut Oils, referring to one of the processes mentioned above, call their coconut oil "Extra Virgin Coconut Oil." But there are no other processes used to make coconut oil other than the ones mentioned above, so this classification is simply arbitrary. There is no official classification or difference between "virgin" and "extra virgin" as there is in the olive oil industry, since the two oils are completely different in fatty acid composition, harvesting procedures, and terminology.

> When I take Virgin Coconut Oil on a regular basis with my food, I have NO memory problems. I am 53 and for many years had been having a very difficult time with short term memory and word associations (i.e., being able to use a word for a common implement like a comb or brush—I knew what the item was but couldn't get the word out of my mouth). Once I used coconut oil systematically, I had 100% recall and no word connection problems. **Ellen** - Centreville, VA

22

Is Coconut Oil Affected by Heat?

As the truth about the health benefits of coconut oil continues to spread, many people are jumping into the coconut oil reselling business and making fantastic claims for their particular brand of coconut oil. Unfortunately, most of these distributors have never lived in the tropics where coconuts are grown, and know very little about the actual processing of coconut oil.

One current claim being propagated through the Internet is that certain coconut oils are more "raw" than others because they supposedly see less heat, and actually contain enzymes that are beneficial. However, this is simply not true. If any coconut oil actually contained any appreciable amounts of enzymes, that oil would quickly deteriorate and have a very short shelf life. That is, after all, the job of enzymes in plants: to break things down and start the process of decomposition. High quality coconut oils, particularly Virgin Coconut Oil, have a very long shelf life (2 years or more) and would not have any appreciable amounts of enzymes in the oil.

When we first started making Virgin Coconut Oil the traditional way, and the demand for such a high-quality product grew very rapidly, we proceeded to investigate every possible way coconut oil was produced in order to provide larger quantities. One of the ways we learned about was from a professor at the University of the Philippines, who had extracted the oil through enzyme action, and then further separated the oil via a centrifuge process. He made it very clear that the enzymes needed to be completely removed.

Others who are very knowledgeable about coconut oil have stated the same thing when we asked them: enzymes are not present in coconut oil. Here is what they told us:

"There are no enzymes in coconut oil, nor any other edible oil for that matter." - **Mary Enig, Ph.D**, a nutritionist/biochemist and the author of *Know Your Fats*.

"If you don't heat the oil high enough to destroy the enzymes and then filter them off, plus filter the oil, that oil becomes unstable and tastes terrible." **Ray Peat, Ph.D**, author of several articles on fats and oils, and coconut oil in particular.

"The good thing about coconut oil is that it isn't damaged by heat. That's why it's so good for cooking. It's the saturation that makes it stable. If coconut oil contains enzymes it would become very perishable - just like all raw foods containing enzymes." **Lita Lee, Ph.D**. - Dr. Lee is a chemist, enzyme nutritionist, nutritional counselor, and has written on coconut oil.

"Coconut oil does not contain enzymes. Many in the raw food movement are misinformed about this." **Dr. Adiel Tel-Oren**, **M.D.**, medical doctor, doctor of chiropractic, licensed nutritionist, certified clinical nutritionist, frequent lecturer on the health benefits of coconut oil, and owner of the Ecopolitan, the largest organic raw food restaurant in Minneapolis.

It is a myth that there are coconut oils on the market that are "live" with enzymes and "see no heat." Coconuts are native to the tropics, where temperatures are very hot. Any coconut oil distributed anywhere in North America has "seen heat." Shipping containers used to ship the coconut oil to the U.S. by sea from the tropics reach temperatures of over 130 degrees. If you have a truck deliver coconut oil to your home in the summer time by any of the major carriers, temperatures inside that truck will reach up to 125 degrees. In the winter time coconut oil turns solid and must be heated in order to be repackaged into retail size containers from drums. Tropical Traditions uses large insulated containers that hold many drums and keep a steady temperature of between 90 to 100 degrees F. in the winter time to keep our stored oil liquid so it can be repackaged. It does take longer to liquefy 55 gallon drums this way (a few days) in the winter, but it more closely resembles ambiance air temperatures in the tropics. Many other repackagers use electric drum bands to melt the coconut oil more quickly, and temperatures inside the drum become much hotter, closer to boiling temperatures. So any coconut oil you buy will have "seen heat." But the good news is that coconuts are designed by our Maker to grow and thrive in hot climates, and the oil is not harmed in any way by these low-level heats.

> My wife and I began using Virgin Coconut Oil about two months ago. We began cooking everything we used to cook using conventional oil with coconut oil, and love it. Not only is the food healthier for us, it tastes fantastic. I never get on the scale, but all of my pants are fitting much looser, requiring a two belt notch move. Additionally, we have noticed our energy level increase dramatically. As this is the ONLY change

we have made to our diets, I have no doubt that Tropical Traditions Virgin Coconut Oil is responsible. We are hooked. **Greg and Deciree** - Graham, TX

In the end, we determined that the traditional method of making coconut oil from fresh coconuts via family producers produced the highest quality Virgin Coconut Oil on the market. We work directly with family farmers, helping them become certified organic according to strict USDA standards. Our family producers hand select each coconut they use to make Virgin Coconut Oil, using only coconuts harvested within 24 hours. Our Virgin Coconut Oil is made from fresh coconut milk, allowed to separate from the water naturally over night, and then lightly heated for a few minutes to remove any remaining water or enzymes that may cause deterioration. Our moisture levels, free fatty acid content, and peroxide value are usually lower than industry standards, and independent laboratory analysis has consistently shown that our fatty acid concentrations have a higher percentage of lauric acid than commercially-refined coconut oil. Even though we now produce larger quantities of Virgin Coconut Oil via our network of family farmers, it is still hand-made the traditional way. No other coconut oil on the market sees more individual attention to details in the processing, as all other coconut oils are mass-produced using technology and machines. We believe this is the highest quality coconut oil one can find anywhere, and many others agree with us!

I have tried all other brands of coconut oil, and Tropical Traditions is the best! **Marilyn Diamond**, best selling author of *Fit for Life.*

You should be absolutely certain, however, of the quality and effectiveness of whatever coconut oil brand you choose. There is a very wide variance in terms of the types of coconuts, the manufacturing processes used to make the oil, and more, which will have a major impact on the healthiness and effectiveness of your coconut oil. Because there is so much uncertainty, my team and I here researched coconut oil extensively until we found the ideal source. I now highly recommend and offer you what is clearly the premier brand of virgin coconut oil in the U.S., Tropical Traditions. I highly recommend the Tropical Traditions Virgin Coconut Oil. **Dr. Mercola**, mercola.com

Tropical Traditions Virgin Coconut Oil is the only coconut oil I use and recommend because it's the freshest, best tasting coconut oil I've found. I've compared it to others and it won my vote. **Cherie Calbom, *The Juice Lady***, nutritionist and best-selling author of *Juicing for Life*

Frequently Asked Questions about Virgin Coconut Oil (VCNO)

1. How much coconut oil should one ingest daily to receive its health benefits?

The health benefits of coconut oil are mainly from the medium chain fatty acids (MCFAs). The best comparison in nature as to percentage of MCFAs being consumed in a diet is human breast milk. To equal the amount of MCFAs a nursing infant would receive in one day, an adult needs about 3.5 tablespoons of VCNO a day according to researchers. Since coconut oil in nature is packaged inside the coconut meat, it is recommended to take this amount throughout the day with food high in fiber and protein.

2. Does VCNO need to be kept in the refrigerator, and how long does it last?

No, VCNO does not need to be kept in the refrigerator. In the Philippines and other tropical climates, where the ambiant air temperature is much higher than in North America, people traditionally have not refrigerated coconut oil. Virgin Coconut Oil is the least susceptible to oxidation of any plant oil. Its natural antioxidants give it the longest shelf life of any plant oil. Tropical Traditions VCNO samples have been shown to show no breakdown in a constant liquid state at temperatures above 80 degrees for over 2 years. We recommend you store the oil out of direct sunlight.

3. Is VCNO liquid or solid?

In the tropics Virgin Coconut Oil is almost always a liquid, since its melting point is about 76 degrees F. In North America it will usually be a solid, butter-like consistency. It can be stored in either form.

4. Is your coconut oil heated in its processing?

Yes, Tropical Traditions VCNO is slightly heated at the end of the processing prior to packaging. This is to ensure that no moisture is present, and to draw all the oil out of the curds that are formed by the fermentation process. This heat is very low (less than boiling temperatures), and is for a very short duration (10-15 minutes). Commercial RBD coconut oils, by contrast, undergo steam deodorization at temperatures of around 400 degrees. Traditional methods of making coconut oil naturally have always used heat in the process, and we are committed to honoring time-tested traditional methods that have nourished populations in the tropics for thousands of years. (See above for more info)

5. Will cooking with VCNO cause it to become hydrogenated and toxic like hydrogenated oils?

No. Hydrogenation is an industrial process where hydrogen molecules are introduced into the oil to make it solid at room temperatures. It chemically alters the oil and creates harmful trans fatty acids. Cooking with VCNO does NOT introduce hydrogen into the oil or hydrogenate it. As stated above, VCNO is a very stable oil at even higher temperatures. However, it is best not to cook beyond the smoke point of VCNO, as this will begin to deteriorate the oil and turn it yellow. Once it has turned dark yellow, the oil should be discarded and no longer used.

6. How does one use VCNO?

There are many ways to use VCNO and incorporate it into one's diet. Since it is a stable cooking oil, one can simply replace unhealthy oils in their diet with VCNO. Since it is a solid most of the time at room temperature or when refrigerated, it can be a butter or margarine substitute for spreads or for baking. Any recipe calling for butter, margarine, or any other oil can use VCNO as a substitute. It is popularly mixed in with "smoothies." Many people do eat it simply by the spoonful. If you refrigerate or freeze it the taste changes completely, and some describe it like a "candy" or "white chocolate." Some people fill up ice cube trays with VCNO and then store them in the freezer. VCNO can also be massaged into the skin for external applications. So some people use it as a spread, many people use it with fruit smoothies, and a lot of people put it into their coffee or tea. For more ideas on using VCNO, join *The Coconut Diet Forums* at www.coconutdiet.com and search the archives.

7. How is VCNO different from other coconut oils found in health food stores?

When purchasing a healthy coconut oil, one must determine between "virgin" and "refined." The determining characteristic of Virgin Coconut Oils is that they are made from fresh coconuts, and they have a distinct aroma and taste of coconuts present. Tasteless coconut oils are probably made from copra, not fresh coconuts. There are also some oils that are made from copra that are not fully deodorized and have a taste to them. But these oils are refined also, despite marketing claims. You will be able to taste the difference when comparing with a Virgin Coconut Oil. There are many ways of refining coconut oil made from copra, some more healthy than others. But Virgin Coconut Oils start out with fresh coconuts, and do not need further refining as their natural antioxidant properties make them very stable oils.

8. Since farmers and families make your VCNO, are sanitary conditions in processing a concern?

No. On the contrary, our VCNO receives much more special care and attention than any mass-produced machine-made coconut oil could ever receive. Every family approved to sell us VCNO must undergo stringent quality control training and have their home or facilities inspected. We set standards that they must abide by, such as how old the coconuts can be that are used (24 hours after harvesting), the type of coconuts, and the instruments used for processing, like graters and presses, etc. Equipment used to produce the oil is dedicated to VCNO production only, and usually provided for by our company. Cement floors are used in the production facilities. Therefore the VCNO is completely kosher and clean. In addition, our producers are small family businesses that live in rural areas away from the pollution of the cities, like on Mt. Banahaw. To assure standards are maintained and that only the best quality oil is produced, all producers are organized into groups that are managed by overseers, which in turn are organized into groups that are managed by area managers. So when VCNO is delivered to our warehouse for packaging, it has already been inspected 3 times before final inspection at the warehouse prior to packaging into drums. Laboratory tests have continually confirmed that our traditional methods of testing the oil by sight (clarity), smell, and taste result in a very high quality oil. Some of the standards tested for in commercial oils, such a peroxide value (PV levels have consistently tested at nil or near 0 levels in our oil) , have actually tested better in our VCNO. Moisture levels are consistently around 0.1% and often lower. This is due to the extreme care that is used from the selection of the coconuts used, to the actual making of the oil, and the removal of almost all moisture. We seriously doubt that any other coconut oil on the market has received such personal care, or could claim to have a higher quality or cleaner handling than our VCNO. And our VCNO is certified organic by USDA standards (see below).

9. Are coconuts a nut, fruit, or vegetable?

Actually, they can be classified as all three in some form. The meat of the coconut is usually referred to as fruit, and the coconut itself is the nut, or seed, that will reproduce into a coconut palm tree if allowed to sprout and grow, and the oil made from coconuts is classified as a "vegetable oil" in terms of commodity trading.

10. Is Tropical Traditions Virgin Coconut Oil organic?

Yes! We have lived in the community where most of the coconut oil is produced, and we can personally guarantee that the coconuts used to produce our oil are completely organic. In addition, our coconuts and Virgin Coconut Oil producers are certified organic by a third party organization based out of the U.S., and meet strict requirements for organic certification according to USDA/NOP standards. Tropical Traditions Virgin Coconut Oil is made from fresh, certified organic coconuts, and the family-based small-scale operation we use to make the Virgin Coconut Oil is also certified organic. Our repackaging facilities in the U.S. are also certified organic by USDA standards.

11. Are all coconuts naturally organic?

No. It is true that most coconuts are grown by small-scale farmers and that pesticides and fertilizers are very uncommon. However, in many coconut-growing places today farmers are starting to practice "intercropping" by growing other crops and fruit trees underneath the tall coconut palms. Many of these crops are sprayed. Also, organic certification according to USDA standards assures that neighboring fields where conventional crops are grown do not contaminate coconut trees. Many coconut farms are next to conventional farming fields where there could be run-off from harmful fertilizers and pesticides, or contaminated in other ways. In addition, we go beyond organic certification standards and implement our own standards, like not using coconuts from heavily populated areas where they are exposed to polluting forces such as diesel and gas fumes from trucks and other vehicles. Most of our trees are from distant mountain sources far away from the cities.

12. What is the amount of Omega 3 fatty acids in VCNO?

None. VCNO is not a source of Omega 3 fatty acids. These need to be supplemented in diet from elsewhere (such as our Cod Liver Oil). The primary health benefits of coconut oil are the medium chain fatty acids.

13. Are there "side effects" to VCNO?

VCNO is a food, not a medication, and therefore it does not have "side effects." Since individuals vary, there could be adverse reactions, especially if your body is used to a low-fat diet regimen. Since lauric acid is antibacterial and anti-viral, there could also be "die-off" effects from the VCNO as these organisms are eliminated from the body. The most common reaction is diarrhea. While 3 tablespoons is recommended as the daily intake by some researchers, it is probably best not to start with that amount, or take it all at once. Spread it out over the course of the day, and reduce your intake if there are unwanted effects. Like any food, some people could possibly have allergic reactions to VCNO as well, although it has traditionally nourished millions if not billions of people throughout Asia for thousands of years.

14. Is VCNO safe for pregnant women?

Since VCNO is a food and is a staple for many living in Asia, it is considered safe for anyone. In coconut producing countries it is considered very healthy for pregnant and lactating women, since it contains lauric acid which is also present in breast milk. However, the cautions of side effects as stated above should be noted. Many in Western countries are used to a low-fat diet, and it is best NOT to begin experimenting with VCNO while pregnant if your body is not used to it. If, however, you have been consuming VCNO regularly without any side effects, there is no reason to discontinue while pregnant, and many good reasons to continue consuming it.

15. What is "Expeller-Pressed" Coconut Oil (EPCO)?

Tropical Traditions Expeller Pressed Coconut Oil is a high quality refined coconut oil. This oil is processed the "old" way by what is called "physical refining." The modern way of processing coconut oil is by chemical extraction, using solvent extracts, which produces higher yields and is quicker and less expensive. Tropical Traditions Expeller Pressed Coconut Oil does not use chemicals or solvent extracts. It is made the "old" way by expeller-pressed mechanical extraction. This oil is also not hydrogenated, and contains no trans fatty acids. It is a very good quality food-grade coconut oil. Tropical Traditions Expeller Pressed Coconut Oil is made from coconuts that have not been treated with chemicals or fertilizers. It is 100% natural. Our Expeller-Pressed coconut oil is high in the medium chain fatty acids, such as Lauric acid. This is the "common" type oil that billions of people in Asia consume on a daily basis, where thyroid disease and obesity is rare as compared to the U.S. We have also seen recently that Asian countries with high refined coconut oil consumption, such as the Philippines, have not seen the kinds of outbreak in SARS that other Asian countries have where vegetable oils are the primary dietary oil. Expeller Pressed Coconut oil is less expensive than Virgin Coconut Oil, and because it goes through a steam deodorizing process the taste is very bland, unlike Virgin Coconut Oil which retains the odor and taste of fresh coconuts. Some people prefer a bland, tasteless oil.

16. Are the Health Benefits of EPCO the same as VCNO?

As far as the comparison between the Expeller Pressed Coconut Oil (EPCO) and the VCNO, the EPCO still has the medium chain fatty acids/tryglicerides (MCTs) that are the major reason for the health benefits of coconut oil, although lauric acid content tends to be slightly lower in EPCO. These MCTs are what studies say increase metabolism, fight against viruses and bacteria, etc. The EPCO is missing some of the nutrients and anti-oxidant properties that are in VCNO, like vitamin E, for example (although coconut oil is not a real significant source of vitamin E: natural/red palm oil is better for that.) How much this affects the body is really unkown. The general rule in nutrition is that the closer to nature/natural the better. What we do know is that many of the studies that have been done on MCTs and report their benefits have been done on regular (non-virgin) coconut oil, or in some cases pure extracted MCTs taken out of coconut oil. We also know that the refined coconut oil is what the Asian population for the most part consumes today, and in countries like the Philippines where it is the common cooking oil you don't see the kinds of thyriod and obesity problems that you see in the U.S. The customer testimonies and feedback we have gotten from our VCNO suggests that it is more potent than refined coconut oil. But many people are reporting good results from the EPCO as well.

17. Do you offer coconut oil in a capsule?

We have received many requests about coconut oil pills, or coconut oil soft gels. And indeed, since so many people have requested this, there are some vendors now offering this on the market.

However, Tropical Traditions has no intention of offering a coconut oil soft gel capsule. For one thing, the largest soft gel one can make is 1000 mg (1 gram). As most people know, the recommended amount of coconut oil to eat each day by many researchers is about 3.5 tablespoons. 1 tablespoon is 14 grams. So to get the equivalent amount of coconut oil that most people are consuming in capsule form, one would need to take about 49 capsules a day. The companies peddling these coconut pills are recommending anywhere from 3 to 6 capsules a day, which is only a few drops of coconut oil. So if you want coconut oil in pill form, you are going to pay 20 or 30 dollars for a jar of 100 or so pills. And what value are those pills? If you do the math, you will see that you are being sold something of very little value that is extremely overpriced.

Not only that: if you were to consume large amounts of soft gel capsules, this raises the question of what else are you consuming besides the oil inside them. These large gelatin capsules are made from bovine (cows), and we don't see anyone advertising organic grass-fed derived gelatin capsules. So all the toxins currently existing in our cattle industry (growth hormones, antibiotics, etc.) will also be in these gelatin capsules. Also, in the encapsulation process it is standard practice to use mineral oil. We talked to one major manufacturer who has been in the business for 25 years making capsules and other products, and while he himself does not do gel caps, he knows many who do and he said that there is definitely mineral oil residue in these gel caps. Mineral oil is basically petroleum.

So to answer all those questions that come in to us on almost a daily basis: no, Tropical Traditions does NOT offer coconut oil in gel caps, and we have no intention of doing so. Coconut oil is a traditional FOOD, not a medicine. We are not going to take advantage of our clients and give them a product that has no value, and is even possibly harmful to them.

> As a certified personal trainer and weight loss program founder, I strongly suggest Virgin Coconut Oil for my class members! Not only does it keep them comfortably satisfied and free of food cravings, so many (myself included!) find their hair and nails healthier! I love the metabolism-booster it has proven to be for me as well as the increased energy I receive for my workouts! I can teach a Spin class even the next day and am able to push myself harder and longer, not burning out after my traditional 40 minutes! The recipes I have, to use the coconut oil, are delicious! From chocolate chip cookie dough to coconut chocolate truffles… I know I will enjoy Tropical Traditions treats for years to come! **Karen** - New Mexico

Chapter 3

The Health Benefits of
Virgin Coconut Oil

Harvesting organic coconuts.

Population Studies

There are quite a few studies that have been done on traditional diets in tropical areas that are high in coconut oil consumption. These studies back up the suggestion that Marianita's experience growing up in the Philippines (see Chapter 1) is common in cultures that derive much of their caloric intake from the saturated fats of coconut oil. In a study published in 1981, the populations of two South Pacific islands (Pukapuka and Tokelau) were examined over a period of time starting in the 1960s, before western foods were prevalent in the diets of either culture. The study was designed to investigate the relative effects of saturated fat and dietary cholesterol in determining serum cholesterol levels. Coconuts were practically a staple in the diets, with up to 60% of their caloric intake coming from the saturated fat of coconut oil. The study found very lean and healthy people who were relatively free from the modern diseases of western cultures, including obesity. Their conclusion: "Vascular disease is uncommon in both populations and there is no evidence of the high saturated fat intake having a harmful effect in these populations."[1]

> My friend Nida's grandmother has continued to prepare coconut oil in the [traditional] manner... She is also a manghihilot (a native Filipino massage therapist). The herbs she adds are, among others, garlic and ginger. She rubs it on herself and her husband every night. They are still healthy. Nida tells of her cousins who were very poor. So poor, in fact, that they ate mostly coconut. Other kids teased them because they ate fresh coconut for breakfast instead of rice and fish, and munched it whenever they were hungry, picking it up from the copra being laid out to dry. These kids ended up being the healthiest in the neighborhood, fat, with smooth, shiny skin and good teeth! As teenagers, they never had skin eruptions. **Luanne** - Mindanao, Philippines

Other studies done among the Pacific islands were conducted back in the 1930s by Dr. Weston Price, a dentist. Dr. Price spent significant time traveling and examining traditional cultures, their diet, and dental and overall health, as compared to those eating more modern diets consisting of refined foods. His work is documented in the book *Nutrition and Physical Degeneration* (1939 Keats Publishing). As he traveled to islands throughout the South Pacific, he found the same thing wherever he went. Those eating a traditional diet consisting of high concentrations of coconut were in very good health, and were not obese even though they had such a high fat content in their diet. Those who through commercial trade with western countries were starting to eat more refined foods were starting to suffer common western diseases, including dental decay.

In India a study was done comparing traditional cooking oils, like coconut oil and ghee which are rich in saturated fats, with modern oils like sunflower or safflower oils which are mostly polyunsaturated, in relation to prevalence of heart disease and Type-II diabetes. The study was done by the Department of Medicine, at Safdarjang Hospital in New Delhi. The study was titled "Choice of cooking oils—myths and realities", and was published in the Journal of the Indian Medical Association in 1998. They found that while saturated fats were portrayed as unhealthy in favor of newer polyunsaturated vegetable oils, that heart disease and diabetes had actually increased after consumption of the traditional oils like coconut oil and ghee decreased.[2] They concluded that these newer "heart-friendly" oils like sunflower or safflower oils possess an undesirable Omega 6 fatty acid ratio to Omega 3 fatty acids, and that there are numerous research data now available to indicate that the sole use or excess intake of these newer vegetable oils are actually detrimental to the health of Indians.

> My wife and I have been using the Virgin Coconut Oil for about 3 months now (a teaspoon in the morning and at night). We have noticed increased energy along with a decrease in the amount of time it takes to overcome viruses. We attribute this to the anti-viral properties of the Virgin Coconut Oil. Also, we use the oil as a moisturizer and have noticed less dryness of our skin in our dry winter climate. **Tom** - Rutland, Vermont

P.K. Thampan, the former Chief Coconut Development officer of Coconut Development Board in India, has found the same thing true in his studies of traditional cultures consuming large amounts of coconut. In his book *Facts and Fallacies about Coconut Oil,* Thampan shows that population studies conducted in countries where coconut oil is a part of the normal diet of the people have revealed that coconut oil consumption is unrelated to coronary heart disease mortality and morbidity, which is contrary to what is being taught in many of these countries. Observations recorded in these countries, where coconut kernel and coconut oil form major dietary components, have shown a longer life expectancy at birth than in countries with negligible intake of coconut products. There are also instances of longer life expectancy in predominantly coconut-consuming areas than in other places within the same country that eat less coconut.[3]

Dr. P. Rethinam and Muhartoyo wrote in the Jakarta Post, on June 18, 2003, that before 1950, heart attacks were not common in Sri Lanka. However, hospital admission rates for heart attacks grew dramatically from 1970 to 1992. On the other hand, the Central Bank of Sri Lanka had determined that the coconut consumption has gone down from 132 nuts per person per year in 1952 to 90 per person per year in 1991. Because of the saturated fat scare of recent years condemning coconut oil, people ate fewer coconuts and heart disease actually increased! Kaunitz wrote in 1986 that the 1978 edition of the Demographic Yearbook of the United Nations reported that Sri Lanka had the lowest death rate from ischemic heart disease, while coconut oil was their main dietary fat.[4]

The Research

So how do people in the tropics do it? How can people on traditional diets consume so much saturated fat and remain slim and healthy?

Researchers have known for quite some time that the secret to health and weight loss associated with coconut oil is related to the length of the fatty acid chains contained in coconut oil. Coconut oil contains what are called medium chain fatty acids, or medium chain triglycerides (MCTs for short). These medium chain fatty acids are different from the common longer chain fatty acids found in other plant-based oils. Most vegetable oils are composed of longer chain fatty acids, or triglycerides (LCTs). LCTs are typically stored in the body as fat, while MCTs are burned for energy. MCTs burn up quickly in the body. They are a lot like adding kindling to a fireplace, rather than a big damp log.

Coconut oil is nature's richest source of MCTs. Not only do MCTs raise the body's metabolism leading to weight loss, but they have special health-giving properties as well. The most predominant MCT in coconut oil, for example, is lauric acid. Lipid researcher Dr. Jon Kabara states "Never before in the history of man is it so important to emphasize the value of Lauric Oils. The medium-chain fats in coconut oil are similar to fats in mother's milk and have similar nutriceutical effects. These health effects were recognized centuries ago in Ayurvedic medicine. Modern research has now found a common link between these two natural health products—their fat or lipid content. The medium chain fatty acids and monoglycerides found primarily in coconut oil and mother's milk have miraculous healing power."[5] Outside of a human mother's breast milk, coconut oil is nature's most abundant source of lauric acid and medium chain fatty acids.

> I have personal experience with using Virgin Coconut Oil (VCO) to richen my milk supply. :-) In fact, this is why I started taking VCO in the first place. My baby was very low weight and I just knew that something

wasn't right. Our pediatrician was no help: he said because she hadn't lost weight, she was fine. I finally went to a naturopathic doctor, and explained my situation (besides the baby gaining only a few ounces, I had postpartum depression - PPD). Since my baby was my 9th and I'd nursed the last 6... he said that I probably didn't have enough good fats in my system. That would account for my milk not being rich enough/full of fat to help her grow, and it also probably had a great deal to do with my hormones being out of whack and me struggling with PPD. I started taking VCO when the baby was 5 months old. By the time she was 7 months old, she'd gained 3 whole pounds! My PPD had disappeared also. :)

We went back for a weight check when the baby was 9 months old, and she had gained another 2 pounds and was not only back on the weight chart, but on the correct curve for her age, etc. I had also noticed that she was developing new skills all at once, that maybe she'd not been able to before. My pediatrician was so impressed he asked me what I'd done... I was a little nervous about telling him, but truthfully, the only thing I'd done differently was to take the VCO! So I told him and he never rolled his eyes or treated me like I'd lost my mind. ;-) He even wrote it in her chart! **Jan** - El Paso, TX

Much of the recent research done on coconut oil has centered on lauric acid, the most predominant fatty acid chain found in coconut oil, and the anti-microbial and anti-viral properties of this unique fatty acid. Today, many strains of bacteria are becoming resistant to antibiotics, and antibiotics are generally ineffective in treating virus infections. When lauric acid is consumed in the diet, either in human breast milk or in coconut oil, lauric acid forms a monoglyceride called monolaurin, which has been shown to destroy several bacteria and viruses, including listeria monocytogenes and helicobacter pylori, and protozoa such as giardia lamblia. Some of the viruses that have been destroyed by monolaurin include HIV, measles, herpes simplex virus-1, vesicular stomatitis virus, influenza and cytomegalovirus.[6] There is also evidence now that the MCTs in coconut oil kill yeast infections, such as Candida.[7] (See Chapter 8)

So now that we know that these wonderful health benefits found in coconut oil that lead to vibrant health are in the fatty acids of coconut oil, the question that begs to be answered is, why hasn't this truth been revealed in the past?

The answer is that is has! The incredible health properties of MCTs was researched and documented by researchers like Dr. Jon Kabara as far back as 1966. MCTs have been part of infant formulas and hospital formulas for many years. The food industry at one time considered coconut oil to be the most superior dietary oil for use in baking and food preparations. At one time, it was a significant part of the American diet.

> Our whole family is really enjoying your Virgin Coconut Oil. The original purpose for the purchase was because we have a special needs child who has quadriplegic cerebral palsy and cortical blindness. Unlike most children in her condition, our daughter is fed pureed foods orally and given liquids via gastrostomy tube. She is able to tolerate very few proteins and fats because of the extremely slow movement of her digestive system. Your Virgin Coconut Oil is gentle on her system and she tolerates it wonderfully. This is such an accomplishment since there are only a few oils available that she is able to obtain nourishment and sustenance from. The taste is pleasant and mild, and we are always pleased to provide her with foods that are whole and unprocessed. Much to the surprise of her many doctors, she continues to gain weight steadily, although she is small for her age. The nutritional consultants at the hospital where she receives all necessary care (recently noted to be one of the top ten in the country) continue to instruct us with regard to her nutrition "just keep doing whatever you are doing because she is thriving wonderfully." They have no explanation for her wonderful skin, great immune system, and weight gain—all areas in which children like her struggle with daily their entire lives. We thank God for such wonderful foods as the coconut, for blessing her with great health, and for companies such as yours who can provide quality products with great integrity. **Carissa** - Independence, Missouri

However, during World War II when the Japanese occupied most of the South Pacific and the Philippines, supplies of coconut oil were cut off for several years. Americans were forced to turn to alternative sources for cooking oils, and this is when many of the polyunsaturated oils began to make their way into the market place.

How Did Coconut Oil Get Such a Bad Reputation?

Beginning in the 1950s, public opinion towards saturated fats in general, and then later towards coconut oil in particular, began to turn negative. This history of the edible oil industry in the U.S. has been well documented by Dr. Mary Enig, Ph.D., and can be read at www.coconutoil.com or at the Weston Price Foundation website (www.westonaprice.org). Her articles "The Oiling of American" and

"Coconut: In Support of Good Health in the 21st Century" provide an in depth analysis of the saturated fat research, and the negative campaigns that have been waged against coconut oil.

The anti saturated fat theory apparently began in the 1950s, with the steep rise of heart disease. While heart disease probably caused no more than 10% of all deaths in the U.S. prior to the 1920s, by the 1950s it had risen to more than 30% of all deaths. Researchers were looking for the cause of this new threat to the nation's health. Some researchers suggested that cholesterol levels were the problem, and that saturated fats raised cholesterol levels. One such study was based on examining the artery plaques found in American soldiers who had died in Korea. With high levels of cholesterol found in artery plaques, some started looking at cholesterol levels found in foods as a possible cause. Cholesterol is found only in animal foods such as meat, fish, cheese, eggs and butter. Soon a "lipid hypothesis" was formed that stated "saturated fat and cholesterol from animal sources raise cholesterol levels in the blood, leading to deposition of cholesterol and fatty material as pathogenic plaques in the arteries." So the traditional foods of butter, eggs, and fat from meats were "out", and the new vegetable oils were seen as heart-healthy replacements. However, research now shows that cholesterol levels in food have little or no effect on blood cholesterol levels, and the whole lipid theory of heart disease has been rejected by many researchers and doctors. Malcom Kendrick M.D., Dr. Mary Enig Ph.D., Uffe Ravnskov M.D., Ph.D (author of The Cholesterol Myths), George Mann M.D., Sc.D, and many other top researchers have written extensively on the flaws of the "cholesterol theory" of heart disease.

So what was the cause of the rapid rise of heart disease in the U.S.? While there are many factors to consider, one thing we know is that after World War II there were some significant dietary changes in the American diet, including that kinds of fats Americans were eating. As Mary Enig reports:

> Butter consumption was declining while the use of vegetable oils, especially oils that had been hardened to resemble butter by a process called hydrogenation, was increasing— dramatically increasing. By 1950 butter consumption had dropped from eighteen pounds per person per year to just over ten. Margarine filled in the gap, rising from about two

pounds per person at the turn of the century to about eight. Consumption of vegetable shortening—used in crackers and baked goods—remained relatively steady at about twelve pounds per person per year but vegetable oil consumption had more than tripled—from just under three pounds per person per year to more than ten.[8]

What we know today, but was not known well in the 1950s, is that hydrogenated and partially hydrogenated vegetable oils create trans fatty acids that have been linked to heart disease. (see below)

Coconut Oil: the Center of Attack

The saturated fats/cholesterol scare soon became mainstream thinking, however, and before long certain groups began taking aim at the saturated fats found in coconut oil. At one time coconut oil was a significant part of the American diet. Suddenly, we were told to avoid anything with tropical oils—from theater popcorn oil to packaged snack foods, which was a complete turn from when the food industry considered coconut oil to be an excellent dietary oil for use in baking and food preparations.

Dr. Mary Enig states:

> The coconut industry has suffered more than three decades of abusive rhetoric from the consumer activist group Center for Science in the Public Interest (CSPI), from the American Soybean Association (ASA) and other members of the edible oil industry, and from those in the medical and scientific community who learned their misinformation from groups like CSPI and ASA. According to one of CSPI's own press releases, "In 1984, CSPI organized the first national campaign to pressure fast-food restaurants and food companies to stop frying with beef fat and tropical oils, which are high in the cholesterol-raising saturated fats that increase the risk of heart disease. After six years of public pressure—including full-page newspaper ads placed by Nebraska millionaire and cholesterol-crusader Phil Sokolof—the industry finally relented in 1990."[9]

Congress held hearings in 1988 to discuss the safety of tropical oils.

Dr. George Blackburn, a Harvard medical researcher, testified that coconut oil has a neutral effect on blood cholesterol, even in situations where coconut oil is the sole source of fat. Surgeon General C. Everett Koop dismissed the entire attacks on coconut oil as "Foolishness," and continued to say "but to get the word to commercial interests terrorizing the public about nothing is another matter." However, with no strong political influence in Washington from the coconut-producing countries, the ASA and CSPI prevailed and soon coconut oil almost vanished from the American diet. At one time a significant part of the American diet, today coconut oil has been replaced by the so called "healthier" vegetable oils.

The Replacement for Saturated fats: Toxic Oils

Today, walk into any major grocery or retail food chain, visit the cooking oil section and you will not find much in the way of saturated fats. What have replaced saturated fats are now liquid vegetable oils, also known as *polyunsaturated oils*.

Unfortunately, polyunsaturated oils are not stable and they are prone to oxidation. These commercial vegetable oils are a recent addition to our diet since World War II, when manufacturers developed a process to make them shelf stable by using hydrogenation. Hydrogenating, or partially hydrogenating these oils, also makes them more solid (mimicking saturated fats) and useful for baking and deep frying.

Research now shows that the processing of these polyunsaturated oils creates a whole new subclass of fats called *trans fatty acids*. These trans fatty acids are not found in nature, and are very toxic. Studies are now showing that trans fatty acids are linked to cardiovascular disease, diabetes, and cancer, among others. In January 2004 Denmark became the first country in the world to ban the manufacture of trans fatty acids in its foods.[10] In Europe, the consumption of trans fatty acids is decreasing. In the U.S., the FDA is requiring all food manufacturers to list trans fatty acids in the nutrition panel of their labels by the year 2006. The FDA website states:

> On July 9, 2003, FDA issued a regulation requiring manufacturers to list trans fatty acids, or trans fat, on the

Nutrition Facts panel of foods and some dietary supplements. With this rule, consumers have more information to make healthier food choices that could lower their consumption of trans fat as part of a heart-healthy diet. Scientific reports have confirmed the relationship between trans fat and an increased risk of coronary heart disease. Food manufacturers have until Jan. 1, 2006, to list trans fat on the nutrition label. FDA estimates that by three years after that date, trans fat labeling will have prevented from 600 to 1,200 cases of coronary heart disease and 250 to 500 deaths each year.[11]

What are the polyunsaturated oils commercially processed in the U.S. containing trans fatty acids? Soy, corn, cottonseed, and safflower are the most common. 90% of all margarines in the U.S. today are made from soy oil, and loaded with trans fatty acids. These are the very fats that CSPI promoted as a replacement for saturated fats back in the 1980s. As Dr. Mary Enig writes:

> The whitewash of trans fatty acids began in 1987 with an article by Elaine Blume, published in CSPI's Nutrition Action newsletter. Wrote Blume: "From margarine to Tater Tots, partially hydrogenated vegetable oils play a major role in our food supply. . . . In fact, hydrogenated oils don't post a dire threat to health. . . . Improving on Nature. . . . Manufacturers hydrogenate. . . these vegetable oils so they won't become rancid while they sit on shelves, or during frying. . . . it seems unlikely that hydrogenation contributes much to our burden of heart disease. . . The fact that hydrogenated oils appear to be relatively benign is cause for thanks, because these fats are everywhere."

> In 1988, CSPI published a booklet called Saturated Fat Attack, which defended trans fatty acids and partially hydrogenated vegetable oils and called for pejorative labeling of "saturated" fats. The booklet contained a section called "Biochemistry 101," which claimed that only tropical oils were dangerous when hydrogenated. "Hydrogenated (or partially hydrogenated) fats are widely used in foods and cause untold consternation among consumers. . . [they] start out as plain old liquid vegetable oils (usually soybean), which are then reacted with hydrogen. . . converting much of the

polyunsaturated fatty acids to monounsaturated fatty acids. . . [with]. . . small amounts. . . converted to saturated fatty acids. . . [e.g.], stearic acid, which seems to have no effect on blood cholesterol levels.

"Overall, hydrogenated fats don't pose a significant risk. . . exceptions are hydrogenated [tropical oils, which are made]. . . even worse after hydrogenation."

Obviously, the individuals writing the booklet were completely ignorant (or pretended to be ignorant) of lipid science. Modern hydrogenation methods create trans fatty acids rather than monounsaturated fatty acids, and very few saturated fatty acids. By 1988, the adverse effects of trans fats were well known. The article points out that stearic acid has no effect on blood cholesterol levels, yet CSPI continued to accuse beef tallow, which is rich in stearic acid, of "raising cholesterol and increasing the risk of heart disease." As for the tropical oils, they do not need to be hydrogenated![12]

By 1990 the dangers of trans fats from hydrogenated vegetable oils was so well documented, that CSPI had to completely change their position. As Dr. Enig writes:

The revisionism began in December 1992 when Ms. Liebman wrote: "We've been crying 'foul' for some time now, as the margarine industry has tried to convince people that eating margarine was as good for their hearts as aerobic exercise. . . . And we warned folks several years ago that trans fatty acids could be a problem. . . . That's especially true now that we know that trans fatty acids are harmful, but we don't know how much trans are in different foods." Of course, CSPI had issued no such warning, but had been defending trans fats for more than five years. And there's no apology for falsely demonizing traditional fats. "Don't switch back from margarine to butter," wrote Ms. Liebman, ". . . try diet or whipped margarine. . . use a liquid margarine."[13]

The Benefits of Saturated Fats

Most of the fats in the diet of our forefathers were saturated fats. This is also true of many traditional cultures. Tropical diets, for example, get much of their fats from coconuts and palm oil, which are rich in saturated fats. As we have seen with our experience in the Philippines, these traditional cultures have not had the obesity and health problems that we are seeing today in our culture, even though they had a diet high in saturated fats.

> At 2 years of age, my daughter was screaming, grunting and pointing and grunting for most things. She had a very small vocabulary (despite us trying to teach her words for things). We discovered that a cousin of hers has NIDS and started researching to find out if our daughter might have NIDS as well. NIDS is NeuroImmune Dysfunction Syndrome. Basically it says there is a virus attacking the brain that causes Autism, ADD, ADHD and CFS and the whole range in-between (including apraxia). Her son was put on a ton of pills in order to help him (antivirals, antibacterials, antifungals and others). Since coconut oil is a known NATURAL antiviral, antibacterial and antifungal, I figured it could not hurt to try it. So I immediately replaced all our cooking oils with coconut oil. I also gave her a supplement of coconut oil (1-2 teaspoons a day).
>
> While I have no scientific proof that coconut oil helped my daughter, within days she was speaking more words. She was also trying harder to communicate. She is now 2 1/2 and speaking 3-4 word sentences! Her speech is still a little delayed (she has difficulty forming the words—I believe she has always had apraxia, but there has been no official diagnosis), and she is sometimes a little difficult to understand (not able to pronounce clearly). But she no longer grunts and points at objects. She even tells me "I love you Mommy." I will continue to give my daughter coconut oil because I truly feel that it is helping her. **Paula** - Colorado Springs, CO

One reason saturated fats have a long history of use in traditional cultures is that they are very stable fats that do not easily oxidize (turn rancid). Virgin Coconut Oil, for example, will not go rancid even at room temperatures in the tropics for a couple of years. Conversely, the refined oils that many Americans use are very unstable and turn rancid (oxidize) quickly. Oxidized oils are very toxic to the body and they can cause wide spread free-radical damage.

In addition to their shelf stability, saturated fats have many important role's in the body's chemistry. For example:

- Saturated fatty acids constitute at least 50 percent of cell membranes. They give our cells necessary firmness and integrity.
- They play a vital role in the health of our bones. For example, at least 50 percent of our dietary fats need to be saturated for calcium to be effectively incorporated into the skeletal structure.[14]
- They lower Lp(a), a substance in the blood that indicates proneness to heart disease.[15]
- They protect the liver from the toxic effects of alcohol and certain drugs.[16]
- They enhance the immune system.[17]
- They are needed for the proper utilization of essential fatty acids. Elongated omega-3 fatty acids are better retained in the tissues when the diet is rich in saturated fats.[18]
- Saturated 18-carbon stearic acid and 16-carbon palmitic acid are the preferred foods for the heart, which is why the fat around the heart muscle is highly saturated.[19] The heart draws on this reserve of fat in times of stress.
- Short- and medium-chain saturated fatty acids have important antimicrobial properties. They protect us against harmful microorganisms in the digestive tract.

When my baby boy, David, was 10 weeks old he had a yeast infection on his bottom. Instead of running to the doctor to get an expensive prescription, I first tried Virgin Coconut Oil (VCO). I was very new to using it, so I wasn't sure what to expect. I liberally applied coconut oil at each diaper change (about 6x/day) allowing it to soak in for a few minutes after each application. I was astounded that within 24 hours there was significant improvement. I continued to apply it, and within 3 days the yeast infection was completely gone. VCO is awesome!! I also used VCO on my baby's "acne" skin and cradle cap that was in his eyebrows. The baby acne took about 3 days to completely heal up. I put it on his eyebrows whenever I noticed they were flaky, and it would clear up in about 24 hours. Similarly, my 7 year old has had a flaky scalp since birth. I liberally applied coconut oil to his scalp one night before bed. The next morning (and for about 3 months now) his scalp is no longer flaky.

In general, our family has been much healthier since starting coconut oil only 3 months ago. I use coconut oil nearly exclusively for all cooking. I bake my own bread and add coconut oil to get as much as we can into our diet as well as using it for frying and using it when a recipe calls for oil or butter. When there's a virus bug going through our family, you can hardly tell because all we have is maybe 1 or 2 days of slight sniffles. With 4 boys age 7 and under that's a great health benefit. **Vanessa** - Gilbert, IA

Chapter 4

How Virgin Coconut Oil has Changed People's Lives

The dehusking of fresh coconuts shortly after harvest.

Testimonies

When we started exporting Virgin Coconut Oil into the U.S., we never dreamed we would see the response and the kinds of healing testimonies that have come in to us over the past few years. Each day now brings us health care practitioners who have been drawn to the Virgin Coconut Oil by the testimonies of their clients and other health care practitioners who have started using Virgin Coconut Oil as part of their healing regimen. Many of them are published in this book. Here are a few more.

I work in the hospital as a Medical Technologist. Our emergency room always gives everyone a prophylactic dose of Ciprofloxacin whenever we process a patient with bacterial meningitis. One of our lab techs had a nasty reaction to the Cipro. She kept getting tired, suffered from chronic insomnia after taking the Cipro for the 1st time. Her liver enzymes went off the scale—almost too high to read. She stayed this way for almost six months until I started her on the Virgin Coconut Oil (VCO). Her tiredness disappeared over night. The insomnia cleared up a little later. At one point, she started to get very ill from taking the VCO. Severe nausea and diarrhea. I had a feeling that it was probably a cleansing reaction, and that the liver was finally dumping the poison from the Cipro. I had her cut back from 4 TBSP per day to 1 TBSP per day. That stopped the discomfort. We ran another set of liver enzyme tests. For the very first time in six months, the results were back to normal. She is now back to 4 TBSP a day without a reaction, with more energy than she has ever had before. We are strong advocates of Virgin Coconut Oil. I use it in everything. **Bob** M.T. (Coconutdiet Forums)

In my practice I have had a few clients who have had detox symptoms after the very first time they used the Virgin Coconut Oil. Although most are able to use it by the tablespoon from the start, I have learned to start very ill and/or sensitive people with a teaspoon or less and work up from there. I have not had anyone so far that wasn't able to tolerate the 4 tablespoons per day, if they work up to it. Die-off symptoms are a very real phenomenon with any effective therapy for yeast, virus, and bacteria. Even my people who have known histories of gallbladder and/ or liver problems tolerate it very well. **Marie** – Nutritionist, Rogersville, MO

Being a massage therapist, I got interested in the effect of oils on people's skin—not to mention my own—and was swept away by the information on coconut oil. I've now switched to the Tropical Traditions Virgin Coconut Oil in my practice here in Los Angeles. In addition I consume at least 4 tablespoons per day, apart from the oil I get from cooking. I've thrown out all other oils except for the really good olive oil I get from San Francisco. I live in such a polluted city I figure the more free radical damage I can avoid the better. Why ingest it through food when we breathe it here every day?!!! **John** - Los Angeles, CA

Virgin Coconut Oil and Viruses

The antiviral, antibacterial, and antifungal properties of the medium chain fatty acids/triglycerides (MCTs) found in coconut oil have been known to researchers since the 1960s. Research has shown that microorganisms that are inactivated include bacteria, yeast, fungi, and enveloped viruses. Much of this research is highlighted in the writings of Dr. Mary Enig Ph.D, and can be found at www.coconutoil.com.

> I haven't had a cold in over 5 years. Just when I feel as though I'm coming down with something, the scratchy, sore throat symptoms.... they're gone the next morning! I also used to get these little blisters on the bottom of my right foot. Someone told me they are some sort of herpes virus. Since using the Virgin Coconut Oil I don't get these annoying little things. Usually they would surface in the summer or when the weather turned warm. But I realized this fall that I hadn't been bothered this past summer. I believe that the coconut oil really helps ward off the virus. I also have hepatitis C and my viral counts are so low that they are almost in the undetected category. I don't even worry about this anymore. **Nancy** (Coconut Diet Forums)

There is growing consensus that man-made antibiotics produced by pharmaceutical companies are over-used today, creating a whole new host of problems for modern societies. Michael Murray N.D. and Joseph Pizzorno N.D. write:

> There is little argument that, when used appropriately, antibiotics save lives. However, there is also little argument that antibiotics are seriously overused. While the appropriate use of antibiotics makes good medical sense, using them for such conditions as acne, recurrent bladder infections, chronic ear infections, chronic sinusitis, chronic bronchitis, and nonbacterial sore throats does not. The antibiotics rarely provide benefit, and these conditions can be effectively treated with natural measures. The widespread use and abuse of antibiotics is becoming increasingly alarming, not only because of the chronic Candidiasis epidemic, but also due to the development of "superbugs" that are resistant to currently available antibiotics. According to many experts, such as the World Health Organization, we are coming dangerously close to arriving at a "postantibiotic era," in which many infectious diseases will once again become almost impossible to treat.[1]

(For more info see Chapter 8 on Candida)

Even if you are not taking antibiotics from your doctor, there is a good chance that you are getting plenty of pharmaceuticals through the foods you eat. There are just as many (if not more) antibiotics sold and given to animals for meat production in the U.S., as there are for human medicine. You say you're vegetarian? Pesticides used on crops today can also cause mutations in micro-organisms similar to antibiotics. Pharmaceutical companies today produce many of the seeds used in agriculture, and they have pesticides manufactured right into them via genetic modification. Ronnie Cummins of the Campaign for Food Safety states:

> When gene engineers splice a foreign gene into a plant or microbe, they often link it to another gene, called an antibiotic resistance marker gene (ARM), that helps determine if the first gene was successfully spliced into the host organism. Some researchers warn that these ARM genes might unexpectedly recombine with disease-causing bacteria or microbes in the environment or in the guts of animals or people who eat GE food, contributing to the growing public health danger of antibiotic resistance—of infections that cannot be cured with traditional antibiotics (for example: new strains of salmonella, e-coli, campylobacter, and enterococci). EU (European Union) authorities are currently considering a ban on all GE foods containing antibiotic resistant marker genes.....Gene-splicing will inevitably result in unanticipated outcomes and dangerous surprises that damage plants and the environment. Researchers conducting experiments at Michigan State University several years ago found that genetically-altering plants to resist viruses can cause the viruses to mutate into new, more virulent forms. Scientists in Oregon found that a genetically engineered soil microorganism, Klebsiella planticola, completely killed essential soil nutrients. Environmental Protection Agency whistle blowers issued similar warnings in 1997, protesting government approval of a GE soil bacteria called Rhizobium melitoli.[2]

Instead of relying on man-made pharmaceuticals for everything, many are now turning to natural methods to boost the body's immune system and resist harmful viruses and micro-organisms naturally. Coconut oil is truly one of nature's best "germ fighters."

> I, too, have had major improvement with cold and sinus symptoms. I used to chronically get bronchitis at least three times a year. Already this year, I have had two bouts of cold symptoms, and increased the amount [of Virgin Coconut Oil] to nearly six tbsp a day thus averting the yucky sickies. I must say that I am truly impressed with this stuff.

I have also seen major improvement my complexion, i.e. blackheads and breakouts. I use it directly on my face twice a day and my skin keeps looking better and better. Cheers to Virgin Coconut Oil!!! **Laurie** (Coconut Diet Forums)

I have Hepatitis C. I was informed some time ago that coconut oil can be a healing agent for this potentially fatal disease. I had undergone the medical treatment with interferon with no success. I was only real sick from the interferon treatment, lost my hair, and became severely anemic. That was about six years ago. In the last four years I began nutritional regimens noted to help/heal Hepatitis C. That includes flax seed oil, milk thistle, multi-vitamins, and, in the last two years, coconut oil. My viral load was initially at five million—high! In the last three years it has gone from that to 1/20th of a million—low! My doctor is amazed. I feel better, with more energy. And most importantly, I now have the belief I can watch my grand-children grow up. I believe that the coconut oil was a major ingredient that boosted this healing. It is also yummy! **Gay** (Coconut Diet Forums)

Lauric Acid

Lauric acid is the most predominant MCT found in coconut oil. Regarding lauric acid, Mary Enig Ph.D writes:

> Lauric acid is a medium chain fatty acid, which has the additional beneficial function of being formed into monolaurin in the human or animal body. Monolaurin is the antiviral, antibacterial, and antiprotozoal monoglyceride used by the human or animal to destroy lipid-coated viruses such as HIV, herpes, cytomegalovirus, influenza, various pathogenic bacteria, including listeria monocytogenes and helicobacter pylori, and protozoa such as giardia lamblia. Some studies have also shown some antimicrobial effects of the free lauric acid.[3]

Lauric acid is also prominent in the saturated fat of human breast milk, giving vital immune-building properties to a child's first stage of life. Outside of human breast milk, nature's most abundant source of lauric acid is coconut oil.

> Just a testimonial: I learned about the purported benefits of coconut oil and lauric acid last summer on the Internet. I began taking it because I had, as it turned out, been misdiagnosed, with Herpes 2. My father is a biochemist who taught medical school and graduate school for

51

thirty-five years before retiring. So before I began taking it, I ran some literature by him. He was impressed. So I have been taking it ever since, but my family hasn't. This October, I received a call from my eldest daughter who is in college. She had been diagnosed the day before (by blood tests) that she had mononucleosis. I checked to see if the virus (Epstein-Barr) was lipid-enveloped, and found that it was. I got on the Internet and found her some [monolaurin] pills and had them overnighted to her. She received them on a Wednesday and began taking the prescribed dose daily. Nine days later—a Friday—she called to tell me she was well. Subsequent blood work the following week confirmed that she was. Her other classmates who had gotten mono and had not taken monolaurin, remained sick for weeks and some were not even well by the end of the semester. I told my dad and he was impressed again. It seems like coconut oil should be the prescribed regimen for mono. **David**, Attorney, Memphis TN

From 1999 to 2000 a study was done at San Lazaro hospital in Manila by Conrado S. Dayrit, MD, on the effect of coconut oil and monolaurin on the viral load of HIV patients. It was found that lauric acid did bring down the viral load of HIV patients. You can read the results of his study online at www.coconutoil.com. Dr. Dayrit is now conducting similar studies on the SARS virus, since the coconut-oil-consuming Philippines population was relatively unaffected by the recent SARS outbreak in China and other countries.

My roommate has been a herpes carrier for years—not the genital herpes, but my understanding is that all cases of herpes are viral, and that is the important common denominator. Virgin Coconut Oil is an anti-viral and breaks down what is called the "lipid envelope" surrounding the herpes cell. She initially got herpes in her eye many years ago, and it was basically dormant for several years after getting the initial episode under control. About 20 years later, it became re-activated when she acquired another herpes infection doing post mortem care on a patient in the hospital. The patient did not have a known diagnosis of herpes, but my roommate remembers cutting her finger on a piece of metal on the bed frame while giving this care. Perhaps the virus had been dormant for years on the bed. (If that is the case, and we will never know, so much for hospital cleanliness!) This time the herpes affected her spine, and she had a long bout of it, with much pain and suffering. This one was harder to get under control, and she had a few minor flare-ups. Since beginning VCO, she has not had so much as a cold sore. Only time will tell for sure, but so far it's looking good, and she is getting other very positive results from the oil. **Debby, R.N.** (Coconut Diet Forums)

HIV - AIDS

Can coconut oil reduce the viral load of HIV-AIDS patients? "Initial trials have confirmed that coconut oil does have an anti-viral effect and can beneficially reduce the viral load of HIV patients," University of the Philippines Emeritus professor of pharmacology, Dr. Conrado S. Dayrit said.[4]

A minimum of 50 ml of coconut oil would contain 20 to 25 grams of lauric acid, which indicates that the oil is metabolized in the body to release monolaurin, which is an antibiotic and an anti-viral agent. "Among the saturated fatty acids, lauric acid has the maximum anti-viral activity," Dr. Dayrit said. Based on this research, the first clinical trial using monolaurin as monotherapy on some of the HIV patients was conducted in 1999-2000. Dr. Dayrit's conclusions after the study: "This initial trial confirmed the anecdotal reports that coconut oil does have an anti-viral effect and can beneficially reduce the viral load of HIV patients. The positive anti-viral action was seen not only with the monoglyceride of lauric acid but with coconut oil itself. This indicates that coconut oil is metabolized to monoglyceride forms of C-8, C-10, and C-12 to which it must owe its anti-pathogenic activity."[5]

The entire results of Dr. Dayrit's study can be read at www.coconutoil. com.

On July 19, 1995, Dr. Mary Enig was quoted in an article published in The HINDU, India's National Newspaper as stating that coconut oil is converted by the body into "monolaurin" a fatty acid with anti-viral properties that might be useful in the treatment of AIDS. The staff reporter for The HINDU wrote about Enig's presentation at a press conference in Kochi and wrote the following:

"There was an instance in the U.S. in which an infant tested HIV positive had become HIV negative. That it was fed with an infant formula with a high coconut oil content gains significance in this context and at present an effort was on to find out how the 'viral load' of an HIV-infected baby came down when fed a diet that helped in the generation of Monolaurin in the body."

The reporter commented on Enig's observations that "monolaurin helped in inactivating other viruses such as measles, herpes, vesicular stomatitis and Cytomegalovirus (CMV) and that research undertaken so far on coconut oil also indicated that it offered a certain measure of protection against cancer-inducing substances."

Enig stated, in an article published in the Indian Coconut Journal, Sept. 1995, that monolaurin, of which the precursor is lauric acid, disrupted the lipid membranes of envelope viruses and also inactivated bacteria, yeast and fungi. She wrote: "Of the saturated fatty acids, lauric acid has greater anti-viral activity than either caprylic acid (C-10) or myristic acid (C-14). The action attributed to monolaurin is that of solubilizing the lipids ..in the envelope of the virus causing the disintegration of the virus envelope."

> Being HIV positive myself, and having things very under control, there are a couple of concerns I have and questions. The Virgin Coconut Oil? Absolutely amazing stuff! It has given me back the energy and good feeling that the antivirals can knock out of you. **Bill** *from The Coconut Diet Forums in answer to someone else's request for information on coconut oil and AIDS.*

Dr. Mary Enig has also written a book entitled *Nutrients and Foods in AIDS*, and one of the chapters is published on her website at www.lauric.org

In a July 1997 newsletter entitled "Keep Hope Alive" by Mark Konlee, an interview with Chris Dafoe was recorded. Chris Dafoe of Cloverdale, IN, thought the end was near in September, 1996, based on his lab numbers. His HIV viral load was over 600,000, CD4 count was 10 and CD8 was 300. He prepaid his funeral and decided to take his last vacation in the jungles of South America with an Indian tribe in the Republic of Surinam. Around October 14, 1996, he began eating daily a dish of cooked coconut which was prepared by the local Indians. By December 27th, 1996, a mere two and a half months later, his viral load was at non-detectable levels and he had gained 32 lbs and was feeling great. He had some other people he knew with HIV try using coconuts in their diet, and they experienced the same results. The entire interview can be read at www.coconutoil.com.

A woman named Betty buys Tropical Traditions Virgin Coconut Oil and uses it in her ministry to the sick. She shares the following story of her friend with HIV, who wishes to remain anonymous:

> My friend B... is an HIV patient. He was dying in the hospital for three years and his body was covered with acne. There was also one dollar-

sized boil on his left hip. When I got my first order of Virgin Coconut Oil, I gave him a quart of the oil to try. The result was amazing! After my friend took it for less than 2 weeks, the acne disappeared. The big boil on his hip started to heal and at this time is completely gone. After more than a month on coconut oil, his skin is now baby silk. You would think he is a different person. His recent blood test showed great improvement. The helper cells (T- cells) which were at level 60 are now at a higher level of 608 after about one and a half months of taking the oil consistently. He is taking the minimum amount of 3.5 tablespoons per day. The viral load is now down to 50. That was almost on the 100 level before he used the oil. My friend is not completely healed yet, but he has come a long way from where he was before because of this amazing oil. I will keep on introducing this amazing oil to my friends!

Nicola from South Africa writes:

I was diagnosed Hiv+ six months ago. I started using VCO (3 tablespoons, three times a day) two months ago. The viral load went down from 15,500 to 6,000. CD4 count went up from 615 to 705. I am obviously very excited about these results. **Nicola - South Africa**, reported on The Coconut Diet Forums

Virgin Coconut Oil and Diabetes

Indeed VCNO has a substantial effect on blood sugar levels. My wife and daughter (both have type-2 diabetes) measure their blood sugar levels at least three times a day. When they eat the wrong foods and their blood sugar levels get to 80-100 points above normal, they don't take extra medication; they take 2-3 tablespoons of the coconut oil directly from the bottle. Within a half hour their blood sugar levels will come back to normal. **Ed** (Coconut Diet Forums**)**

Ed's report is not unique at all. We have received many reports of people finding help with diabetes by using coconut oil, especially when they replace polyunsaturated vegetable oils in their diet with Virgin Coconut Oil. For some, the coconut oil seems to have a direct effect on blood sugar levels as Ed has reported here. For others, the comment has been a reducing of cravings for foods that tend to raise blood sugar levels. Consider Dr. Mark Andrew's testimony:

As a physician of many diabetics, I am constantly telling them how to eat more healthily but was unable to follow my own advice. I knew WHAT to do, but feeling like I had the wherewithal to practice what I preached was a different matter! I knew my patients didn't take my advice seriously enough, since I wasn't treating my own body right and was clinically "morbidly obese". My hunger and cravings have been my downfall for years, leading me to donuts, cookies and other unhealthy foods I knew to stay away from. I was constantly hungry. When I heard that adding [healthy] oils like Tropical Traditions Virgin Coconut Oil could help satisfy my run-away hunger and cravings, I was skeptical. I knew if it could help even ME, then there would be something to the claims! No one was more surprised than me when I felt satisfied for hours after spreading some on my morning toast, or enjoying a tablespoon in my oatmeal. My wife loves to make our family sugar-free chocolate balls using this wonderful oil, and I am still amazed that something so delicious is actually good for me! I have more energy, have been able to exercise for longer periods of time, and have now lost 36 pounds! **Mark** -an M.D. in New Mexico.

Coconut oil's ability to control hunger and cravings is well documented. Coconut oil's medium chain fatty acids promote thermogenesis and lead to increased metabolic rates. For more info, see Chapter 5 on weight loss.

The Virgin Coconut Oil (VCO) also is helping with my diabetes. I have Type-1 juvenile diabetes & take insulin. I've had ups and downs with my control through the years and I've ALWAYS struggled with cravings for sweets and carbohydrates. The VCO has helped with my control (I've noticed more stability) and it has alleviated some cravings. It has not completely alleviated cravings, but I've have noticed a decrease. People with diabetes often crave high-glycemic foods (that we should stay away from!) due to cravings caused by blood sugar swings. The VCO has helped a lot in this area! I'd recommend it to anyone with diabetes. Diabetes can cause low moods and low energy levels, and I've noticed a positive increase / lift in both. **Megan** (Coconut Diet Forums)

Population studies of societies that consume much of their calories from the saturated fats of coconut oil show that diabetes is very rare. A study done in India in 1998, which was referenced earlier in this book, showed that when Indians abandoned traditional fats like ghee and coconut oil, and started using polyunsaturated fats like sunflower or safflower oils, that the rates of diabetes became alarmingly high.[6] Studies carried out in many South Pacific Island countries have revealed the same thing: when the traditional diet, high in coconut oil, is abandoned in favor of more modern foods that are highly processed, including polyunsaturated vegetable oils, there is a direct increase in the rate of diabetes and other western diseases.

I also wanted to pass along a bit of my experience in regard to diabetes. I have been taking Coconut Oil (CO) since about the end of February of this year. I first started cooking with it and replacing the vegetable oils in my home. Then I started taking it by the spoon as well. I was taking about 2 tablespoons daily around the first of March. I was diagnosed as Type-2 diabetic in July of 2001 and immediately put on Amaryl (one in morning and one half in the evening.) I have been looking for a way to reverse this condition since I was diagnosed. I have found a world of info out there on various supplements and diet, BUT not from my doctor who just said, "Welcome to the club," and told me to take my meds. (I was crying and he seemed happy!) The bottom line is this: I have been able to slowly remove myself from the RX and now control my blood sugar by diet, supplements, and with CO! Cool, huh? I do still check my blood sugar levels once or twice daily... and they are as good as and usually BETTER than when I was on the Amaryl RX! And I have been off the RX since the end of March of 2003. I was taking several supplements for a year or so before CO but still had to take the RX. It wasn't until I removed most of the vegetable oils (all of them at home and careful when out to eat) and added the CO that I noticed I was beginning to crash while on the RX at different times during the day... so I would cut down on the RX and still maintain good blood sugar levels. Gradually I was NOT taking the RX anymore!!! (I cook with it and take about 4 Tbs daily) I still take my supplements also and I have never tested if the coconut oil alone would control my blood sugar levels but would be interested to hear if anyone out there has. Hope this may help someone and God Bless all. **Sharon** (Coconut Diet Forums**)**

I've been diagnosed as Type-2 diabetes and have been struggling with a wildly fluctuating blood sugar level for two years. I've used diet, exercise, herbs and vitamins in my attempts to stabilize my levels, with limited success. My MD wanted to put me on prescription meds, but I resisted based on reports I'd read about the long-term side effects of those drugs. One day reading the Mercola newsletter, I ran across an article where Dr. Mercola mentioned that Coconut Oil was used to regulate blood sugar levels, and mentioned your brand as being the best. So on November 7, 2003, I ordered 2 quarts of the Virgin Coconut Oil. I began taking one tablespoon a day at dinner. My yearly blood test was done on January 2, 2004. When I saw my MD on January 13, 2004, he was pleased to see that my blood sugar levels were now in the normal range, and told me that they'd been that way for a few months. I was ecstatic! I've been using Tropical Traditions Coconut oil since, and my blood sugars have stayed in the normal range ever since. Thank you so much for making such a wonderful, healthy food source available to us! **Beth** - Albany, NY

My husband is Type 2 diabetic and we believe the use coconut oil has greatly helped in his control of blood glucose. With a very low carbohydrate diet, and cooking only with coconut oil he has been able to reduce his prescription drugs to the very lowest amount. Hopefully he will be able to eliminate them all together and control his diabetes with just diet. **Suzan** (Coconut Diet Forums)

Chronic Fatigue Syndrome and Fibromyalgia

I had this chronic fatigue problem for the last 2 years or so. I tried taking a lot of medication, but nothing really helped! Finally I started taking 3 tbsp Virgin Coconut Oil a day and praise God I felt my energy level renewed and refreshed within a week! Now it's more than a month and I don't feel tired and run down anymore, as I take 3 tbsp of Coconut oil a day, and no other medication of any sort. I thank God for this wonder-working oil. Now I tell everyone I meet about the positive effects of Coconut oil to our body and ask them to visit this site! ...I'm sure Coconut oil will help you too! God Bless you, **Juliyana** (Coconut Diet Forums)

I CAN say that coconut oil really truly helps with my pain with my fibromyalgia and thyroid problems and gives me more energy. I feel so much better!! **Amy** (Coconut Diet Forums)

There are a number of alternative doctors who believe chronic fatigue syndrome (CFS) and fibromyalgia are really a thyroid disorder. I tend to think there is something to this since I have hypothyroidism and there was a time when my thyroid replacement was too low and I developed many of the classic symptoms of fibromyalgia. When this happened I refused to accept this lame excuse for an explanation, and did some research. I came upon some articles by Dr. Lowe in Colorado, which made me decide to start raising my thyroid medication. Amazingly, within a month my symptoms really improved and I no longer think CFS and fibromyalgia are real diseases but the manifestations of thyroid disease or some type of metabolic problem tied to thyroid function. I don't have these symptoms anymore. Fibromyalgia and CFS were not heard of much until the development of the TSH test and the overall use of Synthroid or other T4-only treatments. Prior to that, people with these symptoms were treated with Armour thyroid, and the dose was adjusted up until symptoms were relieved.

Since the TSH test was implemented for detecting thyroid disease and for adjusting the dose, thyroid replacement doses have dropped to 1/3 of what they were for about 73 years prior to that. I suspect that this is why thyroid treatment has not been very effective for CFS and fibromyalgia patients. The doses are too low to affect any improvement and may result in suppression of the pituitary, leading to the person becoming even more hypothyroid as their own thyroids are not stimulated by the pituitary to keep up their own production to complement the additional replacement. Typical thyroid doses prior to the 1970s were between 3 and 9 grains of Armour a day. Today, they range between 1 and 2 grains.

Performing the Barnes basal body temperature test or keeping a record of your daily temperatures (taken 3 times a day every 3 hours starting in the morning) will tell you whether your metabolic rate is too low. There are other causes of low metabolic rate, but by far thyroid is the most common. Also, if you have high cholesterol, that is another very strong indication of low thyroid function. We are awash, today, in thyroid inhibitors—one of which is trans fatty acids.

Leaky gut can definitely play a role in fatigue and many disorders. Research on celiacs (people with wheat allergy) has shown that they have a high rate of development of thyroid disease. People with leaky gut are at greatly increased risk of developing auto-immune disorders such as thyroid disease, Lupus, and arthritis. People who are hypothyroid get leaky gut because they cannot rebuild the intestinal tract lining at a fast enough rate to keep its integrity.

Hypothyroid people and those with adrenal hypofunction can develop many allergies. It is the adrenals that play a major role in immune response and regulation of immune function, keeping it in a narrow range where it kills the bad things but doesn't attack the host. In hypothyroidism, adrenal function is greatly reduced or they may overproduce trying to replace the lacking thyroid function and increase available T3. So, multiple allergy development is a classic symptom of hypothyroidism. This is what happened to me before my diagnosis. Since beginning treatment a year and nine months ago, I have lost all but two allergies, wheat being the main one that I will probably never loose.

There is also some other research and anecdotal evidence that CFS and fibromyalgia seems to happen to people who have had major trauma such as childhood abuse. It is thought that this type of thing affects the pituitary/hypothalamus area of the brain interfering with proper function. Studies have found that these people have disturbed brain electrical function. Others have called it the "delayed stress effect" and say that trauma builds up in the brain as electrical disturbances and imbalances. Practicing meditation, prayer or some relaxation technique regularly is said to greatly help. Research is being done with EEG training to help these people. EEG trains the brain to balance itself electrically and to relax the body. Research with children raised in abusive situations has found that that they have up to double the output of adrenal stress hormones and tend to be in a heightened alert state all the time. When followed to adulthood, researchers have found that in adulthood they often develop low energy problems or other metabolic disorders. These types of people also do not respond well to thyroid hormone (thyroid hormone resistance). They have a suppressed metabolism, basically. Violent prison inmates from abusive childhood situations were found to have greatly reduced cortisol output. It can be speculated that some abused children later suffer adrenal burnout. Without sufficient adrenal hormones thyroid hormone can't work properly. Dr. David Derry found that traumatized people who develop hypothyroidism often need very high doses of thyroid medication to function normally.

Proper adrenal function is essential for proper thyroid function and blood sugar metabolism. Also, high levels of cortisol, an adrenal stress hormone, can damage pituitary function resulting in altered metabolic function.

I object to the CFS and fibromyalgia label because the doctor who uses it is saying that there is no cure and that you will be miserable all your life. I don't accept this hopeless statement. I think it is very cruel to tell a patient that there is no hope and to give up on them offering only palliative treatment. **Tish** (Coconut Diet Forums)

I too have had very painful Fibromyalgia for the past 15 years or so. I have been using the Virgin Coconut Oil now for two months and have no pain at all. No Pain!!!! And I have a lot more energy. And my skin has never looked so good. For me, I call it my Miracle VCO. I'm so glad it's working for you, too. **Danne** (Coconut Diet Forums)

Coconut Oil Increases Energy Levels

Researchers now know that the increased energy associated with eating coconut oil is related to the length of the fatty acid chains contained in coconut oil. As we have previously mentioned, coconut oil contains what are called medium chain fatty acids, or medium chain triglycerides (MCTs for short). These medium chain fatty acids are different from the common longer chain fatty acids found in other plant-based oils. Most vegetable oils are composed of longer chain fatty acids, or triglycerides (LCTs). LCTs are typically stored in the body as fat, while MCTs are burned for energy. MCTs burn up quickly in the body. Coconut oil is nature's richest source of MCTs that increase metabolic rates and lead to weight loss. MCTs promote what is called thermogenesis. Thermogenesis increases the body's metabolism, producing energy. People in the animal feed business have known this truth for quite some time. If you feed animals vegetable oils, they put on weight and produce more fatty meat. If you feed them coconut oil, they will be very lean.

There are many studies proving this concept of thermogenesis and MCTs in the scientific literature. In 1989 a study was done in the Department of Pediatrics, Vanderbilt University, at Nashville TN. Ten male volunteers (ages 22 to 44) were overfed (150% of estimated energy requirement) liquid formula diets containing 40% of fat as either MCT or LCT. Each patient was studied for one week on each diet in a double-blind, crossover design. The results: "Our results demonstrate that excess dietary energy as MCT stimulates thermogenesis to a greater degree than does excess energy as LCT. This increased energy expenditure, most likely due to lipogenesis in the liver, provides evidence that excess energy derived from MCT is stored with a lesser efficiency than is excess energy derived from dietary LCT."[7]

> Dear Tropical Traditions. For many of us (those over 40 years old and hypothyroid), losing weight is extremely difficult. My personal experience, after having researched possible solutions/diets, showed that I actually could speed up my metabolism. The coconut oil reputation for doing exactly that is continually proven true for me. In one month's time, I have lost 12 lbs. and honest to goodness am no longer lethargic. After years of struggling I am so appreciative. Respectfully, **Irene** - Lehigh Acres, FL

In another study recently conducted at the School of Dietetics and Human Nutrition, McGill University, Ste-Anne-de-Bellevue, Quebec, Canada, the effects of diets rich in medium-chain triglycerides (MCTs) or long-chain triglycerides (LCTs) on body composition, energy expenditure, substrate oxidation, subjective appetite, and ad libitum energy intake in overweight men was studied. Twenty-four healthy, overweight men with body mass indexes between 25 and 31 $kg/m(2)$ consumed diets rich in MCT or LCT for 28 days each in a crossover randomized controlled trial. Their conclusion: "Consumption of a diet rich in MCTs results in greater loss of AT compared with LCTs, perhaps due to increased energy expenditure and fat oxidation observed with MCT intake. Thus, MCTs may be considered as agents that aid in the prevention of obesity or potentially stimulate weight loss."[8]

Crohn's Disease, Irritable Bowel Syndrome, and Coconut Oil for Digestive Health

Many Americans suffer from some kind of digestive disorder that prevents them from properly digesting their food. Without a properly working digestive system, essential vitamins and minerals that are necessary to maintain proper health may not be absorbed adequately from the foods we eat, even if we are eating healthy foods.

Candida is one digestive disorder where the digestive tract is overloaded with yeast because of the lack of probiotics in our digestive system. You can read more about Candida in Chapter 8. Other digestive disorders common today would include disorders such as irritable bowel syndrome, ulcerative colitis, gastritis, diverticulosis and constipation. More severe digestive disorders would include Crohn's Disease, where many people have such a hard time digesting foods properly that they can become severely malnourished.

Whether or not you have a diagnosed digestive disorder, chances are that your digestive system needs some detoxifying and help! This is especially true the older we get. It is reported that about 95 million Americans suffer from some kind of digestive disorder. Americans spend more than $100 billion dollars annually on digestive health care! This is over three times as much as is spent annually on weight loss (about $33 billion dollars). Adding coconut oil to your diet can help overcome these problems that affect our health.

> I've been using coconut oil about a month now, 2 tsp. per day. Mix it in anything possible or just throw it on top of pizza slices. I have IBS and am a compulsive overeater. Within a short time of taking it, I realized I was no longer wanting food. In the past month I have lost 5 lbs. and just as many inches. Instead of being a computer potato, I am up and about, doing things… I just have so much more energy. The biggest change is the IBS. Instead of the runs now, I almost need laxatives. *laughing* It's been since my early 20's that I've felt this way....I'm 42 now. Coconut oil is fantastic!!! **Net B.** (Coconut Diet Forums)

Digestive Disorders and Coconut Oil

Many people have reported great relief from digestive disorders such as Crohn's Disease and Irritable Bowel Syndrome after adding coconut oil into their diet. Pharmacist Joe Graedon and his wife Dr. Teresa

Graedon of The People's Pharmacy tell the following story about coconut macaroons:

> The coconut cookie craze started when we got a letter from Donald ... in Pittsfield, Massachusetts: "I have had Crohn's disease for forty years, and during that time I have had a never-ending battle with diarrhea. Lomotil helps some, but it doesn't eliminate the problem. Three months ago I bought a box of ... Coconut Macaroon cookies. I've been eating two a day and have not experienced diarrhea in that time. If by chance I eat three in a day, I get constipated. Believe me, I have a new life now. My brother-in-law has a friend who just had cancer and suffered diarrhea as a consequence of the operation. We told him about the cookies, and they corrected his diarrhea. I would be delighted if others were helped by my discovery too."
>
> We chuckled when Donald's letter arrived. Cookies for diarrhea, what a joke. Yet Crohn's is no laughing matter. Inflammatory bowel disease can be a life-and-death condition with surgery and removal of portions of the large intestine a not-uncommon complication. This disorder often leads to industrial-strength diarrhea. It is a persistent condition that can last for decades, if not a lifetime. We were rather skeptical that Donald's unorthodox approach would help anyone else... It seemed bizarre, but we could not resist sharing his experience with our readers. To our surprise, the letters started pouring in. One woman speculated that it might be the coconut that was working the magic. We started to hear from other people who tried the macaroons. One man wrote about his experience: "With chronic diarrhea due to Crohn's disease I will try anything for relief. I read about the person who controlled his diarrhea by eating two .... Coconut Macaroon cookies a day and decided to give it a try. Relief is imperfect and somewhat inconsistent, but I've had the problem for twenty-five years. There is substantial improvement, better than from any medicine I have taken."[9]

Coconut Oil and Intestinal Absorption

Macaroons are made up mainly of desiccated (dried) coconut, which is

60-70% fat (coconut oil). Coconut oil is one of nature's richest sources of medium chain triglycerides, or fatty acids (MCTs). These smaller chain fatty acids have been shown to absorb easier and quicker in the digestive tract than longer chain fatty acids found in other fats, like vegetable oils. In fact, studies are now showing that longer chain fatty acids found in polyunsaturated oils (soy, corn, and other vegetable oils) are the most harmful oils for those with intestinal problems like Crohn's disease, as they increase inflamation. A study done in the UK in 2003 reported:

> Enteral nutrition is effective in inducing remission in active Crohn's disease. Speculation on the underlying mechanism of action has moved away from the presentation of nitrogen and towards the fat content of the various enteral feeds. Evidence is accumulating that additional long-chain triglyceride in such feeds impairs the response rate in active Crohn's disease, whereas no deleterious effects of additional medium-chain triglyceride have been identified. It has been proposed that long-chain triglycerides composed from n-6 fatty acids may be the most harmful, since such fatty acids are substrates for inflammatory eicosanoid production.[10]

MCTs on the other hand, are not only more easily absorbed in the digestive tract, they apparently also help other nutrients become absorbed as well. A study done in Denmark in 1998 compared absorption of fat in patients who either had their colon removed or partially removed. The patients were fed a diet of either long-chain fatty acids (LCT) or medium chain fatty acids (MCTs) combined with 50% LCT. Their results showed that those fed LCT deposited most of the fat into the feces and were not absorbed in the bowel. The group fed the MCT diet not only absorbed the MCTs better, but the MCTs apparently helped them absorb the LCT as well: "MCT redoubled fat (MCT+LCT) absorption from 23% to 58% in patients with a colon, and increased overall bomb calorimetric energy absorption from 46% to 58%."[11]

This ability of MCTs to help other nutrients in absorption is also seen in a study done in Belgium in 2002. This study compared the absorption rate of vitamin E (alpha-tocopherol) in formulas with either exclusive LCTs or a 50/50 formula of MCT and LCT. The results showed that serum alpha-tocopherol remained the same in those given exclusively

LCT formulas, but doubled in those given the MCT/LCT formulas.[12] Therefore those suffering from digestive disorders such as Crohn's disease and IBS should see very positive results from consuming coconut oil rich in MCTs, not only for the health benefits of coconut oil itself, but because the fatty acids in coconut oil could help them absorb nutrients from other foods as well.

> For years I suffered from IBS or Crohn's disease. The suffering was not minor, I was in sheer misery most of the time. Often it occurred to me, "Other people have no idea how much pain I endure just to make it through the day." I am now well. I feel completely healed. I trace the beginning of my pain relief, and then recovery, to the day I believe I was divinely led to your coconut oil. Your coconut oil has the additional advantage of being delicious. I tried some other coconut oils that were supposedly excellent, but they did not compare to yours in "deliciosity". Thank you for your excellent product and also the graciousness of your staff, which has always been very helpful. Sincerely, **Doug** - Phoenix, Arizona

Chapter 5

Virgin Coconut Oil for Weight Loss

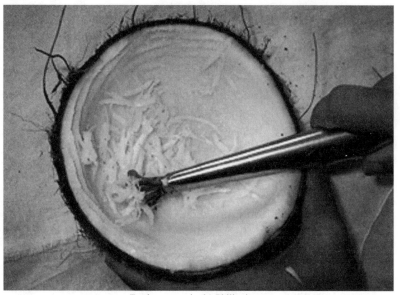

Fresh coconut in the Philippines.

I would like to say that I have been on Virgin Coconut Oil for the past two months (4 tablespoons daily) and feel better than I have in a long time! My energy levels are up and my weight is down. I am never hungry anymore, and have incorporated a daily exercise routine and have lost 20 pounds. **Paula** (Coconut Diet Forums)

The above quote is quite typical of what we are seeing from those who are switching to Virgin Coconut Oil (VCNO) in place of less healthy oils in their diet. Many people are reporting that consumption of VCNO is bringing about increased energy levels, fewer cravings for carbs and sweets, and a more satisfied feeling of being "full" after meals.

> Since beginning to use Tropical Traditions Virgin Coconut Oil, about eight months ago, I have: experienced a noticeable increase in my energy, ridden myself of cravings for carbs, cleared up my complexion (which has always been a problem), gotten the silkiest, most glorious hair from using it internally, AND lost 16 pounds. This oil does all that it promises, and more! **Sharon Elaine, author**

So how does Virgin Coconut Oil provide these weight loss benefits?

Low-fat Diets Don't Work

Before looking at the specific properties of coconut oil, it is helpful to understand that modern nutrition counsel has made a huge mistake in teaching that low-fat diets are healthy and lead to weight loss. For decades now we have been told to cut back on fat in our diet if we want to lose weight. Marketers of low-fat foods have championed this concept. So what has been the result? According to the U.S. Center for Disease Control:

> In 1999–2000, an estimated 30% of U.S adults aged 20 years and older — nearly 59 million people — were obese, defined as having a body mass index (BMI) of 30 or more.
>
> Source: National Health and Nutrition Examination Survey 1999–2000
>
> In 1999–2000, an estimated 64% of U.S adults aged 20 years and older were either overweight or obese, defined as having a body mass index (BMI) of 25 or more.
>
> Source: National Health and Nutrition Examination Survey 1999–2000

Health and Human Services Secretary Tommy G. Thompson states: "We've seen virtually a doubling in the number of obese persons over the past two decades and this has profound health implications. Obesity increases a person's risk for a number of serious conditions, including diabetes, heart disease, stroke, high blood pressure, and some types of cancer."[1]

Obviously, low-fat diets have not helped Americans lose weight, as today nearly two thirds of all adults in the U.S. are classified as overweight. We've been told for years that we should avoid fat as much as possible. Some people have been on a torturous low-fat regimen, trying to avoid all fat in their diet. Now we are learning about the dangers of low-fat diets. Certain fats are necessary and even healthy, but which ones?

> My name is Kelly, and I have been on a quest for health for several years now. At one time I was severely obese. I have since lost 140 pounds. I read about the health benefits of coconut oil over a year ago, and added the oil to my daily regimen. Within a week, I had more energy, and was feeling like a different person. I love Tropical Traditions Virgin Coconut Oil, it is the best I have tried, and I will continue to use this oil forever. The quality cannot be matched. **Kelly** - Lander, WY

Fats in History

Fats have always been a part of human nutrition. Rex Russell, M.D. writes: "It was 1944, and World War II was roaring. A young mother was wasting away with an infection diagnosed as tuberculosis. Antibiotics were unavailable. Her doctor prescribed (1) isolation, (2) bed rest, (3) exercise (eventually) and (4) a diet high in fat. Surprising, but true! High-fat diets were often recommended by the medical profession during those years. Before you scoff, you might want to know that this lady recovered. She is my mother, and she has stayed on this diet through the years. Presently she is enjoying her great-grandchildren"[2] So while the experts claimed "fats are good" prior to World War II, now we hear just the opposite.

So what actually constituted a "high-fat" diet back in the 1800s until the 1940s? Basically butter, eggs, nuts and animal fats such as lard and beef tallow. Margarines, which were introduced in the 1860s, were butter substitutes made with animal fats such as lard and tallow or the saturated fats from coconut oil and palm oils. These high-fat diets, considered then to be healthy, were rich in saturated fats, today seen by many as the worst possible fat one can consume. However, drastically reducing saturated fats from the modern diet has not solved any health problems, and statistics show that obesity rates are at an all-time high. The low-fat advice is losing credibility.

> I gained 80 lbs. with my first [baby] and 60 with my second (who I am still nursing). I was able to lose 50 of the first 80 pounds before

my second one was conceived. This means I started off my second pregnancy 30 pounds heavier. However, we are of a "quiver full" mindset and would not prevent another conception in order for me to lose weight. Since October (when I had my second daughter), I've been able to lose 61 pounds (praise God!). Coconut oil was (and is) a big part of my success. I use it for most of my cooking (occasionally I use Olive Oil and butter) and for body care. I feel like it helped my energy level. It also helped my with some bowel issues I was experiencing. **Holly** (Coconut Diet Forums)

Fats and oils are technically known as "lipids." If a lipid is liquid at room temperature, it is called an "oil." If it is solid, it is called a "fat." Fats can be found in many food sources in nature: animal meats (such as tallow and lard), marine animals (fish oil), vegetables and fruits (such as olives, avocados, coconuts, etc.), nuts and seeds/legumes (soybeans, sesame seeds, peanuts, cashews, grape seeds, etc.), and whole grains (wheat, rice, etc. – must contain the bran and all components to benefit from all the oils present). A diet rich in natural foods will be a naturally high-fat diet! It is virtually impossible to eliminate fats from our diet. And we wouldn't want to! Fats are an essential part of life. Without them, we could not survive.

Four vitamins—A. D, E, and K—are soluble in fat; fat carries fat-soluble vitamins. When fat is removed from a food, many of the fat-soluble compounds are also removed.

Fat also adds satiety to our meal—a feeling of having had enough to eat. Fat-free and low-fat foods are one of the reasons some people over-eat carbohydrates, which really packs on the pounds. They just don't feel like they've had enough to eat, even when the volume has been more than enough.

I have been taking a tablespoon of coconut oil three times daily with meals. Taking the oil with my meals seems to give me a "full feeling" a lot faster. My sweet tooth has practically vanished—and this is from someone who should have bought stock in Hershey's long ago! Ironically, facilitating weight loss was my main reason for trying the coconut oil diet, but with all the wonderful benefits I am experiencing, the weight loss aspect almost seems like an afterthought. About three days into the routine, I had an energy rush on a Saturday morning that kept me going until well after lunch. I can't believe how much I got done that day! My mental state of mind seemed to be much sharper. I was able to focus on the tasks at hand without getting sidetracked. I was not exhausted at the end of running my errands, which included traipsing around a huge mall. It seemed like I was practically running, rather than the leisurely walking that was formerly my habit. In addition to my energy level, my mood has been very stable—no up and down mood swings—even with the onset of PMS! My husband commented yesterday on how soft and silky my skin felt, and I have not used any lotion since I started taking the oil. **Theresa** (Coconut Diet Forums)

Fats for Animal Feeds

One interesting way to study the role of fats and their effect on weight loss or weight gain is to study the animal feed industry. If ever there was a group of people with economic interest in weight gain, it is the livestock industry.

Back in the days when fat was "in," the fatter the pig you could raise the better. Lard was a basic staple for cooking in the days of our forefathers. It was found that feeding pigs polyunsaturated fats (primarily soybean and corn oil) would put more fat on them. This is the reaction of the longer chain fatty acids found in vegetable oils, and is well documented in the scientific literature.

Today however, we've come full circle with our new low-fat mantra, and the consumer demand is now for low-fat meats. So how does one produce a leaner pork? Well according the Department of Animal Science of North Carolina State University, during the "finishing time" before slaughter, you stop feeding them polyunsaturated oils and start feeding them saturated fats.[3] They used beef tallow in their experiment, which they found was a bit hard for the pigs to digest. So some farmers are now actually starting to use coconut oil, a plant-based saturated fat, instead.

So what are the fats found on the shelves of grocery stores today, that make up the majority of the U.S. diet? Polyunsaturated fats: mostly soybean oil, which commonly is referred to as vegetable oil. These are the same fats that have been known to fatten livestock in the animal feed business. The saturated fats, which made up most of the fats in the diet of our forefathers, have been almost banned by modern nutrition advice. The result: lean pigs and obese people!!

Low-Carb Diets: Half the Story

Gary Taubes wrote a startling article in the New York Times in 2002 entitled "What If It Were All a Big Fat Lie!" In it he stated:

> The cause of obesity [is] precisely those refined carbohydrates at the base of the famous Food Guide Pyramid—the pasta, rice and bread—that we are told should be the staple of our healthy low-fat diet, and then add on the sugar or corn syrup in the soft drinks, fruit juices and sports drinks that we have taken to consuming in quantity, if for no other reason than that they are fat free and so appear intrinsically healthy. While the low-fat-is-good-health dogma represents reality as we have come to know it, and the government has spent hundreds of millions of dollars in research trying to prove its worth, the low-carbohydrate message has been relegated to the realm of unscientific fantasy.

> Over the past five years, however, there has been a subtle shift in the scientific consensus. It used to be that even considering the possibility of the alternative hypothesis, let alone researching it, was tantamount to quackery by association. Now a small but growing minority of establishment researchers have come to take seriously what the low-carb-diet doctors have been saying all along. Walter Willett, chairman of the department of nutrition at the Harvard School of Public Health, may be the most visible proponent of testing this heretic hypothesis. Willett is the de facto spokesman of the longest-running, most comprehensive diet and health studies ever performed, which have already cost upward of $100 million and include data on nearly 300,000 individuals. Those data, says Willett, clearly contradict the low-fat-is-good-health message and the idea that all fat is bad for you; the exclusive focus on adverse effects of fat may have contributed to the obesity epidemic.[4]

This started the current low-carb tidal wave because people generally have found that it is true: if you cut back on refined carbohydrates in your diet you will lose weight.

But while these new low-carb diets are now challenging the low-fat hypothesis, there still seems to be mass confusion as to which fats and oils are actually healthy, and which ones are not. And no wonder.

Probably no other food group has been politicized more in American nutrition than *fats*. With all the books and literature written on the subject, and each one practically contradicting each other, there is really only one book written by a lipid expert with no commercial ties to anyone in the edible oil industry. That book is *Know Your Fats: The Complete Primer for Understanding the Nutrition of Fats, Oils, and Cholesterol* by Dr. Mary Enig, a nutritionist/biochemist with her Ph.D. in Nutritional Sciences from the University of Maryland. Much of her work is featured in the Weston Price Foundation that studies traditional foods.

> I just had to tell you that your product has changed my life. For the past ten years I have been fighting hypothyroidism. I have gained over sixty pounds and it seems that lately my doctor is increasing the dosage of my thyroid medication nearly every month. After doing a lot of research, I first learned that it is probably up to me to cure myself, with a high protein - low carb diet. I started my new eating routine about three weeks ago and about a week later, after reading an article in Woman's World Magazine, I purchased a 32 ounce jar of Tropical Traditions Virgin Coconut Oil at a local nutrition store. I mix 2 tablespoons with a low-carb protein drink every morning and the energy I sustain throughout the day is amazing. I have also lost eleven pounds in three weeks and walking on my treadmill for thirty minutes every evening after work is almost effortless. Thank You for this wonderful product. **Cheryl** (Coconut Diet Forums)

Let's face it. The low-fat dietary dictum is a multi-billion dollar industry built upon a foundation of sinking sand. Not only does the scientific research show that the polyunsaturated vegetable oils promote weight gain, it also shows that they are not good as an animal feed either. While they do promote weight gain in livestock, they do so at the expense of another essential fatty acid: conjugated linoleic acid (CLA). CLA is found primarily in beef and dairy products, and cannot be produced in the human body. Research has shown that animals grazed strictly on grass, their natural diet, can have levels of CLA hundreds of times higher than animals raised on grain feeds. Also, in a study done by the Department of Animal Science at Southern Illinois University in 2003, it was found that beef finished off on soybean oil directly reduced the amount of CLA produced by ruminant animals.[5] What are the known benefits of CLA, now that we have almost lost it from our meat and dairy sources? Among its benefits are: it destroys cancer cells, it reduces tumors, and it promotes weight loss while increasing muscle growth.

So while many people are seeing weight loss on low-carb diets because they are cutting back on refined carbohydrates, many do not see weight loss because they are still lacking proper fats in their diet, and most of the popular low-carb diets are giving mixed messages about which fats are healthy and which ones are not. If you choose the wrong fat and consume large quantities of it, such as hydrogenated polyunsaturated fats full of *trans fatty acids*, not only will you not have much success in losing weight, you will probably develop a whole host of other health problems as well.

Flawed "Science"

When a dietary philosophy has been promoted as long as the current low-fat dogma has, and a multi-billion dollar industry feeds off it, we can expect it to die a slow death with much opposition, as America gets fatter and fatter because the popular media continues to propagate the low-fat myth. It is amazing to read new studies conducted that *start* with this myth as fact, and then construct their whole study to support it, never once questioning the "wisdom" behind this myth that is just accepted without question as fact.

In a study published by British Journal of Nutrition, entitled "Effects of including a ruminally protected lipid supplement in the diet on the fatty acid composition of beef muscle," the abstract begins like this: "Enhancing the polyunsaturated fatty acid (PUFA) and decreasing the saturated fatty acid content of beef is an important target in terms of improving the nutritional value of this food for the consumer." With this "truth" declared without any supporting evidence whatsoever, it goes on to show how one can increase the PUFA content of beef while decreasing the saturated fat content by feeding cows soybean, linseed and sunflower-seed oils.[6] And because this entire generation has been brainwashed into believing saturated fats are bad and polyunsaturated fats are good, this is seen as positive!

But wait, it gets even worse. Have you noticed all the news lately about the epidemic of obesity among children? A study was published in 2003 by the Journal of the American Diet Association entitled "Soy-enhanced lunch acceptance by preschoolers." The objective: "To evaluate acceptance of soy-enhanced compared with traditional menus by preschool children, soy-enhanced foods were substituted on a traditional cycle menu, and the amount eaten, energy, and nutrient values for traditional and soy-enhanced lunches were compared." The conclusion? "Soy-enhanced foods were successfully substituted for 23 traditional foods included in the cycle menus. Soy-enhanced foods tended to be higher in energy, protein, and iron. Traditional lunches tended to be higher in fat, saturated fat, and vitamin A." Therefore, "Preschool programs can substitute soy-enhanced for traditional foods, which will add variety to the diet without sacrificing taste, energy, or nutrient value."[7] Great! So since we start with the presupposition that saturated fats are bad and polyunsaturated fats are good, we can now design a study to "prove" we should be feeding preschoolers soy instead of "traditional foods." And people continue to ask why children are so overweight today… Other concerns about soy and children are not even addressed in this study, such as that large amounts of plant hormones (phyto-estrogens) in soy are equal to adult levels and could affect the endocrine system of children.

Traditional Fats are Best

So while we wait for the science to catch up with the truth, here is a better idea. Let's go back and eat the traditional fats our forefathers and other traditional societies have eaten for hundreds and even thousands of years, and were known to be healthy. These fats are rich in saturated fats, and include healthy, traditionally-raised meat, dairy, and eggs. In tropical climates these include coconut oil and palm oil. Coconut oil is unique in nature with medium chain fatty acids that are also found in human breast milk, and with research showing that it leads to greater metabolism and weight loss.

Researchers now know that weight loss associated with coconut oil is related to the length of the fatty acid chains contained in coconut oil. Coconut oil contains what are called medium chain fatty acids, or medium chain triglycerides (MCTs for short). As we have stated previously, these medium chain fatty acids are different from the common longer chain fatty acids found in other plant-based oils. Most vegetable oils are composed of longer chain fatty acids, or triglycerides (LCTs). LCTs are typically stored in the body as fat, while MCTs are burned for energy. MCTs burn up quickly in the body. Coconut oil is nature's richest source of MCTs that increase metabolic rates and lead to weight loss. MCTs promote thermogenesis. Thermogenesis increases the body's metabolism, producing energy. People in the animal feed business have known this truth for quite some time. If you feed animals vegetable oils, they put on weight and produce more fatty meat. If you feed them coconut oil, they will be very lean.

> Before I started taking Virgin Coconut Oil six months ago, I was very low on energy and fighting to lose weight from my last two pregnancies. I was having problems just keeping up with my kids. Now that I have started including coconut oil in my diet, I have lost twenty pounds, so far, and finally have more energy. I am so thankful I found out about Tropical Traditions Coconut oil. Thank you! **Mary** - Centralia, WA

There are many studies validating this concept of thermogenesis and MCTs in the scientific literature. In 1989 a study was done in the Department of Pediatrics, Vanderbilt University, at Nashville TN. Ten male volunteers (ages 22 to 44) were overfed (150% of estimated energy requirement) liquid formula diets containing 40% of fat as either MCT or LCT. Each patient was studied for one week on each diet in a double-blind, crossover design. The results: "Our results demonstrate that excess dietary energy as MCT stimulates thermogenesis to a greater degree than does excess energy as LCT. This increased energy expenditure, most likely due to lipogenesis in the liver, provides evidence that excess energy derived from MCT is stored with a lesser efficiency than is excess energy derived from dietary LCT."[8]

In another study recently conducted at the School of Dietetics and Human Nutrition, McGill University, Ste-Anne-de-Bellevue, Quebec, Canada, the effects of diets rich in medium-chain triglycerides (MCTs) or long-chain triglycerides (LCTs) on body composition, energy expenditure, substrate oxidation, subjective appetite, and ad libitum energy intake in overweight men was studied. Twenty-four healthy, overweight men with body mass indexes between 25 and 31 kg/m(2) consumed diets rich in MCT or LCT for 28 days each in a crossover randomized controlled trial. Their conclusion: "Consumption of a diet rich in MCTs results in greater loss of AT compared with LCTs, perhaps due to increased energy expenditure and fat oxidation observed with MCT intake. Thus, MCTs may be considered as agents that aid in the prevention of obesity or potentially stimulate weight loss."[9]

> Another benefit of coconut consumption is it helps me control my blood sugar levels. Have you ever eaten any carb-intensive food and had a sugar crash? Try eating some coconut oil along with the carb and it may prevent the sugar crashes or at least mitigate them. I try to keep

my blood sugar level steady all day to have a nice energy level, and not ups and downs all day long. I used to always be a little chubby (wonder why?) Eating coconut does help control the chubbiness. So the direct health benefits that I have experienced from coconut oil consumption are: increased thyroid function and the blessings that brings; elimination of yeast infections; and help in controlling blood sugar levels. I am sure the increased thyroid function and controlling the blood sugar accounts for not being chubby anymore, and the stuff tastes good in food. – **Phyllis** (Coconut Diet Forums)

Scientific Studies on the Weight-Loss Effects of Coconut Oil's MCTs

Scientific studies have reported that the fatty acids from MCTs in coconut oil are not easily converted into stored triglycerides, and that MCTs cannot be readily used by the body to make larger fat molecules. One animal-feeding study evaluated body weight and fat storage for three different diets—a low-fat diet, a high-fat diet containing long-chain triglycerides (LCTs), and a high-fat diet containing MCTs. All animals were fed the selected diets for a period of 44 days. At the end of that time, the low-fat diet group had stored an average of 0.47 grams of fat per day; the LCT group stored 0.48 grams/day, while the MCT group deposited only 0.19 grams of fat per day, a 60% reduction in the amount of fat stored. The authors conclude that "the change from a low-fat diet to a MCT-diet is attended by a decrease in the body weight gain."[10]

This study points out two important facts. First, when MCTs are substituted for LCTs in the diet, the body is much less inclined to store fat. Second, when we eat sensibly, a diet containing MCTs is more effective than a low-fat diet at decreasing stored fat.

In a human study, researchers compared the metabolic effects of 400-calorie meals of MCTs and LCTs by measuring metabolic rates prior to and six hours following the test meals. The results showed that the MCT-containing meals caused an average 12 percent increase in basal metabolic rate as compared with a 4 percent increase with the LCT-containing meal. The authors concluded that replacing dietary fats with MCTs could "over long periods of time produce weight loss even in the absence of reduced [caloric] intake."[11]

Coconut oil is nature's richest source of MCTs. Not only do MCTs raise the body's metabolism leading to weight loss, but they have special health-giving properties as well. The most predominant MCT in coconut oil, for example, is lauric acid. Lipid researcher Dr. Jon Kabara, as reported earlier in this book, states "Never before in the history of man is it so important to emphasize the value of Lauric Oils. The medium-chain fats in coconut oil are similar to fats in mother's milk and have similar nutriceutical effects. These health effects were recognized centuries ago in Ayurvedic medicine. Modern research has now found a common link between these two natural health products—their fat or lipid content. The medium chain fatty acids and monoglycerides found primarily in coconut oil and mother's milk have miraculous healing power."[12] Outside of a human mother's breast milk, coconut oil is nature's most abundant source of lauric acid and medium chain fatty acids.

> I've been over 100 lbs. overweight for 5 years. I struggled with ear and sinus infections, headaches, fatigue, and high blood pressure (I've never been diagnosed). Everything in life seemed like work. I was miserable emotionally, mentally and spiritually. Well, I've been consuming about 3-5 tablespoons of coconut oil per day and I feel amazing! I get a slight cold, but never get the secondary infection and beat the fever in 24 hours! I sleep better and wake up with a smile on my face. I'm more flexible. And I feel more at peace with my body. My spiritual life has improved and I am ready to pursue my dream of being a Christian Counselor. This has marked a pivotal change in my entire life including my marriage. This may sound silly. But I gained weight subconsciously because I didn't want to be noticed by men. And by eating better I have allowed myself to be freed from this bondage. I don't know how much I've lost, and choose not to watch the scales. But my clothes fit better, my muscles are stronger and people have noticed the loss. And now, with coconut oil, I actually have hunger pains. Our society is so focused on lowering the appetite, but a healthy appetite is good! I'm now satisfied with less food and not bound by sugar imbalance hunger. **Bridgette** (Coconut Diet Forums)

> Over the past 18 months I've lost 107 pounds, going from 316 to 209 (19 pounds to go) and from size 52 to 36 pants. I lost the weight following a low-carb, no sugar or grain, high saturated fat and high protein diet and eliminating ALL soy products and ALL polyunsaturated vegetable oils. I used about 2 or 3 Tbsp of Virgin Coconut Oil daily. **Chuck** (Coconut Diet Forums)

Does Everyone Lose Weight While Using Coconut Oil?

Does everyone lose weight while using coconut oil? No. We have also had testimonies from people stating that they did not lose weight. Coconut oil is not a magic bullet that one can just add to their diet and sit back and watch the pounds melt away. Some people have actually done that, but most people will not see that happen. For one thing, we have had people report that they could not lose weight until they cut out all polyunsaturated fats from their diet. We have also had many women who take "the pill" report that they actually gain weight if they use coconut oil.

Also, many people have reported that while they did not lose weight, or maybe even put on a few pounds, that somehow their clothes started fitting better. We have heard this many times. Apparently Virgin Coconut Oil does help some people build muscle mass while trimming fat. Here is what one weight lifter, known as MG in the Coconut Diet Forums, reports:

> Last year I was measured at 10.5% body fat. Last month, I hiked up my consumption [of Virgin Coconut Oil] from 4 tbsp/day to 6 tbsp/day. At the same time, I limited my carb intake at dinnertime. In a few weeks time, my bodyweight increased by about 4lbs. but body fat decreased to 9.6% - I did not change my workout intensity or frequency. My trainer is wondering what the heck I am taking (chest and thigh measurements increased). It blows 'em away when I say that I take Virgin Coconut Oil straight up. **MG** (Coconut Diet Forums)

> It's VCO and low carbs. I feel better than I have in a long time, my temp is actually over 98 (not all the time, but it's better than those 94.5 readings). I'm a believer and hope to stick with it! I haven't seen a big weight loss, but my clothes fit better and I know adding an exercise program will impact the weight. **Val** (Coconut Diet Forums)

Chapter 6

Virgin Coconut Oil and Thyroid Health

Freshly harvested organic coconuts that will be used to make Virgin Coconut Oil.

Many Americans suffer from symptoms such as cold hands and feet, low body temperature. sensitivity to cold, a feeling of always being chilled, headaches, insomnia, dry skin, puffy eyes, hair loss, brittle nails, joint aches, constipation, mental dullness, fatigue, frequent infections, hoarse voice, ringing in the ears, dizziness, loss of libido, and weight gain, which is sometimes uncontrollable. Approximately 65 percent of the U. S. population is overweight; 27 percent is clinically obese. Research is pointing to the fact that an under active thyroid might be the number one cause of weight problems, especially among women, in the U.S. today.

Virgin Coconut Oil offers great hope for those suffering from hypothyroidism (low thyroid function) today.

> I didn't even realize how much hypothyroidism was affecting my life until I started on the Virgin Coconut Oil and suddenly had energy like the Energizer Bunny! I also gave up the white toxins (wheat flour, refined sugar, potatoes, and other high-glycemic index foods) and that, in combination with my Virgin Coconut Oil consumption has made a tremendous difference in my hormonal balance, mood stability, stamina and overall energy. And, I'm slowly but steadily losing a little bit of weight without effort. Ya gotta love that! **Julia** (Coconut Diet Forums)

> I began taking coconut oil to address a hypothyroid issue. Recently, especially over the last month, thyroid activity plunged and my temperatures would top out for the day somewhere between 97.2 and 97.8—definitely hypothyroid territory. Now, in just a couple of days the coconut oil has boosted my metabolism back toward the normal range (still subnormal but getting there) and my sleep has been incredible. From past experience with thyroid management, I know that, in my case, greatly improved sleep and feelings of rejuvenation after sleep are related to more normal thyroid activity. Whatever the precise mechanism, it's a welcome development. **Mike** (Coconut Diet Forums)

We have received literally hundreds of comments such as these from those using Virgin Coconut Oil with hypothyroidism.

Hypothyroidism Reaching Epidemic Proportions

In 1995, researchers studied 25,862 participants at the Colorado statewide health fair. They discovered that among patients not taking thyroid medication, 8.9 percent were hypothyroid (under-active thyroid) and 1.1 percent were hyperthyroid (over-active thyroid). This indicates 9.9 percent of the population had a thyroid problem that had most likely gone unrecognized. These figures suggest that nationally, there may be as many as 13 million Americans with an undiagnosed thyroid problem.[1]

In her book *Living Well With Hypothyroidism: What Your Doctor Doesn't Tell You. . . That You Need to Know,* Mary Shomon quotes endocrinologist Kenneth Blanchard, M.D., of Lower Newton Falls, Massachusetts as saying, "The key thing is . . . doctors are always told that TSH is the test that gives us a yes or no answer. And, in fact, I think that's fundamentally wrong. The pituitary TSH is controlled not just by how much T4 and T3 is in circulation, but T4 is getting converted to T3 at the pituitary level. Excess T3 generated at the pituitary level can falsely suppress TSH."[2] Hence, many people who are simply tested for TSH levels and are found to be within "normal" range are, in fact, suffering from thyroid problems that are going undetected.

Ridha Arem, M.D., Associate Professor of Medicine in the Division of Endocrinology and Metabolism at Baylor College of Medicine, agrees. He says that hypothyroidism may exist despite "normal range" TSH levels. In his book *The Thyroid Solution* he says:

> Many people may be suffering from minute imbalances that have not yet resulted in abnormal blood tests. If we included people with low-grade hypothyroidism whose blood tests are normal, the frequency of hypothyroidism would no doubt exceed 10 percent of the population. What is of special concern, though, is that many people whose test results are dismissed as normal could continue to have symptoms of an under active thyroid. Their moods, emotions, and overall well-being are affected by this imbalance, yet they are not receiving the care they need to get to the root of their problems. Even if the TSH level is in the lower segment of normal range, a person may still be suffering from low-grade hypothyroidism.[3]

Thus, if we were to include those who may be suffering from "low-grade hypothyroidism," the number could well be double the 13 million estimate from the Colorado study.

What is Causing This Epidemic?

While more research needs to be done, it is generally accepted that diet plays a major role in thyroid health. For decades we have known that low iodine intake leads to low thyroid function and eventually to goiter. Iodized salt was intended to solve this problem, but it has not been the answer. There are a number of foods known as *goitrogens* that block iodine. Two goitrogens are quite prevalent in the American diet—peanuts and peanut butter and soybeans used most often in prepared foods as textured vegetable protein (a refined soy food) and soybean oil.

The rise of industrialization, corporate farming, and mass production of food has drastically changed our food supply from what our ancestors ate. Many studies show the detrimental effects of refined sugars and grains on our health. These foods are very taxing on the thyroid gland, and we consume them in large quantities.

Environmental stress such as chemical pollutants, pesticides, mercury, and fluoride are also tough on the thyroid. A growing body of evidence suggests that fluoride, which is prevalent in toothpaste and water treatment, may inhibit the functioning of the thyroid gland. Additionally, mercury may diminish thyroid function because it displaces the trace mineral selenium, and selenium is involved in conversion of thyroid hormones T4 to T3.

The Truth About Fats and Oils

Many dietary oils can negatively affect thyroid health. We cook with them almost every day and they are plentiful in commercially prepared foods. Expeller-pressed or solvent-extracted oils only became a major part of the American diet in the last century. It is possible they are among the worst offenders when it comes to the thyroid. They are known as vegetable oils or polyunsaturated oils. The most common source of these oils used in commercially prepared foods is the soybean.

Large-scale cultivation of soybeans in the United States began after World War II and quickly increased to 140 billion pounds per year. Most of the crops are produced for animal feed and soy oil for hydrogenated fats such as margarine and shortening. Today, it is nearly impossible to eat at restaurants or buy packaged foods that don't have soy oil in the ingredients. Often labels simply state "vegetable oil."

Ray Peat Ph.D., a physiologist who has worked with progesterone and related hormones since 1968, says that the sudden surge of polyunsaturated oils into the food chain post World War II has caused many changes in hormones. He writes:

> Their [polyunsaturated oils] best understood effect is their interference with the function of the thyroid gland. Unsaturated oils block thyroid hormone secretion, its movement in the circulatory system, and the response of tissues to the hormone. When the thyroid hormone is deficient, the body is generally exposed to increased levels of estrogen. The thyroid hormone

is essential for making the 'protective hormones' progesterone and pregnenolone, so these hormones are lowered when anything interferes with the function of the thyroid. The thyroid hormone is required for using and eliminating cholesterol, so cholesterol is likely to be raised by anything which blocks the thyroid function.[4]

There is a growing body of research concerning soy's detrimental affect on the thyroid gland. Much of this research centers on the *phytoestrogens* ("phyto" means plant) that are found in soy. In the 1960s when soy was introduced into infant formulas, it was shown that soy was goitrogenic and caused goiters in babies. When iodine was supplemented, the incidence of goiter reduced dramatically. However, a retrospective epidemiological study by Fort, et al. showed that teenaged children with a diagnosis of autoimmune thyroid disease were significantly more likely to have received soy formula as infants (18 out of 59 children; 31 percent) when compared to healthy siblings (nine out of 76, 12 percent) or control group children (seven out of 54; 13 percent).[5]

When healthy individuals without any previous thyroid disease were fed 30 grams of pickled soybeans per day for one month, Ishizuki, et al. reported goiter and elevated individual thyroid stimulating hormone (TSH) levels (although still within the normal range) in thirty-seven healthy, iodine-sufficient adults. One month after stopping soybean consumption, individual TSH values decreased to the original levels and goiters were reduced in size.[6]

Traditionally, polyunsaturated oils such as soybean oil have been used for livestock feed because they cause the animals to gain weight. These oils are made up of what is known as long chain fatty acids—the kind of fatty acids that promote weight gain. In the North Carolina State University's Extension Swine Husbandry 1998-2000 Departmental report, for example, was a study entitled "EFFECT OF DIETARY FAT SOURCE, LEVEL, AND FEEDING INTERVAL ON PORK FATTY ACID COMPOSITION" by M.T. See and J. Odle. Ironically, since the market in its low-fat dogma of recent years is demanding leaner meats, this study showed that one could produce leaner meat and reduce the weight on swine by reducing their intake of soy oil and substituting it with saturated animal fat![7]

According to Dr. Ray Peat, the fattening effect of polyunsaturated oils (primarily soy and corn) is due to the presence of linoleic and linolenic acids, long-chain fatty acids, which have an anti-thyroid effect. Peat says:

> Linoleic and linolenic acids, the "essential fatty acids," and other polyunsaturated fatty acids, which are now fed to pigs to fatten them, in the form of corn and soy beans, cause the animals' fat to be chemically equivalent to vegetable oil. In the late 1940s, chemical toxins were used to suppress the thyroid function of pigs, to make them get fatter while consuming less food. When that was found to be carcinogenic, it was then found that corn and soy beans had the same antithyroid effect, causing the animals to be fattened at low cost. The animals' fat becomes chemically similar to the fats in their food, causing it to be equally toxic, and equally fattening.[8]

Of course in the 1940s the fat from pigs (lard) was highly desirable, as were most saturated fats. Today, saturated fats are fed to pigs to keep them lean, while most people buy polyunsaturated soy and corn oils in the grocery stores as their primary cooking oil! As we stated in the chapter on weight loss, we now have a population characterized by lean pigs and obese people...

Coconut Oil: A-Healthy Choice for the Thyroid

Coconut oil, on the other hand, is a saturated fat made up primarily of medium chain fatty acids, as we have stated many times in previous chapters. As we have seen, these fatty acids are known to increase metabolism and promote weight loss. Coconut oil can also raise basal body temperatures while increasing metabolism. This is good news for people who suffer with low thyroid function. We have seen many testimonies to this effect.

> The "proof is in the pudding." Try it yourself and then you be the judge. All these people certainly can't "be wrong." Everyone will experience different benefits, some more than others, but definitely something. In my own personal experience, I was suffering with hypothyroidism that even prescription medications couldn't help. After a few short weeks of taking Virgin Coconut Oil, my reading was normal for the first time in a year. I use it on my skin after a shower and no longer struggle with the incredibly dry skin that

often goes along with hypothyroidism, and I have used it on my hair as a conditioner. All I can say is that the phrase, "The world's perfect food," is quite accurate. Try it and see for yourself. Warmly, **Melanie** (Coconut Diet Forums)

I am just now jumping on the coconut oil bandwagon (about three weeks now) and I'm really starting to feel GREAT! I have suffered from severe migraines for the past 25 years, the last 15 becoming increasingly severe, coinciding with the addition of soy and the "low-fat mentality" to my diet. Nothing helped! I should be experiencing my pre-menstrual migraine by now and instead I feel like I could climb Mt. Everest! Also I wondered if it decreased the waist to hip ratio because mine has gone from 7.2 all my life to 7 (or something like that). I think I had the sluggish thyroid too, with a low body temperature of between 96 and 96.8. Now it's starting to climb for the first time in years. Thank you... Sincerely, **V. Potter** (Coconut Diet Forums)

For more information on how Virgin Coconut Oil works to promote weight loss, see Chapter 5.

Coconut Oil and Oxidative Stress

One of the reasons the long chain fatty acids in vegetable oils are so damaging to the thyroid is that they oxidize quickly and become rancid. Food manufacturers know about this propensity towards rancidity and, therefore, highly refine their vegetable oils. Considerable research has shown that trans fatty acids, present when vegetable oils are highly refined (hydrogenated or partially hydrogenated), are especially damaging to cell tissue and can have a negative affect on the thyroid as well as health in general. Because the longer chain fatty acids are deposited in cells more often as rancid and oxidizing fat, impairment of the conversion of thyroid hormone T4 to T3 occurs, which is symptomatic of hypothyroidism. To create the enzymes needed to convert fats to energy, T4 must be converted to T3.

Dr. Ray Peat says:

When the oils are stored in our tissues, they are much warmer, and more directly exposed to oxygen than they would be in the seeds, and so their tendency to oxidize is very great. These oxidative processes can damage enzymes and other parts of cells, and especially their ability to produce energy. The enzymes which break down proteins are inhibited by unsaturated fats; these enzymes are needed not only for digestion, but also for production of thyroid hormones, clot removal, immunity, and the general adaptability of cells. The risks of abnormal blood clotting, inflammation, immune deficiency, shock, aging, obesity, and cancer are increased. Thyroid [hormones] and progesterone are decreased.

Since the unsaturated oils block protein digestion in the stomach, we can be malnourished even while "eating well." There are many changes in hormones caused by unsaturated fats. Their best understood effect is their interference with the function of the thyroid gland. Unsaturated oils block thyroid hormone secretion, its movement in the circulatory system, and the response of tissues to the hormone. Coconut oil is unique in its ability to prevent weight-gain or cure obesity, by stimulating metabolism. It is quickly metabolized, and functions in some ways as an antioxidant.[9]

Because coconut oil is saturated and very stable (unrefined coconut oil has a shelf life of over two years at room temperature), the body is not burdened with oxidative stress as it is with the vegetable oils. Coconut oil does not require the enzyme stress that vegetable oils do, preventing T4 to T3 hormone conversion, not only because it is a stable oil, but also because it is processed differently in the body and does not need to be broken down by enzyme dependent processes as do long chain fatty acids. Also, since the liver is the main place where damage occurs from oxidized and rancid oils that cause cell membrane damage, and since the liver is where much of the conversion of T4 to T3 takes place, eliminating long chain fatty acids from the diet and replacing them with medium chain fatty acids found in coconut oil can, in time, help in rebuilding cell membranes and increasing enzyme production that will assist in promoting the conversion of T4 to T3 hormones.

More research in this area is necessary. In the meantime, those switching from polyunsaturated oils to coconut oil are reporting many positive results. For example, Donna has experienced encouraging improvements in her thyroid health. She writes:

I've been on coconut oil since September, 2002 and, although that doesn't seem like long, it has changed my life and the lives of my family and friends. My weight actually went UP when I started on coconut oil but I felt so GREAT! Being hypothyroid, I was on Synthroid and Cytomel and had been for years, but with inconsistent results and feeling worse. Other changes besides the addition of coconut oil were the complete removal of soy (and that is a major challenge in itself!), all trans fatty acids, and refined sugar, and organ cleanses seasonally. My thyroid meds were discontinued with my doctor's knowledge as I was getting too energetic and having trouble sleeping! Imagine this change from being a "sleepaholic" couch potato who was cold! My weight stayed steady until the last three weeks and it has now started the downward move. My goal was health and I just believed the weight would come off when I found the right diet and exercise routine that my life was comfortable with. I've tried removing the coconut oil but my energy drops and I don't feel as good. **Donna** (Coconut Diet Forums)

Another coconut oil user writes:

I have experienced thyroid problems: body temperature not going above 97 degrees, cold hands and feet, can't lose weight, fatigued, slow heart rate, can't sleep some nights, dry skin, etc. My doctor did the thyroid test and it came back normal. I am 46 and peri-menopausal. My Naturopath symptomatically diagnosed me with hypothyroidism. She explained the blood tests currently used by allopathic medicine are not sensitive enough. I started on the coconut oil five weeks ago. In the first week I noticed my body temperature had risen and my resting heart rate had gone from 49 to 88 beats per minute. This has since settled to 66. My energy is now really high and I am slowly losing the weight—three pounds in the past five weeks. I also had been taking flaxseed oil and gamma linoleic acid oil but have stopped eating every other oil but what Dr. Raymond Peat recommends, which is coconut oil, olive oil and butter. I take 3 tablespoons of coconut oil daily. **Cindy** (Coconut Diet Forums)

Chapter 7

Skin Health and Virgin Coconut Oil

Skin care products made from pure Virgin Coconut Oil.

In addition to ingesting the Virgin Coconut Oil, I just have to tell you about another exciting way that coconut oil has helped me! I use it on my face and I can't believe how much it has helped. I used to spend hundreds of dollars on face creams. I won't waste my money on those empty promises again. I look ten years younger! Honestly! My pores are smaller, and my skin tone is much more even. I used to have breakouts once in awhile—not any more thanks to coconut oil. Next March I will be 40 years old and with the help of coconut oil I will not only reach my weight loss/health goal, my face will look younger too! **Kelly** - Lander, WY

Filipinos are well-known for their youthful appearance and soft, wrinkle-free skin, even though they live in a climate that exposes them to the sun's rays year round. Since coconut oil is their main dietary oil, and is also the main ingredient in their skin care products, one must take a closer look at how Virgin Coconut Oil provides skin health.

> I wanted to share my experience with Virgin Coconut Oil. I have been using the oil for about two weeks. My skin looks great, no more dryness—I used to have very dry skin. My hair looks great, soft and shiny—no more frizz. And my scalp is no longer dry. Also, my eyelashes have grown longer and thicker! This is a plus I did not expect. I now make an effort to apply a bit of oil with a clean mascara brush each morning/night. **Lizmarie** (Coconut Diet Forums)

Coconut oil's ability to nourish and heal the skin has been known in the tropics for hundreds of years. Even when the anti-saturated fat campaign waged in the U.S. convinced many even in coconut oil producing countries to switch to polyunsaturated oils, Filipinos and others never stopped using coconut oil on their skin because they have known about its wonderful moisturizing and healing powers for generations. As a saturated fat consisting primarily of medium chain fatty acids, it is not easily oxidized and does not cause harmful free radical damage like polyunsaturated vegetable oils. Most commercial skin care products in the U.S. today are made from polyunsaturated oils which oxidize and turn rancid very quickly causing free radical damage in the skin. There is good evidence that this is not only true for external applications, but also holds true for the oils one consumes. One of the main reasons that we experience so many skin problems in the U.S. today is a switch in our dietary oil. Our forefathers consumed primarily saturated fats, but most people today consume polyunsaturated fats and trans fatty acids.

A Healthy Head!

In India, a whole coconut oil industry has survived in recent years among the anti-saturated fat/coconut oil propaganda almost entirely for one application: the conditioning of hair. This is the number one reason why people in India buy coconut oil today—to condition and nurture their hair.

> In the short time I have internally consumed and topically applied the Virgin Coconut Oil, I, as well as others, have noticed a significant difference in my skin tone, as well as how shiny my hair has become.

Recently my husband asked me what I had done differently to my hair because it was so shiny! The skin on my entire body has become softer and more subtle. I know this is a result of the Virgin Coconut Oil because I haven't been using any body lotion. I couldn't be more thrilled! **C. Morgan** - South Bend, IN

Studies in India have been done on how effective various oils are on treating damaged hair. One study compared mineral oil, sunflower oil, and coconut oil because these were the three most commonly used oils in hair treatment products used in India. The aim of this study was to cover different treatments, and the effect of these treatments on various hair types using these three oils. The number of experiments to be conducted was a very high number and a technique termed as the "Taguchi Design of Experimentation" was used. Their results:

> The findings clearly indicate the strong impact that coconut oil application has to hair as compared to application of both sunflower and mineral oils. Among three oils, coconut oil was the only oil found to reduce the protein loss remarkably for both undamaged and damaged hair when used as a pre-wash and post-wash grooming product. Both sunflower and mineral oils do not help at all in reducing the protein loss from hair. This difference in results could arise from the composition of each of these oils. Coconut oil, being a triglyceride of lauric acid (principal fatty acid), has a high affinity for hair proteins and, because of its low molecular weight and straight linear chain, is able to penetrate inside the hair shaft. Mineral oil, being a hydrocarbon, has no affinity for proteins and therefore is not able to penetrate and yield better results. In the case of sunflower oil, although it is a triglyceride of linoleic acid, because of its bulky structure due to the presence of double bonds, it does not penetrate the fiber, consequently resulting in no favorable impact on protein loss.[1]

Many of our clients have also reported wonderful results from dry scalp conditions.

> I have three children, 4, 2, and 3 months and they ALL get [Virgin Coconut Oil] on their skin. Along with our skin, we use it for our hair and scalp. My youngest son had very dry scalp (cradle cap) and the Virgin Coconut Oil healed it in two days. It was wonderful! **Amy** Falls Church, VA

My mom had been suffering for the past four months with a very red, dry, peeling scalp. It moved to her neck and hands—the pain was so bad she would sometimes cry. She tried using every dandruff/dry scalp shampoo on the market and would put various substances on her scalp nightly in the hopes of hydrating it. She would even leave these items on her head for days at a time. She tried crisco, baby oil, olive oil, jojoba oil, and every dry skin lotion out there but nothing helped—it just got worse. The doctors did not know what it was and were trying to get her to take medicine orally and to experiment with different cremes consisting of steroids. I just happened to be reading up on the coconut oil and suggested that she try it before using the items that the doctors were tying to give her. After ordering your product, I gave some to her. She massaged the coconut oil into her scalp and left it on overnight. When she woke up the next morning, 95% of the dry skin was gone and almost all of the redness. When my mom told the doctor what had helped, he didn't believe her, as her scalp, hands, and forehead were so bad. It has been over a month now, and you can hardly tell she ever had any skin problems. Praise God! **Michelle** - Tucson, AZ

Hope for Skin Problems

Virgin Coconut Oil has been reported to help many other skin problems as well. Depending on what is causing the skin problem, the coconut oil seems to work in a variety of ways. For example, we have had positive reports from people who suffer from yeast infections in the skin, and there is research that shows the MCTs in coconut oil kill yeast infections (see Chapter 8 on Candida.)

I started on coconut oil three weeks ago. I am a large person, hoping that the Virgin Coconut Oil (VCO) will speed up my sluggish thyroid. As a large person I have skin folds and I often suffer(ed) from fungal/yeast infections that made me very sore. The only remedy that I found in the past that worked was an ingested dose of a proprietary remedy for "Thrush." This was both expensive and only ever a partial solution. After taking the VCO for, as I said, three weeks, all my skin fold problems have disappeared. It is wonderful to be clear of them. This current very hot, humid weather that we have recently had was a real test for this. **Liz** (Coconut Diet Forums)

You're right Liz, I deal with this same stubborn yeast/fungal thing, especially in the summertime. While waiting for my second order, I've been reading the research reports on the Tropical Traditions website and the archives over and over as if just knowing the information would help me with my own physical problems. But this week, I am a believer from experience!

One of the big problems with skin yeast and fungal infections is that clothing tends to absorb or else rub off the expensive medicine after application. This time, I wasn't looking forward to applying the strong liquid prescription to it because the kind I have stings—big time—when it hits the red, angry, sore area of the yeast infection in the skin folds. I had some VCO left in a small jar which I was using for smoothing on after a shower. I took that out and just slathered it on. Instantly the pain was soothed away and, for the moment anyway, that was enough. By the end of the day, I could tell that the coconut oil was doing more than just relieving the soreness—the rash was breaking up a little, and there were some small clear areas where before it was just solid red soreness. I applied the coconut oil twice a day, and in three or four days, the whole area is mostly pink and clearing. And it isn't staining clothing, either!

I am marveling over and over about how this coconut oil is working!!! I've been poring over the archived information. By the time I finished my first quart of VCO I could tell my hypoglycemic hunger cravings were subsiding, and my taste for coffee and chocolate was changing. Anything more I could say would just be like a lot of exclamation points, and I've been told that isn't very polite! So just "Thank you, thank you, Tropical Traditions." **Beverly** (in response to Liz on the Coconut Diet Forums)

When my baby boy, David, was 10 weeks old he had a yeast infection on his bottom. Instead of running to the doctor to get an expensive prescription, I first tried VCO. I was very new to using it so I wasn't sure what to expect. I liberally applied coconut oil at each diaper change (about 6x/day) allowing it to soak in for a few minutes after each application. I was astounded that within 24 hours there was significant improvement. I continued to apply it and within three days the yeast infection was completely gone. VCO is awesome!! **Vanessa** - Gilbert, IA

Most of the research on coconut oil's anti-fungal, anti-bacterial, and anti-viral effects have been done on the monoglycerides of MCTs produced inside our bodies when we eat the oil. However, the anecdotal evidence we were seeing from our clients suggested the MCTs had similar effects when applied topically on the skin. Consider Tammy's experience with a fungal skin infection:

I am a 35-year-old female who had red lesions on my face for many years. Unbelievably it finally cleared in three months when I applied Virgin Coconut Oil topically to my face each day.

I had been going to a dermatologist for twelve years with minimal results. I had lesions, which were red, and resembled acne. Ironically, antibiotics made it worse, yet the doctor kept prescribing them for me. I had used six different topicals for acne, which usually ended up hurting my face. The doctor kept saying, "Give it a chance. It will get worse before getting better." I couldn't understand why I had acne since my skin was so dry, itchy and flaky. The retinols were the worst on my skin, followed by the salicylic acid, the glycol's and then the benzyl peroxides.

Frustrated, I then became a nutritional purist for five years, and still saw no clearing. I started using natural remedies, homeopathics, herbals and super foods to change my skin condition. I had already eliminated hydrogenated oils from my diet, so I decided to try to incorporate coconut oil into my diet. I really wasn't consistent about eating the coconut oil, but I was faithful about applying it to my face each night. I had nothing to lose by giving it a try. My theory on why it might work was that the sebum in the skin breaks down the medium chain triglycerides into smaller fatty acids which have antibacterial and anti-fungal activities.

My dermatologist had tried for 12 years to dry up the sebum and kill the bacteria causing the acne, so I decided to go a different route by using the sebum constructively instead of trying to eliminate it. My face cleared and I was so excited that I [went] to my dermatologist and told her about my success. The doctor belittled the theory, saying that I had just grown out of it. [She said that] most likely my hormones had stabilized and that my face clearing at the same time I used the coconut oil was just a coincidence.

Since I believed in my doctor's medical knowledge, I started to doubt my discovery. So, to test my theory, I stopped using the coconut oil on my face and, as well, I didn't go out of my way to eat it either. Additionally, I still avoided hydrogenated oils.

Six months later I had a follow up appointment with that dermatologist and my face was as bad as it had always been. The doctor snidely asked if I was still using that coconut oil because "that heavy oil" had clogged up all my pores. I replied that I had stopped using the oil after our last appointment. However, I intended to use the coconut oil again to see if my theory was right. Unexpectedly, the doctor offered to order blood-work to check my hormones at the beginning and again at the end of my trial. I agreed to the testing. My blood-work showed most of my hormones as normal with the testosterone as a little high. I used the coconut oil on my face every night faithfully; and in three months at my next appointment my face had cleared again with almost no scarring. The doctor ran the follow-up blood work and surprisingly my testosterone level had increased. Too much testosterone has been proven to increase acne. The doctor was surprised, but wasn't ready to rule out other factors. She then wanted to do more testing, including allergy testing and skin scrapings. This meant that I would have to stop using the oil for some of the testing. I hated the thought of losing that great confident feeling and freedom I got from having a clear face, but I agreed to the testing anyway.

The doctor tested for different yeast, fungus, ringworm, bacteria, allergens, and Demodex and Scabies mites. I didn't test positive for any of the allergens either time. When not using the coconut oil, my skin scrapings had increased numbers of Demodex in my sebaceous glands as well as in my hair follicles but there were no Scabies. There were minimal increases in bacteria and the yeast Candidia, but there was a marked increase in the fungus Malassezia Furfur, but not ringworm. This clearly explained why the antibiotics made things worse; I didn't have acne. Any bacteria was secondary, the main culprit was the fungus Malassezia Furfur which caused a condition called Pityrosporum Folliculitis. Using antibiotic reduced the bad as well as the good bacteria allowing the fungus to grow unchallenged. Additionally, although the Demodex mite lives in everyone's skin in small numbers, they multiply greatly in immune deficient host and they thrive on yeast in the body.

Since my experiment was intended to use the excess sebum that is present with acne to combine with the coconut oil to fight the bacteria that causes the acne, I failed to prove my hypothesis because my condition was misdiagnosed as acne and I don't have excess sebum. Hopefully someone reading this with confirmed excess sebum and acne would complete the experiment for me. However, I do believe my theory was mostly right in that the coconut oil mixes with sebum in the skin which breaks the oil down into the healing fatty acids. In my case it just happened to be the anti-fungal activity of the fatty acids that cleared my skin. By eliminating the yeast, many of the mites starved. As my face healed and the irritation was less, the occurrence of bacterial infections decreased.

I truly believe if I stop using coconut oil on my face the fungus will grow out of control and the whole cycle would begin, resulting in the lesions I had been plagued with for over a decade. I am now trying to eat coconut oil every day in order to correct the underlying cause that makes me an ideal host for the Malassezia Furfur fungus. **Tammy** - Salisbury, MD

While Tammy did not have acne, others who did have reported benefits as well.

Yes, coconut oil is great for getting rid of both dry skin and pimples. I have had combination skin for years, but almost immediately, I saw my face free from pimples and free from dry areas. In fact, I had a flaky, itchy patch of skin just below my eyebrow that disappeared and has not returned, since regularly using coconut oil on my face—which has been just over a month now. I put it on before bed, without first washing my face; then I wash it off in the morning. From what I understand, the medium chain triglycerides break down into the useful antimicrobial free fatty acids because of the affects of bacteria on the skin. So I decided to start using the oil on my unwashed face instead of a newly cleansed face, which would have less bacteria and therefore (I assume) a slower breakdown of the oil into fatty acids. My skin looks great, smooth and healthy. And it's definitely softer than it used to be, too. **Melinda** (Coconut Diet Forums)

My son really did not want to use Virgin Coconut Oil, but his Benzemyacin was really not working very well, and the retin A just brutally destroyed his skin (painfully red and dry and cracked). So he used his neutrogena face wash and then applied the oil. It took a little while to soak in, but by the next morning his red skin from the retin A was gone and his face was white again. He uses more at night when no one sees him, and less in the morning before he goes to school. When he gets home from school, he dabs a little just on the spots that are worse. I have used it, and I was afraid, at first, because the thought of oil on your face is the opposite of what we are taught about getting rid of pimples. But I just tried it on a few blemishes, and they were gone the next day—it was amazing. I now use it all over my face! My son's acne is under control now. He has some problem areas, but they are slowly getting better. **Robin** (Coconut Diet Forums)

While not everyone who has tried Virgin Coconut Oil for skin problems has reported success, it is by far the one area where we continue to see the most results. The range of skin problems that have been reported to us as being helped by Virgin Coconut Oil is almost limitless. Here are a few more samples:

Hello! A friend introduced us to Tropical Traditions about six months ago, and I have since been telling everyone I know about it. We have been using the oil in more ways than I had imagined we would! I use it as a facial moisturizer, and I prefer it to the expensive lotion that I have used for years. Several people have even commented on my skin! Probably the most dramatic result we have gotten with the coconut oil is with my 20 month old son. He has had **eczema** on his legs and arms for a long time, and nothing seemed to help it. I even tried costly lotion just for that purpose and it seemed to make the dry, scaly patches worse! Many people noticed it, and I just didn't know what to do. Well, I began putting the coconut oil on his skin nightly and there has been HUGE improvement!! The big, rough, red patches are gone and there is just the tiniest hint of a rough feeling in places, and only when I slack off and don't use it for a while. We do eat the coconut oil, by the way, and have enjoyed it very much (especially the almond bark recipe on your site—yum). But I wanted you to know how much it had helped us in ways that people may not realize it would. THANK YOU. **Louise** - South Carolina

Through Dr. Joseph Mercola's website, I was fortunate to have found the miracle coconut oil. For years I suffered with a skin condition called keratosis polaris (bumpy, itchy skin). I tried many, many treatments and spent hundreds of dollars on creams and cleansers. Nothing worked—until Tropical Traditions Coconut Oil. I have been using the oil for cooking and as a body cream. My skin condition is 100% improved. The products are very inexpensive compared to the cost of most of the useless products I tried in the past. Thank you for this miracle product! **Janet** - Elizabeth, NJ

Last year I started noticing embarrassing little red scaly itchy patches of skin on my hands. I tried just about every lotion for dry and sensitive skin on the [store] shelf, and got very few results. I made an appointment with my doctor and she diagnosed me with **psoriasis**. She sent me to the pharmacy with a prescription for a psoriasis cream and a lotion and instructed me to use them everyday. The lotion and cream stung so bad, it was worse then the itchy skin I had been dealing with for months. By this time I had big patches on my hands, a few on my neck, and on my eyelids. I was getting desperate because more and more people were starting to notice my red flaky skin. While doing some research for a natural solution online I stumbled across the Tropical Traditions website, and read about all the health benefits of Virgin Coconut Oil. I didn't see anything specific about helping to alleviate the dry skin of psoriasis, but it did say it was an excellent skin moisturizer, so I thought I would give it a try. The day I got it I started adding a little to just about everything I ate. I ended up incorporating about 2-3 tablespoons a day into my food, and using it as a moisturizer on my psoriasis patches as well as the rest of my body. In no time at all my psoriasis was gone. As an added bonus my splotchy complexion started evening out, my skin has never been softer, and my body temperature rose to the level where I was no longer cold all the time. I am very grateful I found this perfect oil; it has made a huge difference in the way my skin looks and feels. I am now a lifetime customer of Tropical Traditions Virgin Coconut Oil.

Ashley - La Cygne, KS

Dear Tropical Traditions, I love your Virgin Coconut Oil! I started using it on my skin and in my diet after reading about its healing powers. I am a licensed esthetician and have been working with many clients with rosacea. Nothing was working. A few of my clients even tried prescription medication and expensive laser treatments. As a skin care specialist, I am used to using multiple products on my skin and on my clients, yet I transitioned to only using a mild cleanser and Virgin Coconut Oil on my self. I decided to experiment on my clients. During a skin care treatment on my client with tenacious rosacea, I applied coconut oil and let it absorb for about 15 minutes. I could see results instantly. My client was very pleased and has continued to see more improvement! I look forward to receiving your product so I can have it available to my clients to use everyday. Who would have thought it could be that simple? **Leslie** Licensed Esthetician

Sun Protection

One of the most interesting facts about people who live in tropical climates like the Philippines, where the people are constantly exposed to the rays of the sun year round, is that skin cancer is almost unheard of in these places. Here in the U.S. we are constantly warned about the dangers of exposure to the sun, and yet the sun helps our bodies produce much needed nutrients for our skin, such as vitamin D, which has been shown to *prevent* cancer.[2]

Once again we see that coconut oil is probably one of the main reasons people in tropical climates can spend so much time in the sun and not suffer from skin cancer. Coconut oil has wonderful antioxidant properties that protect the skin from free radical damage. Also, when coconut oil is consumed and used topically on our skin, it helps our bodies absorb other nutrients more effectively as well, such as vitamin E, another powerful antioxidant nutrient that protects the skin.

I am fair skinned but used VCO as a sunscreen in Florida last summer. My family thought I was crazy. I did not burn while everyone else did (with their toxic sunscreen). One day I did get a little too much sun, and was a little red, but I put the VCO on it and it was gone by the next day. So try it and see. Just be sensible about the sun. Nothing can protect you if you stand in the hot sun for a very long time. **Rachel** (Coconut Diet Forums)

I just got back from my 7-day trip to Jamaica. I used VCO exclusively as my sunscreen. I had no burns and my tan is even and golden. I am somewhat fair-skinned. Most of my time was spent in the shade, but I spent a good amount of time floating around on the water each day. My husband is even fairer and he did get pink slightly on his shoulders, at which time he applied both sunscreen and VCO to that area (VCO everywhere else). His tan is also pretty dark. People kept commenting on what nice color we were getting. Ha Ha. **Marnie** (Coconut Diet Forums)

It should be noted that when reports like this are made in our discussion group, invariably some will try using Virgin Coconut Oil exclusively as a sunscreen and go out and get burned! Some have even reported that sometimes the coconut oil works wonderfully as a sunscreen, while at other times they seem to get burned. It seems that the oils you put *into* your body are just as important as what you put *onto* your body in regards to sun protection. We have found that if one eats foods loaded with polyunsaturated oils, generally they will burn more in the sun. It is theorized that when one eats foods cooked in polyunsaturated vegetable oils, often with trans fatty acids, that one is putting oxidized lipids into their skin tissue that are causing free radical damage, and more susceptible to burning in the sun. So if you just got done eating some french fries from a fast food restaurant, you may be more susceptible to sun burn!

Under Arm Protection!

Another amazing result many are reporting from Virgin Coconut Oil is using it directly under their arms as a deodorant! Many have theorized that the MCTs in the oil attack the bacteria in sweat that cause the odors.

I have been using straight VCO as an underarm deodorant since last fall. It works wonders. It works just as good as any anti-perspirant deodorant I have ever used—you just don't have the fragrance from regular deodorant. I have a job that requires a lot of manual labor and my VCO deodorant has not failed me yet, even when I'm over-heated. **Abigail** (Coconut Diet Forums)

I used some VCO on a paper towel and put under my arms. It is like magic—no smell, no sweat—awesome!!!!!!! I just got back from biking and there's not a drop of sweat under my arms! **Jackie** (Coconut Diet Forums)

Chapter 8

Virgin Coconut Oil and Candida Yeast Infections

Young coconuts are transported from remote areas to jeepneys in the Philippines where they will be taken to the local markets.

For the past twenty years I have been affected by a chronic illness that creates a susceptibility to opportunistic imbalances like Candida. It's been five years that I have really been struggling with this (though the imbalance was established long before that). I read that taking Tropical Traditions Virgin Coconut Oil (TTVCO) could help with a Candida imbalance and it really has. Of course, I did experience the dread die-off when I began the TTVCO (Feb '04). This is not pleasant, but I know of nothing that works to balance this situation without creating a die-off. I began using the coconut oil at 1 tsp the first day and increased by 1 tsp each day until I was taking 1 tbsp with each meal (3x/day). I have also used the coconut oil to make suppositories with essential oils. This, too, has been very helpful. In addition, I am using well-chosen super-strain probiotics, enzymes, and nearly impeccable eating habits. Subduing a Candida overgrowth can be very costly. TTVCO is one of the more affordable tools I've come across, and it's a great addition to my curry recipes and the morning oatmeal (with cardamon, cinnamon and coriander). If it can make the difference for me that it does now, I imagine that had I found this five or ten years ago the Candida would never have gotten so out of hand. I recommend to anyone who is dealing with Candida overgrowth that they read about this product and seriously consider employing it. **Elizabeth** – Sacramento, CA

Candida albicans is yeast (or fungus) that normally inhabits our digestive system. In healthy people, Candida does little harm because it's kept in check by beneficial microorganisms, or probiotics. These "good" bacteria, however, can be easily destroyed by antibiotics, prescription medications, birth control pills, poor diet and daily stress, allowing Candida yeast to grow out of control and produce infections. Thought to affect more than 40 million Americans, Candida can cause uncomfortable symptoms such as vaginitis, weight retention, bowel disorders, ear and sinus irritation, intense itching, canker sores, and ringworm.

Yeast-connected health problems occur in people of all ages and both sexes. However, women are more apt to be affected. Yeasts are especially apt to play a role in causing your health problems if you:

1. Feel bad "all over," yet the cause can't be identified and treatment of many kinds hasn't helped.

2. Have taken prolonged courses of broad-spectrum antibiotic drugs, including the tetracyclines, ampicillin, amoxicillin, the cephalosporins, and sulfonamide drugs.

3. Have consumed diets containing a lot of yeast and sugar.

4. Crave sweets, breads, or alcoholic beverages.

5. Notice that sweets make your symptoms worse or give you a "pick-up," followed by a "let-down."

6. Have symptoms of hypoglycemia.

7. Have taken birth control pills, prednisone, Decadron® or other corticosteroid drugs.

8. Have had multiple pregnancies.

9. Have been troubled by recurrent problems related to your reproductive organs, including abdominal pain, vaginal infection or discomfort, premenstrual tension, menstrual irregularities, prostatitis, or impotence.

10. Are bothered by persistent or recurrent symptoms involving your digestive and nervous systems.

11. Have been bothered by persistent or recurrent athlete's foot, fungus infection of the nails, or "jock itch."

12. Feel bad on damp days or in moldy places.

13. Are made ill when exposed to perfumes, tobacco smoke, and other chemicals.[1]

Prolonged antibiotic use is believed to be the most important factor in the development of chronic Candidiasis. Antibiotics suppress the immune system and the normal intestinal bacteria that prevent yeast overgrowth, strongly promoting the proliferation of Candida. Systemic Candidiasis is when Candida spreads throughout the body, outside just the digestive tract, and it can be life-threatening.

> I definitely wanted to report my testimony. I had my baby a couple of years ago at home and went to the hospital to get stitched from a third degree tear. While there, they gave me 1/2 a bottle of antibiotic. When I realized what it was, I took the needle out of my arm and left, but not without a horrible yeast infection which affected both my baby and me. I had it on my breasts and she had it on her tongue and both of us were miserable. I had read about the coconut oil killing yeast so I started applying it topically as well as taking it internally. I ate quite a bit. I would melt it in a shot glass and take shots, put it in recipes, and use it as a weapon against the infection that had waged a war in my body. (I even had yeast in my eyes.) Well, finally it left after much persistence on my part. The other "side effect" I had from the coconut oil during the 3 month battle against yeast, was that my weight went below where it had started at the beginning of the pregnancy. I gained 50 pounds while pregnant and was a size 6 within 3 months of the birth. I am pregnant again and when I saw my midwife for the first time for this pregnancy, she could NOT believe how thin I was. I must say it was the coconut oil, as my exercising fervor went out the window as soon as baby #1 was born. When anyone asks how I got so thin or stay so thin after

pregnancy, I swear by the coconut oil. My shot glass is ready and I will be taking it when baby #2 is born as well. I think it's good for my milk as well—my baby was VERY healthy and continues to be amazingly aware in mind, body, and spirit. Thanks for getting out the good news! **Rachel** - San Antonio, TX

Getting rid of Candida and restoring the proper balance of healthy flora within one's digestive system is no easy task. It takes a multifaceted approach to kill the yeast, promote the healthy microorganisms, and watch one's diet to prevent the yeast from feeding on excessive sugar. The medium chain fatty acids in coconut oil are effective in killing off the yeast, but if this happens too quickly it can cause a "die-off" effect that is referred to as a *Herxheimer* reaction, which is the result of the rapid killing of microorganisms and absorption of large quantities of yeast toxins, cell particles, and antigens. Your symptoms may get worse before they improve. Tom's story illustrates this:

> I have only recently discovered coconut oil and want to relate how it caused a severe Herxheimer reaction. I've been battling a systemic Candida yeast infection for over ten years. I have the mutated (fungal) stage and it's the toughest thing I've ever had to deal with. I recently read research reports out of Harvard and the University of Tennessee that this can be deadly and there are no phamaceuticals for it that are effective. Candida yeast can overgrow in the gut under the right conditions until it mutates and becomes an invading pathogen, moves out of the gut and grows in mass in any part of the body. When it affects a vital organ, then it can be deadly. I've tried everything from conventional drugs to all the natural remedies including caprylic acid but have never experienced a die off reaction as I did when I took the Virgin Coconut Oil and aerobic oxygen for about one week. I have subcutaneous masses on the scalp, face, buttocks, arms, and probably internally, that I can't see. I applied the coconut [oil] heavily and would melt a large hunk in my mouth all during the day. My skin is starting to look better and I know from the reaction that it killed off a lot of Candida. The Herxheimer reaction is a welcome sign that you are doing something right. In cases where people are suffering with a chronic problem there may be a quick and somewhat adverse reaction. The "die-off effect," or Herxheimer reaction, refers to symptoms generated by a detoxification process. As the body begins to deal with dead microbes, one may experience a variety of detox symptoms. I am now recovering from the reaction and will start another round of coconut oil. [This oil] is something I will not be without for the rest of my life. Brian, thanks for all your efforts in bringing this to market. **Tom** (The Coconut Diet Forums)

To determine if you might suffer from Candida, Dr. W. G. Crook has developed a questionnaire that you can fill out. See Appendix 1.

Research

There is good research now that shows the medium chain fatty acids in coconut oil kill Candida yeast. Caprylic acid is one of the fatty acids found in coconut oil that has been used for quite some time in fighting Candida yeast infections. William Crook, M.D., the author of *The Yeast Connection* and the questionnaire above, reports that many physicians have used caprylic acid successfully for yeast infections and that it works especially well for those patients who have adverse reactions to antifungal drugs.

Besides caprylic acid, two other medium chain fatty acids found in coconut oil have been found to kill Candida albicans. A study done at the University of Iceland showed "capric acid, a 10-carbon saturated fatty acid, causes the fastest and most effective killing of all three strains of Candida albicans tested, leaving the cytoplasm disorganized and shrunken because of a disrupted or disintegrated plasma membrane. Lauric acid, a 12-carbon saturated fatty acid, was the most active at lower concentrations and after a longer incubation time."[2] This study shows great promise that all the medium chain fatty acids in coconut oil work together to kill Candida albicans.

> I am a walking testimonial to the benefits of a low carbohydrate/high fat diet with regard to Candida and cystitis. I used to purchase Monistat two or three packages at a time. Now I use lots of coconut oil for cooking and eat plenty of coconut products such as fresh coconut, coconut flakes, and coconut milk. Coconut contains capric/caprylic acid and lauric acid both proven to kill Candida while leaving healthy intestinal flora intact. I was taking a long-term, broad-spectrum antibiotic for chronic cystitis for over two years and now it's been two years since I stopped refilling the prescription with no recurrence! By far the most remarkable transformation occurred when I started using Virgin Coconut Oil and simultaneously eliminated skim milk and all soy products from my diet. And I lost weight! – **Laura** (Coconut Diet Forums)

It is interesting that people who eat a lot of coconuts live in areas where yeast and fungi are extremely plentiful, yet they are rarely troubled by infections. Women in the Philippines who eat their traditional coconut-based diet rarely, if ever, get yeast infections. Eating coconut oil on a regular basis, as the Filipinos do, would help to keep Candida yeast overgrowth at bay.

The Coconut Diet Anti-Yeast Program

In addition to Virgin Coconut Oil, if you suspect that you have a Candida yeast overgrowth, we strongly recommend you supplement your diet with strong probiotics to balance the flora in your intestinal tract and rebuild your immune system. Traditional fermented foods are one of the best additions you can make to your diet, while eliminating refined sugars and simple carbohydrates that the yeasts feed upon.

Fermented milk called "Kefir", a yogurt-like drink, is one traditional food originating from the Caucasus region of Central Asia and Turkey. It is best to make this drink yourself from real Kefir grains, rather than purchasing ready-made Kefir drinks, or kits that only contain "starter cultures" without the actual self-propagating Kefir grains. The best non-commercial website on Kefir, with links on where to obtain real Kefir grains, is: http://users.chariot.net.au/~dna/kefirpage.html run by Dominic N. Anfiteatro in Australia.

Other great traditional fermented foods and beverages would include sauerkraut, kimchee, chutney, and kombucha. Make sure they are not pasteurized, which would kill all the beneficial microorganisms.

As far as supplements go, we highly recommend the homeostatic soil organisms contained in Primal Defense, by Garden of Life. Many Candida sufferers have responded well with this type of probiotic. It is best to begin with the 15-day program called Fungal Defense (Garden of Life), and then follow this up with at least 6 months of probiotic supplementation with Primal Defense.

So to summarize the Coconut Diet Anti-Yeast program:

1. Slowly work up to at least 3.5 tablespoons of Virgin Coconut Oil into one's diet.

2. Add traditional fermented foods to one's diet.

3. Eliminate sugars and simple carbohydrates (white breads, pasta, etc.) as much as possible from your diet.

4. Once your system is used to the Virgin Coconut Oil, begin the 15-day Fungal Defense supplements.

5. Follow-up with Primal Defense supplementation at maximum dosage for at least 6 months.

At each step be aware that there could be "die-off" reactions as described above. Just slow down and decrease the rate of whatever you are doing at that time, or cut back altogether for a while, until your body adjusts.

> I would like to share my story with coconut oil in hope that others will also be able to benefit from the various wonders of this oil!! I have been taking the Virgin Coconut Oil for over six weeks now, 3 tablespoons each day. Previously I was suffering from unstable energy levels, lethargy, low body temperature, and Candida albicans. I noticed, within just a few days, dramatic increases in my mood, my energy, etc. I replaced all the hempseed oil and flax oil in my diet with the Virgin Coconut Oil. I simply love cooking with it and the pleasant taste of it! To date I have marked many positive changes—my energy levels are now more stable and I do not tire easily. I'm feeling much more energized than before. My body temperature has risen from a low 97 degrees to now a mid 98 degrees everyday!! I used to get so cold very easily, but do not experience this anymore. My hair has become so soft and manageable and my nails are growing at such a fast rate! Also my Candida-related symptoms have drastically lowered. I feel like a new person and without a doubt recommend coconut oil to anyone, even for those who are healthy! I've been telling all my friends and family about how wonderful the coconut oil is. I only wish that more people could experience this as well! To good health. **Jennifer** - Canada

Chapter 9

Does Coconut Oil Affect Cholesterol Levels?

Only the best coconuts are selected to make Virgin Coconut Oil.

I use Virgin Coconut Oil, olive oil, and butter in my cooking, and add Virgin Coconut Oil to my smoothies. I also eat coconut oil just by the tablespoon. My total cholesterol went down over 100 points. HDL and LDL were great! My co-workers could not believe I was eating so much fat and watching my cholesterol levels go down. I had to take a fasting [blood] test to prove it to them. I have lost 18 pounds in three months. I have learned a new way of life and it's easy. I'm healthier for it, too. I will never count calories again! **Laurel** (Coconut Diet Forums)

Population Studies

Coconut oil (and all saturated fats) has been blamed for many years as a cause of increased cholesterol levels, which supposedly leads to heart disease. But studies done on traditional tropical populations that consume large amounts of coconut oil show just the opposite. One of the best ways to study the effects of coconut oil on human nutrition is to look at tropical populations that get most of their caloric intake from the saturated fat of coconut oil. Logic would dictate that if the saturated fat/cholesterol theory of heart disease and obesity were correct, those populations with the highest consumption of saturated fats would be the most overweight and have the highest rates of heart disease. Such is not the case.

As we have reported earlier, in a study published in 1981, the populations of two South Pacific islands were examined over a period of time starting in the 1960s, before western foods were prevalent in the diets of either culture. The study was designed to investigate the relative effects of saturated fat and dietary cholesterol in determining serum cholesterol levels. Coconuts were practically a staple in the diets, with up to 60% of their caloric intake coming from the saturated fat of coconut oil. The study found very healthy people who were relatively free from the modern diseases of western cultures, including obesity and heart disease. Their conclusion: "Vascular disease is uncommon in both populations and there is no evidence of the high saturated fat intake having a harmful effect in these populations."[1]

> I had been taking Tropical Traditions Coconut Oil for obvious health benefits when I realized one day that my knees weren't hurting, so I stopped for a day or two and they hurt again. I have one artificial knee, and one that isn't in very good shape, and they used to hurt all the time. When I resume the oil, the pain goes away, so that makes me very happy. Also, my cholesterol went from 242 to 218. I take about 2 teaspoon/day and haven't gained any weight, although I eat anything I want, so it works for me. **Darleen** - Othello, WA

Another study, which we have refereneced earlier in this book, was done on the Indian subcontinent comparing traditional cooking oils with modern oils in relation to prevalence of atherosclerotic heart disease and Type-II diabetes. Their conclusion:

> In contrast to earlier epidemiologic studies showing a low prevalence of atherosclerotic heart disease (AHD) and Type-

II dependent diabetes mellitus (Type-II DM) in the Indian subcontinent, over the recent years, there has been an alarming increase in the prevalence of these diseases in Indians—both abroad and at home, attributable to increased dietary fat intake. Replacing the traditional cooking fats condemned to be atherogenic, with refined vegetable oils promoted as 'heart-friendly' because of their polyunsaturated fatty acid (PUFA) content, unfortunately, has not been able to curtail this trend. Current data on dietary fats indicate that it is not just the presence of PUFA, but the type of PUFA that is important—a high PUFA n-6 content and high n-6/n-3 ratio in dietary fats being atherogenic and diabetogenic. The newer 'heart-friendly' oils like sunflower or safflower oils possess this undesirable PUFA content and there are numerous research data now available to indicate that the sole use or excess intake of these newer vegetable oils are actually detrimental to health and switching to a combination of different types of fats, including the traditional cooking fats like ghee, coconut oil and mustard oil, would actually reduce the risk of dyslipidaemias, AHD and Type-II DM.[2]

When measurements of serum cholesterol (cholesterol levels in the blood) were first done, only the total of both HDL ("good cholesterol") and LDL ("bad cholesterol") were read. Now that testing has become more sophisticated, researchers look more at the balance of these two types of cholesterol. They note whether a substance raises cholesterol levels of HDL or LDL levels. In some cases, certain foods lower total cholesterol, but only by lowering good HDL cholesterol while at the same time actually raising levels of the bad LDL cholesterol. Studies now show that coconut oil actually increases the good HDL cholesterol, while lowering LDL. So total cholesterol levels may actually increase, but in a very favorable ratio.

I have been on Virgin Coconut Oil (VCO) since early June (1 Tbsp per day in oatmeal and using it on my skin). I had a blood test performed at the end of August. My total cholesterol did go up since last year from 168 mg/dL to 187 mg/dL currently as did my Triglycerides from 60 mg/dL to 72 mg/dL (all within normal range). My HDL ("good" cholesterol) jumped from 60 mg/dL to 85 mg/dL! My LDL ("bad" cholesterol) dropped from 96 mg/dL to 87 mg/dL. My Cholesterol/ HDL ratio dropped from 2.8 ratio units to 2.2 ratio units. I live in a dry climate, but my skin is soft and smooth from using VCO. I find that the oil rids my face of wrinkles, as others on the list have experienced. When I have dinner with my son at the restaurant where he works, his co-workers assume that I am a friend his age. They don't believe him when he tells them that I am his mother. I had gained twenty pounds from forced inactivity due to disc problems in my back, but I have lost those and am now a size 4-6 again. I will definitely keep using the VCO. **Gayle** (The Coconut Diet Forums)

Faulty Science

In a lecture given in Viet Nam in 1996, Dr. Mary Enig stated:

> The problems for coconut oil started four decades ago when researchers fed animals hydrogenated coconut oil that was purposely altered to make it completely devoid of any essential fatty acids. The animals fed the hydrogenated coconut oil (as the only fat source) naturally became essential fatty acid deficient; their serum cholesterol increased. Diets that cause an essential fatty acid deficiency always produce an increase in serum cholesterol levels as well as an increase in the atherosclerotic indices. The same effect has also been seen when other highly hydrogenated oils such as cottonseed, soybean or corn oils have been fed; so it is clearly a function of the hydrogenated products, either because the oil is essential fatty acid (EFA) deficient or because of trans fatty acids.[3]

What about studies where animals were fed unprocessed coconut oil? Enig wrote: "Hostmark et al (1980) compared the effects of diets containing 10% coconut oil and 10% sunflower oil on lipoprotein distribution in male Wistar rats. Coconut oil feeding produced significantly lower levels (p=0.05) of pre-beta lipoproteins (VLDL) and significantly higher (p=<0.01) alpha-lipoproteins (HDL) relative to sunflower feeding."[4] She also cited a study by Awad (1981) on Wistar rats fed a diet of either 14% (natural) coconut oil or 14% safflower oil. She stated: "Total tissue cholesterol accumulation for animals on the safflower diet was six times greater than for animals fed the [unhydrogenated] coconut oil. A conclusion that can be drawn from some of the animal research is that feeding hydrogenated coconut oil devoid of essential fatty acids (EFA) potentate the formation of atherosclerosis markers. It is of note that animals fed regular coconut oil have less cholesterol deposited in their livers and other parts of their bodies."[5]

Do Saturated Fats Clog Arteries?

Saturated fats are probably the most maligned fats in the popular media today. They are often blamed for "clogging arteries" and leading to heart disease. However, an examination of the research and science behind saturated fats leads one to a vastly different conclusion, suggesting that the attacks against saturated fats have been primarily political and economical, and not scientific. While we will provide a brief summary of the science behind saturated fats here, we encourage you to examine the research more closely yourself. Much of it is documented at www. coconutoil.com.

First of all, saturated fats are essential to our health. They comprise about 50% of our cell membranes, and some proportion of saturated fats are found in all fats and oils, whether plant-based or animal-based.

In recent years some have made claims that too much saturated fats in our diet can lead to higher cholesterol levels and clogged arteries, which leads to heart disease. So an anti-saturated fat campaign was launched in the U.S. in recent years. As a result, Americans have consumed less saturated fats than any other nation, yet the U.S. is still a world leader in deaths from heart disease. Obesity rates are also at an all-time high. Many are now questioning the "wisdom" behind the low-fat nutritional advice that has dominated the popular media (see Gary Taubes article "The Soft Science of Dietary Fat" at www. coconutoil.com)

Does research support the claim that saturated fats like coconut oil raise cholesterol levels and clog arteries? This "lipid theory" of heart disease, which blames high cholesterol levels as causing heart disease, is being seriously questioned by researchers and doctors. Malcom Kendrick M.D., Dr. Mary Enig Ph.D., Uffe Ravnskov M.D., Ph.D (author of *The Cholesterol Myths*), George Mann M.D., Sc.D, and many other top researchers have written extensively on the flaws of the "cholesterol theory" of heart disease. You can read more about the cholesterol issue at www.coconutoil.com

As to the research on "clogged arteries," a study was done at the Wynn Institute for Metabolic Research, London, examining the composition of human aortic plaques. This study found that the "artery clogging fats" in those who died from heart disease were composed of 26%

saturated fat: the rest (74%) were polyunsaturated fatty acids, such as those found in vegetable oils commonly consumed in today's modern societies. Their conclusion: "No associations were found with saturated fatty acids. These findings imply a direct influence of dietary polyunsaturated fatty acids on aortic plaque formation and suggest that current trends favoring increased intake of polyunsaturated fatty acids should be reconsidered."[6]

> My doctor wanted me to start taking pravachol to lower my cholesterol, which was 219. He said, "Because you are diabetic, I don't want you to have a heart attack once your blood sugars are under control." I told him I wanted to see if I could bring my cholesterol down naturally with VCO and eating right. I began taking VCO last spring when I read about it in Woman's World Magazine. At the time I had a lot of problems with hypothyroid, fibromyalgia, IBS, Candida, super dry skin and skin rashes, etc. I have stopped taking all meds for my gastrointestinal symptoms and my skin is now silky soft and smooth. My blood work done on December 4, 2003 showed my cholesterol was down 31 points to 188 mg/dl. **Ann** (The Coconut Diet Forums)

> Hi. I don't post often but felt I had to on this one. I just got back from the doctor's office and my total cholesterol went [down]. My doc was SO happy. I've been going to her for over 15 years and dreaded every time I got the blood test. It was always the same thing—a lecture. I had always used olive oil for years but started using coconut oil for most of our cooking (olive oil occasionally). My cholesterol results after at least 15 years of being high: triglycerides was 187, now 109. Cholesterol, total was 260, now 185. Chol/hdlc ratio 5.41, now 4.1. Glucose 105, now 94. My doctor was ecstatic. I believe I already mentioned this, but I can now use these statistics for anyone who gives me a hard time [about using Virgin Coconut Oil.] **Sally Ann** (The Coconut Diet Forums)

Chapter 10

Coconut Oil in Pet and Animal Nutrition

Adding coconut oil to your pet's diet is one of the healthiest things you can do for your pet! Read below how other users from The Coconut Diet Forums are using coconut oil for their cats, dogs, birds and horses! This is just a sample of the testimonies about what coconut oil is doing for pets and animals.

For Dogs

> Actually, I give all my animals Virgin Coconut Oil on their food. The two most dramatic improvements to their health are:

> Casey is a Chihuahua mix we were given as a gift when she was young.

Her hind knees are a bit knobby and the vet said we would have to watch them as she has a loose ligament in them and she may eventually need surgery. She was hesitant to jump up on the couch or bed and we often assisted her by picking her up. Even though she was a young dog, she acted much older. I began putting Virgin Coconut Oil on her food and in no time she began springing up onto everything! The vet was amazed.

Belkie is a long-haired Chihuahua mix and he was in very poor condition when we rescued him. You could feel every bone in his body. He had several bad teeth that needed pulling and his coat was very coarse. He cowered around and was very sad. After having him about a month and having some dental work done, his health and attitude improved. However, I still could not get him to stop itching. He did not have one flea on him, but he still itched! I added Virgin Coconut Oil to his food and in no time, he stopped itching and his coat is shiny, soft, and bright. He is the happiest little guy you ever saw!

My neighbor also has a female Doberman that they adore. She became very ill and could not stand. Their vet said Dobermans often develop "Wobblers" and there was not much they could do—it was degenerative and she may have about a month to live. He and his wife were, of course, crushed. I, of course, never give up and told him to add Virgin Coconut Oil to her food. I sent my neighbor home with a small jar of the precious oil. He was willing to try anything. They were having to force feed her a liquid diet at the time. In 24 hours the dog was up! Over the course of the week she continued to improve. He now puts it in her food daily. She no longer wobbles when she walks and all is right with the world! My neighbor was amazed. **Susan** (The Coconut Diet Forums)

I have begun adding Virgin/Expeller-pressed coconut oil (whichever I happen to have) to my dogs' food several times a week. They have been eating this way for two months now and the results are nothing less than spectacular. My purebred Bernese Mountain Dog is now growing in a lustrous, soft, gorgeous coat. And I've never seen him scratch! I can't wait to see how it looks when it has grown in completely! My CollieX rescue lost the spare tire he was carrying around his middle and has gained lots of energy. His coat is also shiny, soft, and with no hint of itchiness or flakes. They are both in incredible weight and condition— enough so that I have begun to take my Virgin Coconut Oil religiously again! They lost weight, so can I! **Irene** (The Coconut Diet Forums)

I feed my dog a tablespoon of Virgin Coconut Oil every morning and I put some in her food. She loves it and her coat is shiny. The other day she got stung by a bee and her mouth was swollen. I rubbed some Virgin Coconut Oil plus gave her a tablespoon and within an hour the swelling had gone down and she was up and about. **Michelle** (The Coconut Diet Forums)

We make our own dog food. We were feeding the dog a very expensive canned lamb and rice diet, the one our holistic vet recommended. But when his health turned for the worse, we decided to make the food ourselves and we now spend much less. We buy organic brown and long grain rice in bulk and cook a cup at a time. To that we add cooked organically grown, ground lamb, or bison or sometimes ground turkey. We cut up vegetables and add that to the meat and sauté in coconut oil. We divide the mixture in half and freeze one part. (He's a small dog; we feed him about 1 cup a day—divided into two meals.) He's 12 and his health has greatly improved—soared actually! He has great energy, a beautiful coat, shining eyes, and a great resistance to illness. **Cherie Calbom** M.S. *The Juice Lady*

How much to give?

All of our dogs (6) get coconut oil every day, and they line up to get it when they see me get the jar of it out. Needless to say, their coats are sleek and shiny. The amount of coconut oil I give my dogs is primarily based on the reason I am giving it. I don't know of any other guide for doing it. One is quite overweight with a known thyroid condition—about 90 lbs., so he gets at least a couple of Tbsp. Two of the others have some dry "dandruffy" skin and weigh less, so they get about 3-4 tsp. per day. Another has absolutely nothing wrong with her, so I give it preventatively and to keep her coat good—about 1-2 Tbsp. as she is about 80 lbs. The little one, about 20 lbs. gets at least a teaspoon—often more. She has very dry skin and I adjust it to her scratching. The outdoor dog (outside because she doesn't get along with one of the others in the house, and she came last) gets about a Tbsp. just because she is out in the weather.

I also give it as needed as the occasion(s) arises. For instance, a couple of them recently had some parasites. My holistic vet recommended some other stuff for them, but by the time he got it in the mail to me, I only needed part of it because the coconut oil had already had a good head start in getting the problem resolved.

These amounts are all subject to change, of course, depending on needs, but I just use common sense. I don't worry much about giving them too much, as long as what I give seems reasonable. I am also in the process of making my own dog food, as the more I read about the processed stuff, the more I'm not willing to feed that stuff to my dogs. If I'm not willing to eat something, I'm not willing to feed it to my dogs. I am using coconut oil in all of their food. **Debby** (The Coconut Diet Forums)

For Cats

I put Virgin Coconut Oil in my kitty's homemade cat food, and her coat is gorgeous. Even the vet commented on how beautiful it was! I also keep a glob (its cold in NY so it stays hard) next to her food bowl, and she nibbles whenever she needs it. Sometimes she doesn't touch it for a while.. then she will eat a lot the next week. I believe she just eats it when her body needs it. **Rachel** (The Coconut Diet Forums)

My testimonial is for my beloved cat, Sara. Sara is over 13 years old and is absolutely spoiled rotten!!! She's all black with green eyes rimmed in yellow, with a few stray white hairs on her chest. For the past 3 years Sara had been coughing. She'd stick her neck out close to the ground and cough, as if she had a fur ball. Most of the time while in the house she would not produce anything. It kept getting worse and worse. Once in a while we'd see some fur balls she had coughed up on our deck outside. I had talked to the vet about it many times. They ruled out any lung problems, tested her for thyroid disorders and diabetes...nothing. They determined it was fur balls and gave me a tube of hairball remedy. She licked it off the vet's finger while at the office. I put it on my finger the next day and she would not lick it off. I then put it in her dish. She left it there to rot. I then put it on her paw—so she would lick it off. She flung it on the carpet and it stained! How frustrating & her cough kept getting worse. I thought, "What am I going to do?" Then I thought of coconut oil—it could soothe her throat and improve her fur. Why not? It's very healthy—I use coconut oil in baking and cooking. I first heated up the oil and mixed it in her food and she would eat it. I noticed while she ate she would deliberately lick the coconut oil first—then eat her food. So now every morning I clean her little bowl and heat up a little coconut oil and I put about a teaspoon in her dish and she licks it right away! She now looks for it every morning and I haven't heard her cough in months! Her coat is absolutely beautiful—so soft and shiny! The coconut oil ended the fur ball coughing. What a relief! Sincerely, **Susan** (The Coconut Diet Forums)

For Horses

Coconut is a brilliant food for horses giving them extra energy and a shiny coat. I would not hesitate to say that it would do wonders applied externally to the skin of a horse also. In coconut communities coconut oil is a universal treatment for human cuts, abrasions, skin infections of all kinds. **Mike** (The Coconut Diet Forums)

My horse had some kind of irritation on it's face. The vet said it wasn't a fungus. I've been putting Virgin Coconut Oil on it almost everyday and it is definitely clearing. My friend's horse had a cyst on it's face. She has been putting Virgin Coconut Oil on it and the cyst went away. My mare's face is 98% clear now. I also use it on one of my horses' bald face to avoid sunburn. His white nose area used to be bright pink when he came in from the pasture. I was putting suntan lotion on him but he would pull away. He loves the Virgin Coconut Oil on his face. They know what is good :). **Lori** (The Coconut Diet Forums)

The horses really do like the coconut oil! We are having to feed our horses hay cubes to prepare them for a week at a horse ranch where all they feed is hay cubes. My daughter's horse particularly, does not like the cubes! I suggested to her to put some coconut oil on them to see if that would help him eat the cubes and it worked! He started eating them. My only concern now is being able to afford the coconut oil for both our horses and us!! **Mary** (The Coconut Diet Forums)

This information is supplied by a user for horses. I have not had direct experience. He told me that the horses in training for racing are fed between 50 grams and 100 grams [of coconut oil] per day. They develop greater stamina for both galloping and trotting races, and the shiny coat and general good health is a bonus. **Mike** (The Coconut Diet Forums)

For Birds

I MUST share this with you as YOUR product REALLY worked wonderfully and I wanted you to know! I am glad that you have looked further into the coconut oil. I AM NOT attempting to SELL anything BUT please bear with me with one previous instance which frightened me to death. The other morning I awoke to lots of blood in TIKI's aviary (my Ducorps Cockatoo). Evidently somehow she had cracked her beak quite seriously, unbeknownst to me. After bathing her because her feathers were quite bloody from her preening, which I did not know at the time, I realized the blood was from her beak. The beak was seriously fractured AND still bleeding. Of course it was the weekend with NO avian vets available. I was at a loss. So after cleaning TIKI, seeing she was calm, I took the coconut oil in my hands and abundantly on my fingers. TIKI rested her beak upon my fingers—as if it were comforting, as if the bird KNEW this was going to help. For 15 to 20 minutes we continued applying more coconut oil and the bleeding subsided, to BOTH our relief!!!!! Then, as I worried I decided that it would be best to only offer TIKI soft foods & liquids with ALOE & coconut oil only, which TIKI nibbled at slowly but surely. Each day TIKI healed remarkably. TODAY, four days later, there is little evidence of TIKI's cracked beak, although I continue to feed TIKI oatmeal & veggies with coconut oil each morning—very warmed and she eats very well. SO, I am convinced that the coconut oil indeed helped HEAL TIKI. TIKI is totally back to normal now. I even had calls to several vets who merely said IF I controlled the bleeding there was little they could do UNLESS infection set in—then antibiotics would be necessary. WELL, thank goodness. COCONUT OIL IS INDEED antiviral & antibacterial. I BELIEVE this is TRUE now—with our specific situation. TIKI continues to rub her beak into coconut oil daily as if the bird KNOWS she NEEDS it!! NOW that is remarkable I THINK!! **Sandy** (The Coconut Diet Forums)

References

Chapter 2: What is Virgin Coconut Oil?

1. Nevin KG, Rajamohan T. "Beneficial effects of virgin coconut oil on lipid parameters and in vitro LDL oxidation." Clinical Biochemistry. 2004 Sep;37(9):830-5.

Chapter 3: The Health Benefits of Virgin Coconut Oil

1. IA Prior, F Davidson, CE Salmond, Z Czochanska. "Cholesterol, coconuts, and diet on Polynesian atolls: a natural experiment: the Pukapuka and Tokelau island studies." American Journal of Clinical Nutrition. 1981 Aug;34(8):1552-61.

2. S Sircar, U Kansra Department of Medicine, Safdarjang Hospital, New Delhi. "Choice of cooking oils—myths and realities." Journal Indian Medical Association. 1998 Oct;96(10):304-7.

3. P.K Thampan,. "Facts and Fallacies about Coconut Oil," Asian and Pacific Coconut Community, Jakarta, 1994.

4. H. Kaunitz J "Medium chain triglycerides (MCT) in aging and arteriosclerosis." Journal of Environmental Pathology, Toxicology, and Oncology. 1986 Mar-Apr;6(3-4):115-21.

5. J. J. Kabara "Health Oils From the Tree of Life" (Nutritional and Health Aspects of Coconut Oil). Indian Coconut Journal 2000;31(8):2-8.

6. Mary G. Enig, PhD. "Health and Nutritional Benefits from Coconut Oil: An Important Functional Food for the 21st Century" Presented at the AVOC Lauric Oils Symposium, Ho Chi Min City, Vietnam, April, 25, 1996.

7. G Bergsson, J Arnfinnsson, O Steingrimsson, H Thormar. "In vitro killing of Candida albicans by fatty acids and monoglycerides." Antimicrob Agents Chemother 2001 Nov;45(11):3209-12

8. Mary Enig, Ph.D Trans Fatty Acids in the Food Supply: A Comprehensive Report Covering 60 Years of Research , 2nd Edition, 1995, Enig Associates, Inc., Silver Spring, MD, pp 4-8

9. Mary G Enig, Ph.D "Coconut: In Support of Good Health in the 21st Century." Presented at the Asian Pacific Coconut Community's 36th Session, 1999.

10. S Stender, J Dyerberg "Denmark is the first county in the world to forbid the use of industrially produced fatty acids" Ugeskr Laeger, 2004 Jan 5;166(1-2):29-32.

11. FDA website: http://www.fda.gov/oc/initiatives/transfat/

12. Mary G Enig, Ph.D "The Tragic Legacy of CSPI" Wise Traditions in Food, Farming and the Healing Arts, the quarterly magazine of the Weston A. Price Foundation, Fall 2003

13. Mary G Enig, Ph.D "The Tragic Legacy of CSPI"

14. Watkins, B A, et al, "Importance of Vitamin E in Bone Formation and in Chrondrocyte Function" Purdue University, Lafayette, IN, AOCS Proceedings, 1996; Watkins, B A, and M F Seifert, "Food Lipids and Bone Health," Food Lipids and Health, R E McDonald and D B Min, eds, (Marcel Dekker, Inc, New York, 1996) p 101.

15. Dahlen, G H, et al, J Intern Med, Nov 1998, 244(5):417-24; Khosla, P, and K C Hayes, Journal American College Nutrition, 1996, 15:325-339;

16. Nanji, A A, et al, Gastroenterology, Aug 1995, 109(2):547-54; Cha, Y S, and D S Sachan, Journal American College Nutrition, Aug 1994, 13(4):338-43; Hargrove, H L, et al, FASEB Journal, Meeting Abstracts, Mar 1999, #204.1, p A222.

17. Kabara, J J, The Pharmacological Effects of Lipids, The American Oil Chemists Society, Champaign, IL, 1978, 1-14; Cohen, L A, et al, Journal National Cancer Institue, 1986, 77:43.

18. Garg, M L, et al, FASEB Journal, 1988, 2:4:A852; Oliart Ros, R M, et al, "Meeting Abstracts," AOCS Proceedings, May 1998, 7, Chicago, IL.

19. Lawson, L D and F Kummerow, Lipids, 1979, 14:501-503; Garg, M L, Lipids, Apr 1989, 24(4):334-9.

Chapter 4: How Virgin Coconut Oil has Changed People's Lives

1. Michael Murray, N.D. and Joseph Pizzorno, N.D. Encyclopedia of Natural Medicine (Prima Publishing, Rocklin, CA 1998) p.301

2. Ronnie Cummins, "Hazards of Genetically Engineered Foods and Crops: Why We Need A Global Moratorium " Motion Magazine, August 29, 1999

3. Mary G. Enig, Ph.D. "Health and Nutritional Benefits from Coconut Oil: An Important Functional Food for the 21st Century" Presented at the AVOC Lauric Oils Symposium, Ho Chi Min City, Vietnam, 25 April 1996

4. Conrado S. Dayrit, MD "COCONUT OIL IN HEALTH AND DISEASE: ITS AND MONOLAURIN'S POTENTIAL AS CURE FOR HIV/AIDS", Philippine Department of Health, San Lazaro Hospital, 2000

5. Conrado S. Dayrit, MD

6. S Sircar, U Kansra Department of Medicine, Safdarjang Hospital, New Delhi. "Choice of cooking oils—myths and realities." Journal Indian Medical Association. 1998 Oct;96(10):304-7.

7. Hill JO, Peters JC, Yang D, Sharp T, Kaler M, Abumrad NN, Greene HL "Thermo-genesis in humans during overfeeding with medium-chain triglycerides." Metabolism. July.1989;38(7):641-8.

8. St-Onge MP, Ross R, Parsons WD, Jones PJ "Medium-chain triglycerides increase energy expenditure and decrease adiposity in overweight men." Obesity Research. 2003 Mar;11(3):395-402.

9. Joe Graedon and Teresa Graedon, "The People's Pharmacy Guide to Home and Herbal Remedies" (St. Martin's Press, New York 1999) p.193-195

10. Gorard DA, "Enteral nutrition in Crohn's disease: fat in the formula." European Journal Gastroenterol Hepatology. 2003 Apr;15(4):459

11. Jeppesen PB, Mortensen PB, "The influence of a preserved colon on the absorption of medium chain fat in patients with small bowel resection." Gut. 1998 Oct;43(4):478-83.

12. Manuel-y-Keenoy B, Nonneman L, et.al. "Effects of intravenous supplementa-tion with alpha-tocopherol in patients receiving total parenteral nutrition containing medium- and long-chain triglycerides." European Journal Clinical Nutrition 2002 Feb;56(2):121-8.

Chapter 5: Virgin Coconut Oil for Weight Loss

1. U.S. Department of Health and Human Services, "Obesity Still on the Rise, New Data Show," Tuesday, October 8, 2002 Published on the Centers for Disease Control website: http://www.cdc.gov/nchs/releases/02news/obesityonrise.htm

2. Rex Russell, M.D. "What the Bible Says About Healthy Living" (Regal Books, Ventura, CA 1996) p.125

3. M.T. See and J. Odle, "EFFECT OF DIETARY FAT SOURCE, LEVEL, AND FEEDING INTERVAL ON PORK FATTY ACID COMPOSITION" 1998-2000 De-partmental Report, Department of Animal Science, ANS Report No. 248 - North Carolina State University

4. Gary Taubes "What If It Were All a Big Fat Lie!" New York Times July 7, 2002

5. Griswold KE, Apgar GA, et. al. "Effectiveness of short-term feeding strategies for altering conjugated linoleic acid content of beef." Journal Animal Science, 2003 Jul;81(7):1862-71.

6. Scollan ND, Enser M, et. al., "Effects of including a ruminally protected lipid sup-plement in the diet on the fatty acid composition of beef muscle." British Journal Nutrition. 2003 Sep;90(3):709-16.

7. Endres J, Barter S, Theodora P, Welch P., "Soy-enhanced lunch acceptance by pre-schoolers." Journal American Diet Association. 2003 Mar;103(3):346-51.

8. Hill JO, Peters JC, Yang D, Sharp T, Kaler M, Abumrad NN, Greene HL "Thermogenesis in humans during overfeeding with medium-chain triglycerides." Metabolism. July.1989;38(7):641-8.

9. St-Onge MP, Ross R, Parsons WD, Jones PJ "Medium-chain triglycerides increase energy expenditure and decrease adiposity in overweight men." Obesity Research. 2003 Mar;11(3):395-402.

10. G. Crozier, B. Bois-Joyeux, M Chanex, et. al. "Overfeeding with medium-chain triglycerides in the rat." Metabolism 1987;36:807-814.

11. T. B. Seaton, S. L. Welles, M. K. Warenko, et al. "Thermic effects of medium-chain and long-chain triglycerides in man." American Journal Clinical Nutrition, 1986;44:630-634.

12. J. J. Kabara "Health Oils From the Tree of Life" (Nutritional and Health Aspects of Coconut Oil). Indian Coconut Journal 2000;31(8):2-8.

Chapter 6: Virgin Coconut Oil and Thyroid Health

1. Gay J. Canaris, MD, MSPH; Neil R. Manowitz, PhD; Gilbert Mayor, MD; E. Chester Ridgway, MD "The Colorado Thyroid Disease Prevalence Study" Archives Internal Medicine. 2000;160:526-534.

2. Mary Shomon, "Living Well With Hypothyroidism: What Your Doctor Doesn't Tell You. . . That You Need to Know" (New York Harper Collins, 2002)

3. Ridha Arem, "The Thyroid Solution : A Mind-Body Program for Beating Depression and Regaining Your Emotional and Physical Health" (New York: Ballantine Books,1999)

4. Raymond Peat Newsletter "Unsaturated Vegetable Oils Toxic" 1996

5. P. Fort, N. Moses, M. Fasano, T. Goldberg and F. Lifshitz "Breast and soy–formula feeding in early infancy and the prevalence of autoimmune thyroid disease in children"'Journal American College Nutrition. 1990;(9):164-167.

6. Daniel R. Doerge, Hebron C. Chang, "Inactivation of thyroid peroxidase by soy isoflavones in vitro and in vivo" Journal of Chromatography B Vol. 777 (1, 2); 25; September 2002: 269-79

7. M.T. See and J. Odle, "EFFECT OF DIETARY FAT SOURCE, LEVEL, AND FEEDING INTERVAL ON PORK FATTY ACID COMPOSITION" 1998-2000 Departmental Report, Department of Animal Science, ANS Report No. 248 - North Carolina State University

8. Raymond Peat Newsletter "Unsaturated Vegetable Oils Toxic" 1996

9. Raymond Peat Newsletter "Unsaturated Vegetable Oils Toxic" 1996

Chapter 7: Skin Health and Virgin Coconut Oil

1. Rele AS, Mohile RB. "Effect of mineral oil, sunflower oil, and coconut oil on prevention of hair damage." Journal Cosmetology Science 2003 Mar-Apr;54(2):175-92.

2. Cedric F Garland, "Sun avoidance will increase incidence of cancers overall" British Medical Journal November 22, 2003;327:1228

Chapter 8: Virgin Coconut Oil and Candida Yeast Infections

1. William G. Crook, M.D., "The Yeast Connection" (Vintage Books, 1986) - What This Book Is All About section

2. Gudmundur Bergsson, et. al., "In Vitro Killing of Candida albicans by Fatty Acids and Monoglycerides," Antimicrobial Agents and Chemotherapy, November 2001, p. 3209-3212, Vol. 45, No. 11

Chapter 9: Does Coconut Oil Affect Cholesterol Levels?

1. Prior IA, Davidson F, et. al. "Cholesterol, coconuts, and diet on Polynesian atolls: a natural experiment: the Pukapuka and Tokelau island studies." American Journal of Clinical Nutrition. 1981 Aug;34(8):1552-61.

2. Sircar S, Kansra U. "Choice of cooking oils—myths and realities." Journal Indian Medical Association. 1998 Oct;96(10):304-7.

3. Mary G. Enig, Ph.D. "Health and Nutritional Benefits from Coconut Oil: An Important Functional Food for the 21st Century" Presented at the AVOC Lauric Oils Symposium, Ho Chi Min City, Vietnam, 25 April 1996

4. Mary G. Enig, Ph.D

5. Mary G. Enig, Ph.D

6. Felton CV, Crook D, Davies MJ, Oliver MF. Wynn Institute for Metabolic Research, London, UK. "Dietary polyunsaturated fatty acids and composition of human aortic plaques." Lancet. Oct,1994; 29;344(8931):1195-6.

Recipes for The Coconut Diet

Virgin Coconut Oil and Coconut Cream Concentrate are the two primary ingredients in the recipes for the Coconut Diet.

The Coconut Diet

The Coconut Diet, in its simplest form, is simply replacing all trans fatty acids and other unhealthy polyunsaturated oils in your diet with Coconut Oil. The only other cooking oils we recommend are natural/red palm oil, extra virgin olive oil, and organic grass-fed butter. To experience the weight-loss effects and other health benefits of Virgin Coconut Oil, most people ingest between 2-4 tablespoons a day. There are many ways to incorporate coconut oil into your diet, and in this section we provide some foundational recipes that will help you incorporate coconut oil into your diet.

It has also been our experience that most people enjoy greater weight loss on a low-carb (or at least a reduced-carb) diet. Refined grains, especially, are one of the major culprits of obesity in the U.S. today. Therefore, the Coconut Diet can be incorporated into many popular diets on the market today. While most people starting a low-carb diet feel drained of energy, the increase in metabolism that coconut oil often brings gives unexpected energy to those on the Coconut Diet.

> With other low-carb programs I would be "dragging" by this time, with no weight loss. This is so different. Also, I'm not hungry at all. If anything I could eat less. At this time I have to say I am very pleased with the Coconut Diet, and expect to lose all the weight I want and be a lot healthier. - **Janice** (The Coconut Diet Forums)

When introducing high quality Virgin Coconut Oil (VCNO) into one's diet, it is important to start slow, because there are certain detoxification effects that could come into play since coconut oil is anti-bacterial, anti-fungal, and anti-viral. Also, many people are used to low-fat diets, and it takes a while to get used to consuming more fats. The most common side effects, when starting out, are diarrhea or stomach cramps. Since coconut oil in nature is packaged within the meat of the coconut, which is high in fiber and protein, it is recommended that you eat VCNO with high fiber and high protein foods to avoid potential side effects in the beginning. See our full FAQ in Chapter 2. One may also want to consider starting out with Coconut Cream Concentrate by Tropical Traditions, as this contains the whole coconut, including the fiber.

Food Sources

The recipes in this book were not designed for any particular dietary plan, but are meant to be the foundation for any dietary plan you may be following, where you want to now start incorporating coconut oil. We have many professional chefs and cooks now using Tropical Traditions Virgin Coconut Oil, and we are in the process of developing a database of recipes that will be able to be sorted according to a variety of food qualities—such as number of carbs, no-grain, no-dairy, vegetarian, etc. Sign up for the Coconut Diet forums at www.coconutdiet.com to watch for announcements regarding this project. In this section, we do include a complete nutritional analysis of each recipe so you can decide which ones are suitable for your eating style. We put the recommended daily allowance (RDA) percentages in also, for those who like to use that as a base, but obviously we feel the RDAs for saturated fats are too low, and the RDAs for polyunsaturated fats are too high! The whole purpose of these recipes is to help you incorporate Virgin Coconut Oil into your diet as much as possible. Each recipe states how much coconut oil is in each serving.

Many of the recipes use Coconut Cream Concentrate, which contains about 70 percent pure coconut oil but also contains the whole coconut, including all the fiber. It is used extensively for sauces and soups.

For recipes that do call for grains, we recommend organic whole grains. The best way to supply whole grains into your diet is to buy them whole and grind them yourselves as you need them. Whole grains deteriorate quickly once they are milled.

For sweeteners, recipes calling for sugar should use organic raw sugar as much as possible. For salt, a good quality sea salt with all the minerals in tact is best.

For those recipes calling for dairy or meat, we recommend organic and, when possible, grass-fed sources. Some of these sources can be located at www.tropicaltraditions.com and www.mercola.com. Search the Internet for local sources in the area where you live.

We don't use any soy except soy sauce in a few places for seasoning. When choosing a soy sauce, look for organic and traditionally fermented soy sauce.

The Recipes

All of these recipes have been created and tested in the kitchen. We didn't just pull recipes out of books and add coconut oil. Most of them were developed by Pete McCracken, a professional chef in California. In this book we have concentrated on "foundational" recipes that are designed to be used in many different kinds of meals and dishes, and to let you easily get a generous amount of coconut oil into your diet. Therefore, we concentrated the most on developing sauces, spreads, and vinaigrettes that can easily be added to many different meal plans. We included some vegetable dishes as well, some of which make use of the sauces. We also created a few main dishes and soups just to show

how easy it is to make delicious meals with coconut! Putting Virgin Coconut Oil and Coconut Cream Concentrate into your smoothies is another great way to add coconut oil to your diet. There are additional recipes at www.coconutdiet.com, such as smoothies, breads, desserts, etc.

These foundational recipes will be built upon in future Coconut Diet recipe books, and will eventually be available online where you can adjust portions and search for recipes according to your particular dietary needs or philosophy. So join the Coconut Diet Forums at www. coconutdiet.com to watch for future announcements.

Note: Keep in mind that coconut oil is solid below 76 degrees F. In many recipes, you will need to warm it to make it liquid.

Measurements: When calculating how much Virgin Coconut Oil you want to consume per serving, keep the following *approximate* measurement conversions in mind.

1 ounce = 2 tablespoons
1 tablespoon = 3 teaspoons
1 tablespoon = 15 grams

Coconut Diet Sauces, Spreads, and Dressings

Aioli Sauce

Ingredients

- 1 slice stale whole wheat bread
- 3 tablespoons milk, or wine vinegar
- 8 cloves garlic, mashed
- 1 large egg yolk
- ¼ teaspoon salt
- 1½ cups Virgin Coconut Oil
- 3 tablespoons boiling water, may need 4, or use fish stock
- 2 tablespoons fresh lemon juice, may need 3 tablespoons

1. Remove crusts and break the bread into a small bowl. Stir in the milk (or wine vinegar) and soak for 5-10 minutes into a soft pulp. Twist the pulp in the corner of a towel to extract the liquid.

2. Place the bread pulp and mashed garlic in a mortar and pound with the pestle for at least 5 minutes to mash the garlic and bread into a very smooth paste. A blender or food processor will NOT produce the necessary smoothness.

3. Add the egg yolk and salt, and continue pounding until mixture is thick and sticky.

4. Then, drop by drop, pound and blend in the Virgin Coconut Oil. When the sauce has thickened into a heavy cream, switch from the pestle to a wire whip and add the Virgin Coconut Oil a little faster.

5. Thin out sauce, as necessary, with drops of boiling water or fish stock, and lemon juice. Sauce should remain quite heavy, so it holds its shape in a spoon.

Nutritional Data

Calories (kcal): 196
% Calories from Fat: 91.0%
% Calories from Carbohydrates: 7.8%
% Calories from Protein: 1.2%

Per Serving Nutritional Information

Total Fat (g): 21g 32%
Saturated Fat (g): 18g 89%
Monounsaturated Fat (g): 1g 6%
Polyunsaturated Fat (g): trace 2%
Total Carbohydrate (g): 4g 1%
Dietary Fiber (g): trace 1%
Protein (g): 1g 1%
Sodium (mg): 44mg 2%
Potassium (mg): 51mg 1%
Calcium (mg): 12mg 1%
Iron (mg): trace 1%
Zinc (mg): trace 1%
Vitamin C (mg): 15mg 24%
Vitamin A (i.u.): 30IU 1%
Vitamin A (r.e.): 8RE 1%
Vitamin B6 (mg): trace 2%
Vitamin B12 (mcg): trace 1%
Thiamin B1 (mg): trace 1%
Riboflavin B2 (mg): trace 1%
Folacin (mcg): 7mcg 2%
Niacin (mg): trace 1%

Percent Daily Values are based on a 2000 calorie diet.

Servings: 16

Yield: 2 Cups

Notes: Contains 12 ounces (24 tablespoons) of Virgin Coconut Oil, equivalent to 1½ tablespoons per serving.

Baba Ghanoush

Ingredients

- 1 large eggplant
- 3 tablespoons Virgin Coconut Oil
- salt and pepper, to taste
- 3 tablespoons fresh lemon juice
- 2 garlic cloves
- 2⅓ fluid ounces tahini
- 1⅓ fluid ounces Virgin Coconut Oil

1. Cut the eggplants in half and score the cut surface of each half from edge to edge in a crosshatch pattern approximately ½ inch (1.2 centimeters) deep.

2. Brush the cut surfaces with 2 fluid ounces (60 milliliters) of Virgin Coconut Oil, season with salt and pepper and place cut side down on a sheet pan. Roast in a 350°F (180°C) oven until very soft, approximately 45 minutes.

3. Cool the eggplants and scoop out the flesh. Purée the flesh in a food processor with the lemon juice, garlic, tahini, salt and pepper. Add the remaining Virgin Coconut Oil and blend in. Adjust the seasonings. Serve in a bowl, drizzled with additional olive oil, if desired, and accompanied by pita bread or crudités.

Servings: 15
Yield: 1⅔ cups

Nutritional Data

Calories (kcal): 93
% Calories from Fat: 67.1%
% Calories from Carbohydrates: 27.8%
% Calories from Protein: 5.1%

Per Serving Nutritional Information

Total Fat (g): 8g 12%
Saturated Fat (g): 5g 24%
Monounsaturated Fat (g): 1g 6%
Polyunsaturated Fat (g): 1g 5%
Total Carbohydrate (g): 7g 2%
Dietary Fiber (g): 1g 6%
Protein (g): 1g 3%
Sodium (mg): 7mg 0%
Potassium (mg): 148mg 4%
Calcium (mg): 26mg 3%
Iron (mg): 1mg 3%
Zinc (mg): trace 2%
Vitamin C (mg): 23mg 38%
Vitamin A (i.u.): 39IU 1%
Vitamin A (r.e.): 3 1/2RE 0%
Vitamin B6 (mg): .1mg 3%
Vitamin B12 (mcg): 0mcg 0%
Thiamin B1 (mg): .1mg 6%
Riboflavin B2 (mg): trace 2%
Folacin (mcg): 17mcg 4%
Niacin (mg): trace 2%

* Percent Daily Values are based on a 2000 calorie diet.

Notes: Contains 4⅓ tablespoons (2 1/6 ounces) of Virgin Coconut Oil equivalent to 13/15 teaspoon per serving.

Basic Meat Sauce

Ingredients

- 1 cup Virgin Coconut Oil
- 3 large yellow onions, chopped
- 2 large carrots, chopped
- 1 stalk celery, chopped
- 6 cloves garlic, chopped
- 4 teaspoons sea salt
- 1½ teaspoons freshly ground pepper
- 2 pounds beef chuck, chopped
- 3 bay leaves
- 2 teaspoons dried oregano
- 2 teaspoons sugar
- 3 28-ounce cans crushed tomatoes
- 1 6-ounce can tomato paste

1. In a large stockpot, heat ½ cup plus 2 tablespoons of the Virgin Coconut Oil over medium heat. When it is hot, add the onions, carrots and celery. Cook, stirring occasionally, until lightly browned, about 10 minutes. Push the vegetables to the side a bit and add the garlic. Season the vegetables with 2 teaspoons of salt and ¾ teaspoon of the pepper, and cook for another 2 minutes.

2. While the vegetables are cooking, heat the remaining two tablespoons of the Virgin Coconut Oil in a large saute pan over high heat. When it is very hot, add half of the meat and cook, breaking up the clumps, until browned, about 8 minutes. Transfer the meat to the pot with the cooked vegetables. Repeat with the other half of meat.

3. Add the bay leaves, oregano, 1 cup of water, the sugar, tomatoes and their liquid, and tomato paste to the meat and vegetables. Mix well and bring to a boil. Season with the remaining 2 teaspoons of salt and ¾ teaspoon of pepper. Reduce the heat to low or medium low and cook for 45 minutes. Adjust the seasonings. Serve with pasta of your choice or use in making lasagna.

Nutritional Data

Calories (kcal): 618
% Calories from Fat: 64.1%
% Calories from Carbohydrates: 20.8%
% Calories from Protein: 15.1%

Per Serving Nutritional Information

Total Fat (g): 46g 71%
Saturated Fat (g): 31g 154%
Monounsaturated Fat (g): 9g 42%
Polyunsaturated Fat (g): 2g 7%
Total Carbohydrate (g): 34g 11%
Dietary Fiber (g): 8g 33%
Protein (g): 24g 49%
Sodium (mg): 1696mg 71%
Potassium (mg): 1526mg 44%
Calcium (mg): 150mg 15%
Iron (mg): 7mg 38%
Zinc (mg): 5mg 33%
Vitamin C (mg): 42mg 70%
Vitamin A (i.u.): 7700IU 154%
Vitamin A (r.e.): 770RE 77%
Vitamin B6 (mg): 1.0mg 48%
Vitamin B12 (mcg): 2.9mcg 49%
Thiamin B1 (mg): .4mg 24%
Riboflavin B2 (mg): .4mg 22%
Folacin (mcg): 63mcg 16%
Niacin (mg): 8mg 38%

* Percent Daily Values are based on a 2000 calorie diet.

Servings: 8

Notes: Contains 8 ounces Virgin Coconut Oil equivalent to 1 ounce per serving.

Basic Tomato Sauce

Ingredients

- 1 spanish onion, cut ¼" dice
- 4 garlic cloves, thinly sliced
- 3 ounces Virgin Coconut Oil
- 4 tablespoons fresh thyme, = (or 2 tbs dried thyme)
- ½ medium carrot, finely shredded
- 2 28-ounce cans crushed tomatoes, with their juices
- salt, to taste

1. Sauté the onion and garlic in the Virgin Coconut Oil over medium heat until translucent, but not brown (about 10 minutes). Add the thyme and carrot and cook 5 minutes more.

2. Add the tomatoes. Bring to a boil. Lower the heat to just bubbling, stirring occasionally for 30 minutes. Season with salt to taste.

3. Serve immediately, or set aside for future use. The sauce may be refrigerated for up to one week or frozen for up to 6 months.

4. This recipe yields 6 cups of sauce.

Yield: 6 cups

Notes: Contains 1 tablespoon of Virgin Coconut Oil per cup of sauce.

Nutritional Data

Calories (kcal): 1345
% Calories from Fat: 54.5%
% Calories from Carbohydrates: 37.5%
% Calories from Protein: 7.9%

Per Serving Nutritional Information

Total Fat (g): 90g 138%
Saturated Fat (g): 74g 371%
Monounsaturated Fat (g): 5g 25%
Polyunsaturated Fat (g): 3g 14%
Total Carbohydrate (g): 139g 46%
Dietary Fiber (g): 35g 142%
Protein (g): 29g 59%
Sodium (mg): 2116mg 88%
Potassium (mg): 5126mg 146%
Calcium (mg): 642mg 64%
Iron (mg): 23mg 127%
Zinc (mg): 5mg 32%
Vitamin C (mg): 179mg 298%
Vitamin A (i.u.): 21680IU 434%
Vitamin A (r.e.): 2169RE 217%
Vitamin B6 (mg): 2.7mg 135%
Vitamin B12 (mcg): 0mcg 0%
Thiamin B1 (mg): 1.1mg 75%
Riboflavin B2 (mg): .8mg 49%
Folacin (mcg): 247mcg 62%
Niacin (mg): 20mg 100%

Percent Daily Values are based on a 2000 calorie diet.

Béchamel Type Sauce

Ingredients

- 1 tablespoon Virgin Coconut Oil
- 1 tablespoon minced onions
- 1 quart milk
- 1 pint Coconut Cream Concentrate
- ½ teaspoon sea salt, to taste
- ¼ teaspoon fresh ground black pepper, to taste
- ¼ teaspoon fresh nutmeg, grated (optional)

1. Sweat minced onion in Virgin Coconut Oil until translucent and tender, no color.

2. Add Coconut Cream Concentrate and heat until bubbling.

3. Add milk to pan gradually, whisking or stirring. Bring to a full boil, then reduce heat and simmer until sauce is smooth and thickened.

4. Adjust seasonings to taste.

5. Strain through a double thickness of rinsed cheesecloth.

6. Sauce is ready for use or it may be cooled and refrigerated for later use.

Notes: Each cup of sauce contains ½ cup (4 ounces) of Coconut Cream Concentrate which is equivalent to 2.8 ounces (approx 5 tablespoons) of Virgin Coconut Oil. Amount per serving will vary with serving size.

Nutritional Data

Calories (kcal): 3720
% Calories from Fat: 90.6%
% Calories from Carbohydrates: 6.7%
% Calories from Protein: 2.7%

Per Serving Nutritional Information

Total Fat (g): 920g 1415%
Saturated Fat (g): 810g 4049%
Monounsaturated Fat (g): 106g 478%
Polyunsaturated Fat (g): 1g 7%
Total Carbohydrate (g): 153g 51%
Dietary Fiber (g): 42g 167%
Protein (g): 61g 122%
Sodium (mg): 1582mg 66%
Potassium (mg): 1503mg 43%
Calcium (mg): 1171mg 117%
Iron (mg): 35mg 196%
Zinc (mg): 4mg 25%
Vitamin C (mg): 10mg 17%
Vitamin A (i.u.): 1231IU 25%
Vitamin A (r.e.): 371RE 37%
Vitamin B6 (mg): .4mg 21%
Vitamin B12 (mcg): 3.5mcg 58%
Thiamin B1 (mg): .4mg 24%
Riboflavin B2 (mg): 1.6mg 92%
Folacin (mcg): 51mcg 13%
Niacin (mg): 1mg 4%

Percent Daily Values are based on a 2000 calorie diet.

Yield: 4 Cups

Serving Ideas: Use as base for cheese, mornay, or other béchamel-based sauces.

Good for lasagna, casseroles, any "white sauce" uses.

Cheddar Cheese Sauce

Ingredients

- 1 cup milk
- ½ cup Coconut Cream Concentrate
- 1 cup grated Cheddar cheese
- ½ teaspoon sea salt
- ¼ teaspoon fresh ground black pepper

1. Combine milk and Coconut Cream Concentrate in saucepan.

2. Heat to 180°F (just until bubbles appear around the edge, DO NOT BOIL!)

3. Add grated cheese and salt & pepper to taste.

Yield: 1½ cups

Notes: Recipe contains ½ cup (4 ounces) Coconut Cream Concentrate which is the equivalent of 2.8 ounces (approx 3 tablespoons) of Virgin Coconut Oil, serving size will vary from ¼ to ½ cup per serving equating to ½ to 1 tablespoon per serving.

Nutritional Data

Calories (kcal): 1357
% Calories from Fat: 87.7%
% Calories from Carbohydrates: 5.8%
% Calories from Protein: 6.4%

Per Serving Nutritional Information

Total Fat (g): 264g 406%
Saturated Fat (g): 223g 1117%
Monounsaturated Fat (g): 37g 166%
Polyunsaturated Fat (g): 1g 6%
Total Carbohydrate (g): 40g 13%
Dietary Fiber (g): 10g 42%
Protein (g): 44g 87%
Sodium (mg): 1804mg 75%
Potassium (mg): 488mg 14%
Calcium (mg): 1112mg 111%
Iron (mg): 10mg 54%
Zinc (mg): 4mg 30%
Vitamin C (mg): 2mg 4%
Vitamin A (i.u.): 1509IU 30%
Vitamin A (r.e.): 453 1/2RE 45%
Vitamin B6 (mg): .2mg 9%
Vitamin B12 (mcg): 1.8mcg 30%
Thiamin B1 (mg): .1mg 8%
Riboflavin B2 (mg): .8mg 48%
Folacin (mcg): 33mcg 8%
Niacin (mg): trace 1%

Percent Daily Values are based on a 2000 calorie diet.

Four Cheese Sauce

Ingredients

- 1 cup milk
- ½ cup Coconut Cream Concentrate
- ¼ cup shredded Mozzarella cheese
- ¼ cup shredded Parmesan cheese
- ¼ cup shredded Romano cheese
- ¼ cup shredded Provolone cheese
- ½ teaspoon sea salt
- ¼ teaspoon fresh ground black pepper

1. Combine milk and Coconut Cream Concentrate in saucepan.

2. Heat to 180°F (just until bubbles appear around the edge, DO NOT BOIL!)

3. Add grated cheese and salt and pepper to taste.

Yield: 1½ cups

Notes: Recipe contains ½ cup (4 ounces) Coconut Cream Concentrate which is the equivalent of 2.8 ounces (approx 3 tablespoons) of Virgin Coconut Oil. Serving size will vary from ¼ to ½ cup per serving equating to ½ to 1 tablespoon per serving.

Nutritional Data

Calories (kcal): 1541
% Calories from Fat: 85.3%
% Calories from Carbohydrates: 6.0%
% Calories from Protein: 8.7%

Per Serving Nutritional Information

Total Fat (g): 274g 422%
Saturated Fat (g): 230g 1148%
Monounsaturated Fat (g): 40g 180%
Polyunsaturated Fat (g): 2g 8%
Total Carbohydrate (g): 43g 14%
Dietary Fiber (g): 10g 42%
Protein (g): 63g 126%
Sodium (mg): 2421mg 101%
Potassium (mg): 527mg 15%
Calcium (mg): 1662mg 166%
Iron (mg): 10mg 53%
Zinc (mg): 6mg 38%
Vitamin C (mg): 2mg 4%
Vitamin A (i.u.): 1902IU 38%
Vitamin A (r.e.): 571RE 57%
Vitamin B6 (mg): .2mg 10%
Vitamin B12 (mcg): 2.5mcg 42%
Thiamin B1 (mg): .1mg 7%
Riboflavin B2 (mg): .9mg 51%
Folacin (mcg): 27mcg 7%
Niacin (mg): trace 2%

* Percent Daily Values are based on a 2000 calorie diet.

Grain Mustard Sauce

Ingredients

- 1 large shallot, minced
- ½ cup white wine
- ½ cup fish stock, highly gelatinous
- ½ cup clam juice
- 2 sprigs fresh thyme
- 1 large bay leaf, whole
- ¼ cup heavy cream
- 6 tablespoons Virgin Coconut Oil
- 1 teaspoon dijon-style mustard, preferably whole grained
- 1 teaspoon horseradish
- 1 tablespoon crème fraiche
- ½ teaspoon fresh dill, minced
- ½ teaspoon chives, sliced thin

1. In heavy-bottomed stainless steel pan, reduce first six ingredients of Grain Mustard Sauce by about ⅔. Add cream and bring to heavy foam. Whisk in Virgin Coconut Oil slowly. Season with salt and strain through a chinois or a fine mesh strainer, pressing firmly on shallots to extract maximum flavor.

2. Hold the sauce in a warm water bath.

3. In a small bowl, mix together the grain mustard, horseradish, and crème fraiche. Whisk sauce in to the prepared mixture. Return mustard in the warm water bath. Add the fresh herbs just before serving.

Servings: 6

Nutritional Data

Calories (kcal): 192
% Calories from Fat: 91.4%
% Calories from Carbohydrates: 7.5%
% Calories from Protein: 1.2%

Per Serving Nutritional Information

Total Fat (g): 19g 29%
Saturated Fat (g): 15g 74%
Monounsaturated Fat (g): 2g 10%
Polyunsaturated Fat (g): trace 2%
Total Carbohydrate (g): 3g 1%
Dietary Fiber (g): trace 1%
Protein (g): 1g 1%
Sodium (mg): 118mg 5%
Potassium (mg): 64mg 2%
Calcium (mg): 18mg 2%
Iron (mg): trace 2%
Zinc (mg): trace 2%
Vitamin C (mg): 2mg 3%
Vitamin A (i.u.): 450IU 9%
Vitamin A (r.e.): 77 1/2RE 8%
Vitamin B6 (mg): trace 1%
Vitamin B12 (mcg): 6.2mcg 103%
Thiamin B1 (mg): trace 1%
Riboflavin B2 (mg): trace 1%
Folacin (mcg): 5mcg 1%
Niacin (mg): trace 0%

Percent Daily Values are based on a 2000 calorie diet.

Notes: Contains 3 ounces (6 tablespoons) Virgin Coconut Oil, equivalent to 1½ tablespoons Virgin Coconut Oil per serving.

Hummus

Ingredients

- 1 pound chickpeas, cooked
- 8 ounces tahini paste
- 2 teaspoons garlic, chopped
- ½ teaspoon cumin
- 4 ounces lemon juice
- 1 teaspoon salt
- cayenne pepper, to taste
- 2 ounces Virgin Coconut Oil, more if desired
- 2 teaspoons fresh parsley, chopped

1. Combine the chickpeas, tahini, garlic, cumin and lemon juice in a food processor. Process until smooth. Season with salt and cayenne.

2. Spoon the hummus onto a serving platter and smooth the surface. Drizzle the Virgin Coconut Oil over the hummus and garnish with the chopped parsley. Serve with warm pita bread that has been cut into quarters.

Servings: 16
Yield: 1 Quart

Notes: Contains 2 tablespoons Virgin Coconut Oil equivalent to 1/16 ounce per serving.

Nutritional Data

Calories (kcal): 221
% Calories from Fat: 50.1%
% Calories from Carbohydrates: 36.2%
% Calories from Protein: 13.7%

Per Serving Nutritional Information

Total Fat (g): 13g 20%
Saturated Fat (g): 4g 22%
Monounsaturated Fat (g): 3g 16%
Polyunsaturated Fat (g): 4g 19%
Total Carbohydrate (g): 21g 7%
Dietary Fiber (g): 6g 25%
Protein (g): 8g 16%
Sodium (mg): 157mg 7%
Potassium (mg): 319mg 9%
Calcium (mg): 93mg 9%
Iron (mg): 3mg 17%
Zinc (mg): 2mg 11%
Vitamin C (mg): 5mg 8%
Vitamin A (i.u.): 39IU 1%
Vitamin A (r.e.): 4RE 0%
Vitamin B6 (mg): .2mg 9%
Vitamin B12 (mcg): 0mcg 0%
Thiamin B1 (mg): .3mg 20%
Riboflavin B2 (mg): .1mg 7%
Folacin (mcg): 173mcg 43%
Niacin (mg): 1mg 6%

Percent Daily Values are based on a 2000 calorie diet.

Italian Tomato Gravy

Ingredients

- ½ cup Virgin Coconut Oil
- 3 garlic cloves, chopped
- 1 pinch red pepper flakes
- 2 tablespoons chopped fresh basil
- 2 tablespoons chopped fresh oregano
- 1 tablespoon fresh thyme leaves
- 2 bay leaves
- 1 medium onion, diced
- 1 medium carrot, finely chopped
- ¼ cup red wine
- 2 28-ounce cans plum tomato, whole
- 1 pinch sugar
- salt, to taste
- freshly-ground black pepper, to taste

1. Heat Virgin Coconut Oil in a large saucepan over low heat. Sauté the garlic, red pepper flakes, and herbs for 2 minutes until the herbs are fragrant and garlic is golden (but not overly brown).

2. Raise the heat to medium. Add onion and carrot. Cook for 5 minutes until they break down and are soft. Deglaze with red wine and reduce to evaporate the alcohol.

3. Hand crush the canned tomatoes and add to the pot, along with its liquid. Add a pinch of sugar to cut down on the acidity from the tomatoes. Season with salt and pepper. Let simmer for 30 minutes, uncovered.

Nutritional Data

Calories (kcal): 230
% Calories from Fat: 71.1%
% Calories from Carbohydrates: 24.7%
% Calories from Protein: 4.2%

Per Serving Nutritional Information

Total Fat (g): 19g 29%
Saturated Fat (g): 16g 79%
Monounsaturated Fat (g): 1g 5%
Polyunsaturated Fat (g): 1g 3%
Total Carbohydrate (g): 15g 5%
Dietary Fiber (g): 4g 14%
Protein (g): 3g 5%
Sodium (mg): 33mg 1%
Potassium (mg): 629mg 18%
Calcium (mg): 28mg 3%
Iron (mg): 1mg 7%
Zinc (mg): trace 2%
Vitamin C (mg): 50mg 83%
Vitamin A (i.u.): 4944IU 99%
Vitamin A (r.e.): 493 1/2RE 49%
Vitamin B6 (mg): .2mg 11%
Vitamin B12 (mcg): 0mcg 0%
Thiamin B1 (mg): .1mg 9%
Riboflavin B2 (mg): .1mg 5%
Folacin (mcg): 42mcg 11%
Niacin (mg): 2mg 8%

Percent Daily Values are based on a 2000 calorie diet.

Servings: 6

Notes: 1⅓ tablespoons Virgin Coconut Oil per serving.

Jalapeno Orange Sauce

Ingredients

- 1 tablespoon Virgin Coconut Oil
- 2 tablespoons dijon mustard
- 3 tablespoons orange marmalade
- 2 tablespoons jalapeno pepper, seeded and minced
- 1 cup white wine, chicken stock or any combination of the two
- 2 teaspoons fresh lime juice
- 1 teaspoon sliced black olives
- 2 tablespoons Coconut Cream Concentrate

1. Seed the jalapeno, being careful to keep away from eyes. Combine the mustard, marmalade, and lime juice. Add a pinch of cayenne pepper if you want it hotter.

2. Heat Virgin Coconut Oil over medium/high heat until hot. Add jalapenos and sauté for 15-30 seconds. Do not burn. Immediately deglaze pan with white wine or chicken stock and reduce by ⅓.

3. Add mustard mixture to pan. Reduce until desired consistency is reached

4. Add 2 tablespoons of Coconut Cream Concentrate at this point to finish sauce.

Servings: 4

Notes: Estimated to contain the equivalent of 2 tablespoons Virgin Coconut Oil, equivalent to ½ tablespoon per serving.

Nutritional Data
Calories (kcal): 161
% Calories from Fat: 73.9%
% Calories from Carbohydrates: 24.4%
% Calories from Protein: 1.8%

Per Serving Nutritional Information
Total Fat (g): 17g 27%
Saturated Fat (g): 15g 76%
Monounsaturated Fat (g): 2g 9%
Polyunsaturated Fat (g): trace 1%
Total Carbohydrate (g): 13g 4%
Dietary Fiber (g): 2g 7%
Protein (g): 1g 2%
Sodium (mg): 114mg 5%
Potassium (mg): 71mg 2%
Calcium (mg): 18mg 2%
Iron (mg): 1mg 5%
Zinc (mg): trace 1%
Vitamin C (mg): 3mg 4%
Vitamin A (i.u.): 16IU 0%
Vitamin A (r.e.): 1 1/2RE 0%
Vitamin B6 (mg): trace 1%
Vitamin B12 (mcg): 0mcg 0%
Thiamin B1 (mg): trace 1%
Riboflavin B2 (mg): trace 1%
Folacin (mcg): 8mcg 2%
Niacin (mg): trace 1%

* Percent Daily Values are based on a 2000 calorie diet.

Lemon Caper Sauce

Ingredients

- ⅔ cup dry white wine, may substitute chicken stock
- 2 tablespoons fresh lemon juice
- 2 teaspoons capers, drained
- 1 teaspoon Virgin Coconut Oil, chilled

1. Add wine and lemon juice to a small saucepan. Bring to a boil. Cook and stir 1 to 2 minutes or until slightly thickened. Remove from heat. Stir in capers and chilled Virgin Coconut Oil.

2. Serve immediately.

Servings: 4

Notes: ⅓ tablespoon Virgin Coconut Oil per serving.

Nutritional Data

Calories (kcal): 67
% Calories from Fat: 18.4%
% Calories from Carbohydrates: 78.1%
% Calories from Protein: 3.5%

Per Serving Nutritional Information

Total Fat (g): 1g 2%
Saturated Fat (g): 1g 5%
Monounsaturated Fat (g): trace 0%
Polyunsaturated Fat (g): trace 0%
Total Carbohydrate (g): 11g 4%
Dietary Fiber (g): trace 2%
Protein (g): trace 1%
Sodium (mg): 16mg 1%
Potassium (mg): 183mg 5%
Calcium (mg): 12mg 1%
Iron (mg): trace 1%
Zinc (mg): trace 1%
Vitamin C (mg): 56mg 94%
Vitamin A (i.u.): 24IU 0%
Vitamin A (r.e.): 2 1/2RE 0%
Vitamin B6 (mg): .1mg 3%
Vitamin B12 (mcg): 0mcg 0%
Thiamin B1 (mg): trace 2%
Riboflavin B2 (mg): trace 1%
Folacin (mcg): 16mcg 4%
Niacin (mg): trace 1%

* Percent Daily Values are based on a 2000 calorie diet.

Lime Cumin Sauce

Ingredients

- 1 teaspoon lime zest
- 1 tablespoon fresh lime juice
- ½ teaspoon ground cumin
- ½ teaspoon salt
- 1 dash Tabasco sauce, to taste
- 3 tablespoons Virgin Coconut Oil
- ¼ cup minced red onion

1. Whisk first four ingredients of lime-cumin sauce (pepper sauce to taste) in small bowl. Whisk in Virgin Coconut Oil until dressing is smooth; stir in onion.

2. Serve immediately.

Servings: 4

Notes: Contains 1½ ounces (3 tablespoons) Virgin Coconut Oil, equivalent to ¾ tablespoon Virgin Coconut Oil per serving.

Nutritional Data

Calories (kcal): 94
% Calories from Fat: 93.5%
% Calories from Carbohydrates: 5.8%
% Calories from Protein: 0.8%

Per Serving Nutritional Information

Total Fat (g): 10g 16%
Saturated Fat (g): 9g 44%
Monounsaturated Fat (g): 1g 3%
Polyunsaturated Fat (g): trace 1%
Total Carbohydrate (g): 1g 0%
Dietary Fiber (g): trace 1%
Protein (g): trace 0%
Sodium (mg): 268mg 11%
Potassium (mg): 26mg 1%
Calcium (mg): 7mg 1%
Iron (mg): trace 1%
Zinc (mg): trace 0%
Vitamin C (mg): 3mg 4%
Vitamin A (i.u.): 5IU 0%
Vitamin A (r.e.): 1/2RE 0%
Vitamin B6 (mg): trace 1%
Vitamin B12 (mcg): 0mcg 0%
Thiamin B1 (mg): trace 0%
Riboflavin B2 (mg): trace 0%
Folacin (mcg): 2mcg 1%
Niacin (mg): trace 0%

* Percent Daily Values are based on a 2000 calorie diet.

Madeira Sauce

Ingredients

- 1 tablespoon Virgin Coconut Oil
- 2 shallots, minced
- 1 pound sliced mushrooms
- 2 cups madeira
- 2 cups demi-glace
- 2 tablespoons Virgin Coconut Oil, chilled and cut into tablespoon cubes

1. Heat 1 tablespoon Virgin Coconut Oil in small skillet. Add shallots and mushrooms to pan and sauté briefly.

2. Deglaze pan with madeira and reduce until almost dry.

3. Add demi-glace and bring to a simmer

4. Finish sauce with chilled Virgin Coconut Oil and salt and pepper to taste.

Servings: 8

Notes: Contains 1½ ounces Virgin Coconut Oil, equivalent to ⅜ tablespoons Virgin Coconut Oil per serving.

Nutritional Data

Calories (kcal): 152
% Calories from Fat: 69.3%
% Calories from Carbohydrates: 21.9%
% Calories from Protein: 8.9%

Per Serving Nutritional Information

Total Fat (g): 5g 8%
Saturated Fat (g): 4g 22%
Monounsaturated Fat (g): trace 1%
Polyunsaturated Fat (g): trace 1%
Total Carbohydrate (g): 4g 1%
Dietary Fiber (g): 1g 3%
Protein (g): 2g 3%
Sodium (mg): 295mg 12%
Potassium (mg): 277mg 8%
Calcium (mg): 8mg 1%
Iron (mg): 1mg 5%
Zinc (mg): trace 3%
Vitamin C (mg): 2mg 4%
Vitamin A (i.u.): 313IU 6%
Vitamin A (r.e.): 31 1/2RE 3%
Vitamin B6 (mg): .1mg 3%
Vitamin B12 (mcg): 0mcg 0%
Thiamin B1 (mg): .1mg 4%
Riboflavin B2 (mg): .3mg 15%
Folacin (mcg): 14mcg 3%
Niacin (mg): 2mg 12%

* Percent Daily Values are based on a 2000 calorie diet.

Mayonnaise

Ingredients

- 1 egg yolk
- ½ teaspoon salt, the finer the better
- ½ teaspoon dry mustard
- 2 pinches sugar, for balance, not sweetness
- 2 teaspoons fresh lemon juice
- 1 tablespoon white wine vinegar
- 1 cup Virgin Coconut Oil

1. In a glass bowl, whisk together egg yolk and dry ingredients. Combine lemon juice and vinegar in a separate bowl. Then thoroughly whisk half into the yolk mixture.

2. Start whisking briskly. Then start adding the Virgin Coconut Oil a few drops at a time until the liquid seems to thicken and lighten a bit (which means you've got an emulsion on your hands).

3. Once you reach that point you can relax your arm a little (but just a little) and increase the Virgin Coconut Oil flow to a constant (albeit thin) stream. Once half of the Virgin Coconut Oil is in, add the rest of the lemon juice mixture.

4. Continue whisking until all of the Virgin Coconut Oil is incorporated. Leave at room temperature for 1 to 2 hours then refrigerate for up to 1 week.

Nutritional Data

Calories (kcal): 125
% Calories from Fat: 96.1%
% Calories from Carbohydrates: 3.1%
% Calories from Protein: 0.8%

Per Serving Nutritional Information

Total Fat (g): 14g 22%
Saturated Fat (g): 12g 59%
Monounsaturated Fat (g): 1g 4%
Polyunsaturated Fat (g): trace 1%
Total Carbohydrate (g): 1g 0%
Dietary Fiber (g): trace 0%
Protein (g): trace 1%
Sodium (mg): 67mg 3%
Potassium (mg): 16mg 0%
Calcium (mg): 3mg 0%
Iron (mg): trace 0%
Zinc (mg): trace 0%
Vitamin C (mg): 5mg 8%
Vitamin A (i.u.): 23IU 0%
Vitamin A (r.e.): 6 1/2RE 1%
Vitamin B6 (mg): trace 0%
Vitamin B12 (mcg): trace 1%
Thiamin B1 (mg): trace 0%
Riboflavin B2 (mg): trace 0%
Folacin (mcg): 3mcg 1%
Niacin (mg): trace 0%

Percent Daily Values are based on a 2000 calorie diet.

Servings: 16
Yield: 1 Cup

Notes: Contains 1 tablespoon of Virgin Coconut Oil per serving

Mayonnaise Verte

Ingredients

Mayonnaise
- 1 ½ egg yolk
- teaspoon salt, the finer the better
- ¾ teaspoon dry mustard
- 3 pinches sugar, for balance, not sweetness
- 3 teaspoons fresh lemon juice
- 1 ½ tablespoons white wine vinegar
- 1 ½ cups Virgin Coconut Oil

Verte
- 8 each spinach leaves
- 2 tablespoons shallots, chopped, or green onions, chopped
- ¼ cup watercress, leaves only, discard stems
- ¼ cup parsley, leaves only, discard stems
- 1 tablespoon fresh tarragon, or ½ tablespoon dried tarragon
- 2 tablespoons fresh chervil, optional

Prepare mayonnaise:

1. In a glass bowl, whisk together egg yolk and dry ingredients. Combine lemon juice and vinegar in a separate bowl then thoroughly whisk half into the yolk mixture.

2. Start whisking briskly, then start adding the Virgin Coconut Oil a few drops at a time until the liquid seems to thicken and lighten a bit, (which means you've got an emulsion on your hands).

3. Once you reach that point you can relax your arm a little (but just a little) and increase the Virgin Coconut Oil flow to a constant (albeit thin) stream. Once half of the Virgin Coconut Oil is in add the rest of the lemon juice mixture.

4. Continue whisking until all of the Virgin Coconut Oil is incorporated. Leave at room temperature for 1 to 2 hours then refrigerate for up to 1 week.

Nutritional Data

Calories (kcal): 127
% Calories from Fat: 94.4%
% Calories from Carbohydrates: 4.2%
% Calories from Protein: 1.3%

Per Serving Nutritional Information

Total Fat (g): 14g 22%
Saturated Fat (g): 12g 59%
Monounsaturated Fat (g): 1g 4%
Polyunsaturated Fat (g): trace 1%
Total Carbohydrate (g): 1g 0%
Dietary Fiber (g): trace 1%
Protein (g): trace 1%
Sodium (mg): 71mg 3%
Potassium (mg): 50mg 1%
Calcium (mg): 10mg 1%
Iron (mg): trace 1%
Zinc (mg): trace 1%
Vitamin C (mg): 7mg 11%
Vitamin A (i.u.): 410IU 8%
Vitamin A (r.e.): 45RE 5%
Vitamin B6 (mg): trace 1%
Vitamin B12 (mcg): trace 1%
Thiamin B1 (mg): trace 0%
Riboflavin B2 (mg): trace 1%
Folacin (mcg): 11mcg 3%
Niacin (mg): trace 0%

* Percent Daily Values are based on a 2000 calorie diet.

Prepare Verte

5. Bring 1 cup of water to boil in a small saucepan. Add spinach and shallots (or green onions) and boil 2 minutes

6. Add remaining ingredients and boil 1 minute more. Strain, rinse in cold water, and pat dry with towel.

7. Purée herbs in blender or by hand and blend into mayonnaise.

Servings: 24
Yield: 1 ½ Cups

Notes: Contains 12 ounces of Virgin Coconut Oil equivalent to 1 tablespoon per serving.

Mayonnaise With Green Herbs

Ingredients

- 1 egg yolk
- ½ teaspoon salt, the finer the better
- ½ teaspoon dry mustard
- 2 pinches sugar, for balance, not sweetness
- 2 teaspoons fresh lemon juice
- 1 tablespoon white wine vinegar
- 1 cup Virgin Coconut Oil
- 2 tablespoons fresh herbs (see note)

1. In a glass bowl, whisk together egg yolk and dry ingredients. Combine lemon juice and vinegar in a separate bowl. Then thoroughly whisk half into the yolk mixture.

2. Start whisking briskly. Then start adding the Virgin Coconut Oil a few drops at a time until the liquid seems to thicken and lighten a bit (which means you've got an emulsion on your hands).

3. Once you reach that point you can relax your arm a little (but just a little) and increase the Virgin Coconut Oil flow to a constant (albeit thin) stream. Once half of the Virgin Coconut Oil is in, add the rest of the lemon juice mixture.

4. Continue whisking until all of the Virgin Coconut Oil is incorporated. Leave at room temperature for 1 to 2 hours then refrigerate for up to 1 week.

5. Blanch the herbs for 1 minute in boiling water. Drain. Run cold water over them or immerse in ice water bath, and pat dry. Once dry, mince finely.

6. Combine with mayonnaise.

7. Store in air-tight container in refrigerator for 4-7 days.

Nutritional Data

Calories (kcal): 2004
% Calories from Fat: 95.7%
% Calories from Carbohydrates: 3.4%
% Calories from Protein: 0.9%

Per Serving Nutritional Information

Total Fat (g): 224g 345%
Saturated Fat (g): 190g 951%
Monounsaturated Fat (g): 15g 66%
Polyunsaturated Fat (g): 5g 21%
Total Carbohydrate (g): 18g 6%
Dietary Fiber (g): 1g 4%
Protein (g): 5g 10%
Sodium (mg): 1087mg 45%
Potassium (mg): 359mg 10%
Calcium (mg): 90mg 9%
Iron (mg): 4mg 20%
Zinc (mg): 1mg 6%
Vitamin C (mg): 78mg 131%
Vitamin A (i.u.): 974IU 19%
Vitamin A (r.e.): 162RE 16%
Vitamin B6 (mg): .2mg 8%
Vitamin B12 (mcg): .5mcg 9%
Thiamin B1 (mg): .1mg 4%
Riboflavin B2 (mg): .1mg 8%
Folacin (mcg): 45mcg 11%
Niacin (mg): 1mg 3%

* Percent Daily Values are based on a 2000 calorie diet.

Servings: 16
Yield: 1 Cup

Notes: Use a mixture of whatever you enjoy: tarragon, basil, chervil, chives, parsley, oregano, etc.

Contains 1 tablespoon of Virgin Coconut Oil per serving.

Mornay Sauce

Ingredients

- 1 teaspoon Virgin Coconut Oil
- 1 teaspoon minced onion
- ½ cup Coconut Cream Concentrate
- 1 cup milk
- ½ cup gruyere cheese, grated
- ½ cup grated parmesan cheese
- ⅛ teaspoon fresh nutmeg
- ½ teaspoon sea salt
- ¼ teaspoon fresh ground black pepper

1. Heat teaspoon of Virgin Coconut Oil in saucepan, add minced onions and "sweat" over low heat until translucent and tender (no color)

2. Combine milk and Coconut Cream Concentrate and add to saucepan.

3. Heat to 180°F (just until bubbles appear around the edge, DO NOT BOIL!)

4. Add grated cheeses, nutmeg, and salt and pepper to taste.

Yield: 1½ cups

Notes: Recipe contains ½ cup (4 ounces) Coconut Cream Concentrate which is the equivalent of 2.8 ounces (approx 3 tablespoons) of Virgin Coconut Oil, serving size will vary from ¼ to ½ cup per serving equating to ½ to 1 tablespoon per serving.

Nutritional Data

Calories (kcal): 1347
% Calories from Fat: 86.9%
% Calories from Carbohydrates: 6.0%
% Calories from Protein: 7.1%

Per Serving Nutritional Information

Total Fat (g): 261g 401%
Saturated Fat (g): 221g 1106%
Monounsaturated Fat (g): 35g 160%
Polyunsaturated Fat (g): 2g 7%
Total Carbohydrate (g): 40g 13%
Dietary Fiber (g): 11g 42%
Protein (g): 48g 96%
Sodium (mg): 2027mg 84%
Potassium (mg): 469mg 13%
Calcium (mg): 1391mg 139%
Iron (mg): 9mg 52%
Zinc (mg): 4mg 28%
Vitamin C (mg): 3mg 4%
Vitamin A (i.u.): 1247IU 25%
Vitamin A (r.e.): 375RE 37%
Vitamin B6 (mg): .1mg 7%
Vitamin B12 (mcg): 2.3mcg 38%
Thiamin B1 (mg): .1mg 8%
Riboflavin B2 (mg): .6mg 37%
Folacin (mcg): 22mcg 5%
Niacin (mg): trace 2%

Percent Daily Values are based on a 2000 calorie diet.

Orange Ginger Sauce

Ingredients

- 1 tablespoon Virgin Coconut Oil
- 1 tablespoon soy sauce
- 1 tablespoon honey
- 1 tablespoon orange zest
- 3 tablespoons fresh orange juice
- 1 medium garlic clove, peeled and chopped
- 1 piece fresh ginger root (about 1 inch) peeled and chopped
- ¼ teaspoon salt

1. Process all ingredients for Orange Ginger sauce in work bowl of food processor or blender, scraping down sides as needed, until dressing is smooth.

2. Serve immediately.

Servings: 4

Notes: Contains ½ ounce (1 tablespoons) Virgin Coconut Oil, equivalent to ⅛ ounce per serving.

Nutritional Data

Calories (kcal): 60
% Calories from Fat: 49.5%
% Calories from Carbohydrates: 47.3%
% Calories from Protein: 3.2%

Per Serving Nutritional Information

Total Fat (g): 3g 5%
Saturated Fat (g): 3g 15%
Monounsaturated Fat (g): trace 1%
Polyunsaturated Fat (g): trace 0%
Total Carbohydrate (g): 7g 2%
Dietary Fiber (g): trace 1%
Protein (g): 1g 1%
Sodium (mg): 392mg 16%
Potassium (mg): 65mg 2%
Calcium (mg): 8mg 1%
Iron (mg): trace 1%
Zinc (mg): trace 0%
Vitamin C (mg): 8mg 14%
Vitamin A (i.u.): 30IU 1%
Vitamin A (r.e.): 3RE 0%
Vitamin B6 (mg): trace 2%
Vitamin B12 (mcg): 0mcg 0%
Thiamin B1 (mg): trace 1%
Riboflavin B2 (mg): trace 1%
Folacin (mcg): 8mcg 2%
Niacin (mg): trace 1%

* Percent Daily Values are based on a 2000 calorie diet.

Pico de Gallo

Ingredients

- 2 pounds tomatoes, diced
- 1 medium yellow onion, diced
- 6 tablespoons fresh cilantro (packed) chopped
- 2 tablespoons fresh lime juice
- 1 teaspoon lime zest, fresh
- 2 large cloves garlic, minced
- 1 large jalapeno, seeded and minced
- 2 tablespoons Virgin Coconut Oil

Toss all ingredients in a medium bowl until well blended. Refrigerate until ready for use.

Servings: 32

Yield: 2 cups

Notes: Contains approximately 1/32 ounces (⅞ gram) Virgin Coconut Oil per tablespoon serving.

Nutritional Data

Calories (kcal): 15
% Calories from Fat: 51.9%
% Calories from Carbohydrates: 41.1%
% Calories from Protein: 6.9%

Per Serving Nutritional Information

Total Fat (g): 1g 1%
Saturated Fat (g): 1g 4%
Monounsaturated Fat (g): trace 0%
Polyunsaturated Fat (g): trace 0%
Total Carbohydrate (g): 2g 1%
Dietary Fiber (g): trace 2%
Protein (g): trace 1%
Sodium (mg): 3mg 0%
Potassium (mg): 67mg 2%
Calcium (mg): 3mg 0%
Iron (mg): trace 1%
Zinc (mg): trace 0%
Vitamin C (mg): 6mg 10%
Vitamin A (i.u.): 174IU 3%
Vitamin A (r.e.): 17 1/2RE 2%
Vitamin B6 (mg): trace 1%
Vitamin B12 (mcg): 0mcg 0%
Thiamin B1 (mg): trace 1%
Riboflavin B2 (mg): trace 1%
Folacin (mcg): 5mcg 1%
Niacin (mg): trace 1%

Percent Daily Values are based on a 2000 calorie diet.

Spanish Green Herb Sauce

Ingredients

- 2 medium garlic cloves, peeled
- ½ cup tightly-packed fresh cilantro leaves
- ½ cup tightly-packed fresh parsley
- 3 tablespoons Virgin Coconut Oil
- 1 tablespoon fresh lemon juice
- ½ teaspoon salt

1. Process Spanish Green Herb sauce ingredients in work bowl of food processor or blender, scraping down sides of bowl as needed, until sauce is smooth.

2. Serve immediately.

Servings: 4

Notes: Contains 1½ ounces (3 tablespoons) Virgin Coconut Oil, equivalent to ¾ tablespoon Virgin Coconut Oil per serving.

Nutritional Data

Calories (kcal): 108
% Calories from Fat: 77.3%
% Calories from Carbohydrates: 20.8%
% Calories from Protein: 1.8%

Per Serving Nutritional Information

Total Fat (g): 10g 16%
Saturated Fat (g): 9g 44%
Monounsaturated Fat (g): 1g 3%
Polyunsaturated Fat (g): trace 1%
Total Carbohydrate (g): 6g 2%
Dietary Fiber (g): 1g 2%
Protein (g): 1g 1%
Sodium (mg): 272mg 11%
Potassium (mg): 124mg 4%
Calcium (mg): 19mg 2%
Iron (mg): 1mg 3%
Zinc (mg): trace 1%
Vitamin C (mg): 39mg 64%
Vitamin A (i.u.): 410IU 8%
Vitamin A (r.e.): 41RE 4%
Vitamin B6 (mg): .1mg 3%
Vitamin B12 (mcg): 0mcg 0%
Thiamin B1 (mg): trace 2%
Riboflavin B2 (mg): trace 1%
Folacin (mcg): 19mcg 5%
Niacin (mg): trace 1%

Percent Daily Values are based on a 2000 calorie diet.

Spicy Balsamic Sauce

Ingredients

- 2 teaspoons balsamic vinegar
- 2 teaspoons red wine vinegar
- 1 medium garlic clove, minced
- ½ teaspoon red pepper flakes, or to taste
- ¼ teaspoon salt
- ¼ cup Virgin Coconut Oil

1. Whisk first five ingredients for Spicy Balsamic Sauce in small bowl; whisk in Virgin Coconut Oil until dressing is smooth.

2. Serve immediately.

Servings: 4

Notes: Contains 4 tablespoons Virgin Coconut Oil, equivalent to 1 tablespoon per serving.

Nutritional Data

Calories (kcal): 119
% Calories from Fat: 98.0%
% Calories from Carbohydrates: 1.8%
% Calories from Protein: 0.2%

Per Serving Nutritional Information

Total Fat (g): 14g 21%
Saturated Fat (g): 12g 59%
Monounsaturated Fat (g): 1g 4%
Polyunsaturated Fat (g): trace 1%
Total Carbohydrate (g): 1g 0%
Dietary Fiber (g): trace 0%
Protein (g): trace 0%
Sodium (mg): 133mg 6%
Potassium (mg): 9mg 0%
Calcium (mg): 3mg 0%
Iron (mg): trace 0%
Zinc (mg): trace 0%
Vitamin C (mg): 1mg 1%
Vitamin A (i.u.): 13IU 0%
Vitamin A (r.e.): 1 1/2RE 0%
Vitamin B6 (mg): trace 0%
Vitamin B12 (mcg): 0mcg 0%
Thiamin B1 (mg): 0mg 0%
Riboflavin B2 (mg): 0mg 0%
Folacin (mcg): trace 0%
Niacin (mg): trace 0%

Percent Daily Values are based on a 2000 calorie diet.

Strawberry Salsa

Ingredients

- 2 pounds fresh strawberries, diced
- 1 medium yellow onion, diced
- 6 tablespoons fresh cilantro (packed) chopped
- 2 tablespoons fresh lime juice
- 1 teaspoon lime zest, fresh
- 2 large cloves garlic, minced
- 1 large jalapeno, seeded and minced
- 2 tablespoons Virgin Coconut Oil

Toss all ingredients in a medium bowl until well blended. Refrigerate until ready for use.

Servings: 32

Yield: 2 cups

Notes: Contains approximately 1/32 ounces Virgin Coconut Oil per tablespoon serving.

Nutritional Data

Calories (kcal): 17
% Calories from Fat: 45.3%
% Calories from Carbohydrates: 50.0%
% Calories from Protein: 4.7%

Per Serving Nutritional Information

Total Fat (g): 1g 1%
Saturated Fat (g): 1g 4%
Monounsaturated Fat (g): trace 0%
Polyunsaturated Fat (g): trace 0%
Total Carbohydrate (g): 2g 1%
Dietary Fiber (g): 1g 3%
Protein (g): trace 0%
Sodium (mg): 1mg 0%
Potassium (mg): 54mg 2%
Calcium (mg): 5mg 1%
Iron (mg): trace 1%
Zinc (mg): trace 0%
Vitamin C (mg): 16mg 27%
Vitamin A (i.u.): 20IU 0%
Vitamin A (r.e.): 2RE 0%
Vitamin B6 (mg): trace 0%
Vitamin B12 (mcg): 0mcg 0%
Thiamin B1 (mg): trace 0%
Riboflavin B2 (mg): trace 0%
Folacin (mcg): 6mcg 1%
Niacin (mg): trace 0%

* Percent Daily Values are based on a 2000 calorie diet.

Tomato Sauce

Ingredients

- 20 roma tomatoes, halved and seeded
- ¼ cup Virgin Coconut Oil
- ½ teaspoon sea salt
- 1 teaspoon fresh ground black pepper
- 1 cup diced onion
- 2 teaspoons minced garlic
- 1 tablespoon fresh oregano, finely-chopped
- 1 tablespoon fresh thyme leaves, finely-chopped
- 1 cup white wine

1. Preheat oven to 325 degrees.

2. In two (13- by 9-inch) pans place tomato halves cut-side up. Sprinkle with Virgin Coconut Oil, salt and pepper, onion, garlic, and herbs. Bake tomatoes for 2 hours. Check the tomatoes after 1 hour and turn down the heat if they seem to be cooking too quickly.

3. Then turn the oven to 400 degrees and bake another 30 minutes. Remove from the oven and process tomatoes through a food mill on medium die setting over a small saucepan. Discard skins. Add white wine. Bring to a boil. Reduce heat to low and cook for 5 minutes.

Servings: 8
Yield: 4 cups

Nutritional Data

Calories (kcal): 153
% Calories from Fat: 47.4%
% Calories from Carbohydrates: 44.7%
% Calories from Protein: 7.9%

Per Serving Nutritional Information

Total Fat (g): 8g 12%
Saturated Fat (g): 6g 30%
Monounsaturated Fat (g): 1g 2%
Polyunsaturated Fat (g): 1g 2%
Total Carbohydrate (g): 17g 6%
Dietary Fiber (g): 4g 16%
Protein (g): 3g 6%
Sodium (mg): 148mg 6%
Potassium (mg): 747mg 21%
Calcium (mg): 27mg 3%
Iron (mg): 2mg 9%
Zinc (mg): trace 2%
Vitamin C (mg): 61mg 102%
Vitamin A (i.u.): 1935IU 39%
Vitamin A (r.e.): 192 1/2RE 19%
Vitamin B6 (mg): .3mg 13%
Vitamin B12 (mcg): 0mcg 0%
Thiamin B1 (mg): .2mg 12%
Riboflavin B2 (mg): .1mg 8%
Folacin (mcg): 50mcg 13%
Niacin (mg): 2mg 10%

* Percent Daily Values are based on a 2000 calorie diet.

Notes: Contains 2 ounces (4 tablespoons) Virgin Coconut Oil, equivalent to ½ tablespoon Virgin Coconut Oil per serving.

Vinaigrette, Basic

Ingredients

- ¼ cup red wine vinegar
- ½ teaspoon kosher salt
- ¼ teaspoon fresh ground black pepper
- ☐ cup extra virgin olive oil
- ☐ cup Virgin Coconut Oil

1. In a small bowl, combine vinegar, salt, and pepper. Whisk until salt dissolves.

2. Combine olive oil and Virgin Coconut Oil until liquid

3. Whisk in oil slowly. Allow to stand 5 minutes. Whisk again, then taste and adjust seasonings, if needed.

4. Basic dressing can be stored on shelf or refrigerated, covered, up to one week. If refrigerated, allow to warm to room temperature before using, whisk, or shake, before using.

Servings: 16
Yield: 1 Cup

Notes: Contains approximately 3/16 ounce Virgin Coconut Oil per serving

Nutritional Data

Calories (kcal): 89
% Calories from Fat: 98.9%
% Calories from Carbohydrates: 1.0%
% Calories from Protein: 0.0%

Per Serving Nutritional Information

Total Fat (g): 10g 16%
Saturated Fat (g): 5g 26%
Monounsaturated Fat (g): 4g 18%
Polyunsaturated Fat (g): 1g 2%
Total Carbohydrate (g): trace 0%
Dietary Fiber (g): trace 0%
Protein (g): trace 0%
Sodium (mg): 59mg 2%
Potassium (mg): 4mg 0%
Calcium (mg): trace 0%
Iron (mg): trace 0%
Zinc (mg): trace 0%
Vitamin C (mg): trace 0%
Vitamin A (i.u.): trace 0%
Vitamin A (r.e.): 0RE 0%
Vitamin B6 (mg): 0mg 0%
Vitamin B12 (mcg): 0mcg 0%
Thiamin B1 (mg): 0mg 0%
Riboflavin B2 (mg): trace 0%
Folacin (mcg): trace 0%
Niacin (mg): trace 0%

Percent Daily Values are based on a 2000 calorie diet.

Vinaigrette, Caper & Egg

Ingredients

- ¼ cup red wine vinegar
- ½ teaspoon sea salt
- ¼ teaspoon fresh ground black pepper
- 1 tablespoon capers, drained
- 2 tablespoons fresh parsley, chopped
- ⅜ cup extra virgin olive oil
- ⅜ cup Virgin Coconut Oil
- 1 egg, hard-boiled, chopped fine

1. In a small bowl, combine vinegar, salt, and pepper. Whisk until salt dissolves. Add capers and chopped parsley.

2. Combine olive oil and Virgin Coconut Oil, and stir until liquid.

3. Whisk in oil slowly. Allow to stand 5 minutes. Whisk again. Then taste and adjust seasonings, if needed. Stir in chopped egg.

4. Basic dressing can be stored on shelf or refrigerated, covered, up to one week. Allow to warm to room temperature and whisk before using.

Servings: 16

Notes: Contains approximately 3/16 ounce Virgin Coconut Oil per serving.

Nutritional Data

Calories (kcal): 94
% Calories from Fat: 97.1%
% Calories from Carbohydrates: 1.3%
% Calories from Protein: 1.7%

Per Serving Nutritional Information

Total Fat (g): 11g 16%
Saturated Fat (g): 5g 26%
Monounsaturated Fat (g): 4g 19%
Polyunsaturated Fat (g): 1g 3%
Total Carbohydrate (g): trace 0%
Dietary Fiber (g): trace 0%
Protein (g): trace 1%
Sodium (mg): 68mg 3%
Potassium (mg): 11mg 0%
Calcium (mg): 3mg 0%
Iron (mg): trace 1%
Zinc (mg): trace 0%
Vitamin C (mg): 1mg 1%
Vitamin A (i.u.): 42IU 1%
Vitamin A (r.e.): 7 1/2RE 1%
Vitamin B6 (mg): trace 0%
Vitamin B12 (mcg): trace 1%
Thiamin B1 (mg): trace 0%
Riboflavin B2 (mg): trace 1%
Folacin (mcg): 2mcg 1%
Niacin (mg): trace 0%

Percent Daily Values are based on a 2000 calorie diet.

Vinaigrette, Garlic

Ingredients

- ¼ cup red wine vinegar
- ½ teaspoon sea salt
- fresh ground black pepper
- ½ tablespoon minced garlic
- ☐ cup extra virgin olive oil
- ☐ cup Virgin Coconut Oil

1. Combine olive oil and Virgin Coconut Oil, and stir until liquid.

2. Cover minced garlic with ¾ cup combined oil and let stand 30 minutes.

3. In a small bowl, combine vinegar, salt, and pepper. Whisk until salt dissolves.

4. Whisk in oil slowly. Allow to stand 5 minutes. Whisk again. Then taste and adjust seasonings, if needed.

5. Use dressing within a day or two. Can be stored on shelf or in refrigerator. If refrigerated, warm to room temperature. Whisk before using.

Servings: 16

Notes: Contains approximately 3/16 ounce Virgin Coconut Oil per serving.

Nutritional Data

Calories (kcal): 90
% Calories from Fat: 98.6%
% Calories from Carbohydrates: 1.3%
% Calories from Protein: 0.1%

Per Serving Nutritional Information

Total Fat (g): 10g 16%
Saturated Fat (g): 5g 26%
Monounsaturated Fat (g): 4g 18%
Polyunsaturated Fat (g): 1g 2%
Total Carbohydrate (g): trace 0%
Dietary Fiber (g): trace 0%
Protein (g): trace 0%
Sodium (mg): trace 0%
Potassium (mg): 5mg 0%
Calcium (mg): 1mg 0%
Iron (mg): trace 0%
Zinc (mg): trace 0%
Vitamin C (mg): trace 0%
Vitamin A (i.u.): 0IU 0%
Vitamin A (r.e.): 0RE 0%
Vitamin B6 (mg): trace 0%
Vitamin B12 (mcg): 0mcg 0%
Thiamin B1 (mg): 0mg 0%
Riboflavin B2 (mg): 0mg 0%
Folacin (mcg): trace 0%
Niacin (mg): trace 0%

* Percent Daily Values are based on a 2000 calorie diet.

Vinaigrette, Lemon-chive

Ingredients

- ¼ cup fresh lemon juice
- ½ teaspoon lemon zest
- 2 tablespoons minced fresh chives
- ½ teaspoon sea salt
- fresh ground black pepper
- ⅜ cup extra virgin olive oil
- ⅜ cup Virgin Coconut Oil

1. In a small bowl, combine lemon juice, salt, and pepper. Whisk until salt dissolves.

2. Combine Virgin Coconut Oil and olive oil and stir until liquid.

3. Whisk in oil slowly. Allow to stand 5 minutes. Whisk again. Then taste and adjust seasonings, if needed. Stir in minced chives.

4. Basic dressing can be stored on shelf or refrigerated, covered, up to one week. Allow to warm to room temperature and whisk before using.

Servings: 16
Yield: 1 Cup

Notes: Contains approximately 3/16 ounce Virgin Coconut Oil per serving.

Nutritional Data

Calories (kcal): 104
% Calories from Fat: 80.5%
% Calories from Carbohydrates: 18.6%
% Calories from Protein: 0.9%

Per Serving Nutritional Information

Total Fat (g): 10g 16%
Saturated Fat (g): 5g 26%
Monounsaturated Fat (g): 4g 18%
Polyunsaturated Fat (g): 1g 2%
Total Carbohydrate (g): 5g 2%
Dietary Fiber (g): trace 1%
Protein (g): trace 0%
Sodium (mg): 1mg 0%
Potassium (mg): 77mg 2%
Calcium (mg): 5mg 0%
Iron (mg): trace 0%
Zinc (mg): trace 0%
Vitamin C (mg): 28mg 47%
Vitamin A (i.u.): 29IU 1%
Vitamin A (r.e.): 3RE 0%
Vitamin B6 (mg): trace 2%
Vitamin B12 (mcg): 0mcg 0%
Thiamin B1 (mg): trace 1%
Riboflavin B2 (mg): trace 0%
Folacin (mcg): 8mcg 2%
Niacin (mg): trace 0%

Percent Daily Values are based on a 2000 calorie diet.

Vinaigrette, Mustard

Ingredients

- ¼ cup red wine vinegar
- 2 teaspoons dijon mustard
- ½ teaspoon sea salt
- fresh ground black pepper
- ⅜ cup extra virgin olive oil
- ⅜ cup Virgin Coconut Oil

1. In a small bowl, combine vinegar, dijon mustard, salt, and pepper. Whisk until salt dissolves.

2. Combine Virgin Coconut Oil and olive oil and stir until liquid.

3. Whisk in oil slowly. Allow to stand 5 minutes. Whisk again. Then taste and adjust seasonings, if needed.

4. Basic dressing can be refrigerated, covered, up to one week. Whisk before using and allow to warm to room temperature.

Servings: 16
Yield: 1 Cup

Notes: Contains approximately 3/16 ounce Virgin Coconut Oil per serving.

Nutritional Data

Calories (kcal): 90
% Calories from Fat: 98.8%
% Calories from Carbohydrates: 1.1%
% Calories from Protein: 0.1%

Per Serving Nutritional Information

Total Fat (g): 10g 16%
Saturated Fat (g): 5g 26%
Monounsaturated Fat (g): 4g 18%
Polyunsaturated Fat (g): 1g 2%
Total Carbohydrate (g): trace 0%
Dietary Fiber (g): trace 0%
Protein (g): trace 0%
Sodium (mg): 8mg 0%
Potassium (mg): 5mg 0%
Calcium (mg): 1mg 0%
Iron (mg): trace 0%
Zinc (mg): trace 0%
Vitamin C (mg): 0mg 0%
Vitamin A (i.u.): 0IU 0%
Vitamin A (r.e.): 0RE 0%
Vitamin B6 (mg): trace 0%
Vitamin B12 (mcg): 0mcg 0%
Thiamin B1 (mg): trace 0%
Riboflavin B2 (mg): 0mg 0%
Folacin (mcg): trace 0%
Niacin (mg): trace 0%

Percent Daily Values are based on a 2000 calorie diet.

Vinaigrette, Tarragon

Ingredients

- ¼ cup white wine vinegar
- ½ teaspoon sea salt
- fresh ground black pepper
- 1 tablespoon fresh tarragon, minced fine
- ⅜ cup extra virgin olive oil
- ⅜ cup Virgin Coconut Oil

1. In a small bowl, combine vinegar, salt, and pepper. Whisk until salt dissolves.

2. Combine Virgin Coconut Oil and olive oil and stir until liquid.

3. Whisk in oil slowly. Allow to stand 5 minutes. Whisk again. Then taste and adjust seasonings, if needed. Stir in minced tarragon.

4. Basic dressing can be refrigerated, covered, up to one week. Whisk before using and allow to warm to room temperature.

Servings: 16
Yield: 1 Cup

Notes: Contains approximately 3/16 ounce Virgin Coconut Oil per serving.

Nutritional Data

Calories (kcal): 89
% Calories from Fat: 99.0%
% Calories from Carbohydrates: 1.0%
% Calories from Protein: 0.0%

Per Serving Nutritional Information

Total Fat (g): 10g 16%
Saturated Fat (g): 5g 26%
Monounsaturated Fat (g): 4g 18%
Polyunsaturated Fat (g): 1g 2%
Total Carbohydrate (g): trace 0%
Dietary Fiber (g): 0g 0%
Protein (g): trace 0%
Sodium (mg): trace 0%
Potassium (mg): 5mg 0%
Calcium (mg): 1mg 0%
Iron (mg): trace 0%
Zinc (mg): trace 0%
Vitamin C (mg): trace 0%
Vitamin A (i.u.): 1IU 0%
Vitamin A (r.e.): 0RE 0%
Vitamin B6 (mg): 0mg 0%
Vitamin B12 (mcg): 0mcg 0%
Thiamin B1 (mg): 0mg 0%
Riboflavin B2 (mg): 0mg 0%
Folacin (mcg): 0mcg 0%
Niacin (mg): 0mg 0%

Percent Daily Values are based on a 2000 calorie diet.

Vinaigrette, Tomato-herb

Ingredients

- 2 tablespoons apple cider vinegar
- 1 tablespoon fresh lemon juice
- 1 teaspoon dijon mustard
- 2 tablespoons minced fresh flat-leaf parsley
- ⅜ cup extra virgin olive oil
- ⅜ cup Virgin Coconut Oil
- ½ cup diced tomato
- 2 teaspoons minced fresh chives
- ½ teaspoon sea salt
- fresh ground black pepper

1. Whisk together vinegar, lemon juice, mustard, and parsley in a medium bowl.

2. Combine Virgin Coconut Oil and olive oil and stir until liquid.

3. Add oil in slow, steady stream, whisking constantly: mixture should be thick and creamy.

4. Stir in tomatoes and chives. Season with salt and pepper to taste.

5. Use within a day or two.

Servings: 20

Notes: Contains approximately 3/16 ounce Virgin Coconut Oil per serving.

Nutritional Data

Calories (kcal): 76
% Calories from Fat: 92.4%
% Calories from Carbohydrates: 7.0%
% Calories from Protein: 0.6%

Per Serving Nutritional Information

Total Fat (g): 8g 13%
Saturated Fat (g): 4g 20%
Monounsaturated Fat (g): 3g 15%
Polyunsaturated Fat (g): trace 2%
Total Carbohydrate (g): 1g 0%
Dietary Fiber (g): trace 0%
Protein (g): trace 0%
Sodium (mg): 4mg 0%
Potassium (mg): 29mg 1%
Calcium (mg): 2mg 0%
Iron (mg): trace 0%
Zinc (mg): trace 0%
Vitamin C (mg): 7mg 12%
Vitamin A (i.u.): 54IU 1%
Vitamin A (r.e.): 5 1/2RE 1%
Vitamin B6 (mg): trace 0%
Vitamin B12 (mcg): 0mcg 0%
Thiamin B1 (mg): trace 0%
Riboflavin B2 (mg): trace 0%
Folacin (mcg): 3mcg 1%
Niacin (mg): trace 0%

Percent Daily Values are based on a 2000 calorie diet.

Coconut Diet Soups

African Vegetable Stew

Ingredients

- 2 tablespoons Virgin Coconut Oil
- 1 large onion, chopped
- 1 bunch swiss chard, stemmed, green part chopped
- 1 15 oz. can garbanzo beans (known also as chick peas, cece, etc.)
- ½ cup raisins
- ½ cup brown rice, uncooked
- 1 28 oz. can canned tomatoes
- 1 clove garlic (or more to taste)
- 2 medium yams
- salt and pepper, to taste
- tabasco sauce, to taste

1. Fry onion, garlic, and white stems of chard until barely limp. Add chopped greens and fry a bit.

2. Either peel the yams or scrub them well with a vegetable brush. Then slice them into thick slices. Add garbanzos, raisins, yams, tomatoes, salt, and pepper. Cook a couple of minutes.

3. Make a well in the center of the mixture in the pot. Put the rice in the well and pat it down until it's wet. Cover and cook until rice is done—about 25-40 minutes.

4. Add Tabasco sauce to taste.

Servings: 4

Nutritional Data

Calories (kcal): 725
% Calories from Fat: 17.2%
% Calories from Carbohydrates: 68.8%
% Calories from Protein: 14.0%

Per Serving Nutritional Information

Total Fat (g): 14g 22%
Saturated Fat (g): 7g 34%
Monounsaturated Fat (g): 2g 9%
Polyunsaturated Fat (g): 3g 15%
Total Carbohydrate (g): 129g 43%
Dietary Fiber (g): 25g 101%
Protein (g): 26g 53%
Sodium (mg): 340mg 14%
Potassium (mg): 2244mg 64%
Calcium (mg): 210mg 21%
Iron (mg): 9mg 51%
Zinc (mg): 5mg 32%
Vitamin C (mg): 49mg 82%
Vitamin A (i.u.): 1402IU 28%
Vitamin A (r.e.): 141 1/2RE 14%
Vitamin B6 (mg): 1.1mg 57%
Vitamin B12 (mcg): 0mcg 0%
Thiamin B1 (mg): .8mg 53%
Riboflavin B2 (mg): .3mg 19%
Folacin (mcg): 636mcg 159%
Niacin (mg): 5mg 24%

Percent Daily Values are based on a 2000 calorie diet.

Notes: Contains ½ tablespoon Virgin Coconut Oil per serving.

Albondingas (Mexican Meatball Soup)

Ingredients

- 2 qt. beef stock
- 2 cups carrot, sliced
- 1 pound chayote squash, ¾" cubes
- ½ lb. new potato, peeled, ¾" cubes
- 5 sprigs fresh mint sprig
- 1 cup radiatorre (pasta shells), or
- small shells, stars, etc.
- salt, to taste
- fresh ground black pepper, to taste

Mexican Meatballs

- 2 tablespoons Virgin Coconut Oil
- ¼ cup onion, finely chopped
- ½ teaspoon garlic, minced
- ½ lb. lean ground beef
- 1 large egg, lightly beaten
- ¼ cup tomato, finely chopped
- 1 tablespoon fresh mint, minced
- 1 teaspoon ground cumin
- ½ teaspoon salt
- ¼ cup fresh bread crumbs
- 1 qt. beef stock

1. Heat the Virgin Coconut Oil in a small skillet over medium-high heat. Add the onion and sauté until soft, about 5 minutes.

2. Add the garlic and sauté 1 minute longer.

3. Transfer to a bowl and stir in the remaining ingredients.

4. Working with about 1 tsp. of the mixture at a time; roll it between the palms of your hands to form balls. Place on a plate, cover loosely, and refrigerate for about 20 minutes before cooking.

5. In a saucepan, bring 4 cups of the stock to a boil over medium-high heat.

6. Add as many meatballs at a time as will fit comfortably in the pan and cook, skimming off foam as necessary, until done, about 5 minutes. Remove the meatballs with a slotted spoon and set aside; cook the remaining meatballs in the same way. Strain and reserve the cooking liquid for another use.

7. In a soup pot or large saucepan, combine the 2 quarts stock, carrot, chayote, potatoes, and mint. Bring to a boil over medium-high heat,

and then reduce to low and simmer, uncovered, until the vegetables are tender, about 25 minutes.

8. Meanwhile, cook the pasta in a large pot of boiling water until al dente. Drain and set aside.

9. About 5 minutes before the vegetables are done, add the meatballs and pasta to heat thoroughly. Season to taste with salt and pepper. Ladle into preheated bowls and garnish with herb sprigs. Alternatively, pour into a container and refrigerate, uncovered, until cool. Then tightly cover and store up to 3 days. Slowly reheat before garnishing and serving.

Servings: 4

Notes: Contains approximately 2 tablespoons (1 ounce) of Virgin Coconut Oil or 1½ teaspoons per serving.

Nutritional Data

Calories (kcal): 494
% Calories from Fat: 42.5%
% Calories from Carbohydrates: 39.9%
% Calories from Protein: 17.6%

Per Serving Nutritional Information

Total Fat (g): 22g 33%
Saturated Fat (g): 11g 57%
Monounsaturated Fat (g): 6g 28%
Polyunsaturated Fat (g): 1g 5%
Total Carbohydrate (g): 46g 15%
Dietary Fiber (g): 5g 19%
Protein (g): 20g 40%
Sodium (mg): 6738mg 281%
Potassium (mg): 1065mg 30%
Calcium (mg): 63mg 6%
Iron (mg): 8mg 45%
Zinc (mg): 3mg 21%
Vitamin C (mg): 21mg 35%
Vitamin A (i.u.): 20515IU 410%
Vitamin A (r.e.): 2064RE 206%
Vitamin B6 (mg): .5mg 23%
Vitamin B12 (mcg): 1.4mcg 24%
Thiamin B1 (mg): 3.3mg 221%
Riboflavin B2 (mg): .8mg 46%
Folacin (mcg): 46mcg 12%
Niacin (mg): 7mg 34%

* Percent Daily Values are based on a 2000 calorie diet.

Avocado Soup

Ingredients

- 2 avocados
- ½ teaspoon fresh lemon juice
- 2 cups chicken broth
- 2 tablespoons dry sherry
- 1 cup Coconut Cream Concentrate
- ½ teaspoon salt
- 2 pinches cayenne pepper

1. Peel and pit avocados. Puree in a blender with lemon juice.

2. Blend in chicken broth and sherry.

3. Pour into a bowl and whisk in Coconut Cream Concentrate.

4. Season to taste with salt and cayenne. Chill.

Servings: 6

Notes: Contains 1½ ounces Coconut Cream Concentrate per serving, equivalent to approximately 2 tablespoons Virgin Coconut Oil per serving.

Nutritional Data

Calories (kcal): 378
% Calories from Fat: 90.3%
% Calories from Carbohydrates: 7.1%
% Calories from Protein: 2.6%

Per Serving Nutritional Information

Total Fat (g): 84g 128%
Saturated Fat (g): 67g 333%
Monounsaturated Fat (g): 15g 66%
Polyunsaturated Fat (g): 1g 6%
Total Carbohydrate (g): 15g 5%
Dietary Fiber (g): 5g 21%
Protein (g): 5g 11%
Sodium (mg): 453mg 19%
Potassium (mg): 482mg 14%
Calcium (mg): 13mg 1%
Iron (mg): 4mg 21%
Zinc (mg): trace 2%
Vitamin C (mg): 8mg 14%
Vitamin A (i.u.): 427IU 9%
Vitamin A (r.e.): 42 1/2RE 4%
Vitamin B6 (mg): .2mg 10%
Vitamin B12 (mcg): .1mcg 1%
Thiamin B1 (mg): .1mg 5%
Riboflavin B2 (mg): .1mg 6%
Folacin (mcg): 44mcg 11%
Niacin (mg): 2mg 12%

Percent Daily Values are based on a 2000 calorie diet.

Beefy Broth

Ingredients

- Virgin Coconut Oil, as needed
- salt, to taste
- freshly-ground black pepper, to taste
- 3 pounds combined beef shank and oxtail pieces
- 2 onions, quartered
- 2 celery ribs, halved
- 2 carrots, halved
- 3 garlic cloves
- 1 bunch parsley
- 1 teaspoon black peppercorns
- 2 quarts water
- 1 cup Coconut Cream Concentrate

1. Place pressure cooker over high heat. Oil and salt the oxtail and shank pieces then sear in batches. Add remaining ingredients and cover with water, being careful not to fill above the cooker's "maximum fill" line. (If your pressure cooker does not have a water line, fill the pot ⅔ full). Bring to a boil and skim off any foam that gathers at the surface. Cover and lock lid. Once pressure builds up inside the cooker, reduce the heat so that you barely hear hissing from the pot. Cook for 50 minutes.

2. Release pressure using your cookers release device (read that manual) or cool the cooker by running cold water over the lid for 5 minutes. Carefully open the lid and strain squeezing the solids before feeding to the compost pile, or the dogs. Strain through a fine sieve or several layers of cheesecloth.

3. Season and stir in Coconut Cream Concentrate and serve or use as a base for other soup recipes.

Nutritional Data

Calories (kcal): 550
% Calories from Fat: 79.5%
% Calories from Carbohydrates: 6.7%
% Calories from Protein: 13.8%

Per Serving Nutritional Information

Total Fat (g): 88g 135%
Saturated Fat (g): 71g 353%
Monounsaturated Fat (g): 15g 66%
Polyunsaturated Fat (g): 1g 3%
Total Carbohydrate (g): 17g 6%
Dietary Fiber (g): 6g 23%
Protein (g): 34g 69%
Sodium (mg): 140mg 6%
Potassium (mg): 784mg 22%
Calcium (mg): 75mg 7%
Iron (mg): 7mg 41%
Zinc (mg): 10mg 66%
Vitamin C (mg): 19mg 32%
Vitamin A (i.u.): 7291IU 146%
Vitamin A (r.e.): 729RE 73%
Vitamin B6 (mg): .8mg 38%
Vitamin B12 (mcg): 4.7mcg 79%
Thiamin B1 (mg): .2mg 12%
Riboflavin B2 (mg): .3mg 20%
Folacin (mcg): 41mcg 10%
Niacin (mg): 8mg 42%

* Percent Daily Values are based on a 2000 calorie diet.

Servings: 6

Notes: Amount of Virgin Coconut Oil content varies with amount of oil used. Approximately 2⅔ to 4 tablespoons of Coconut Cream Concentrate per serving which equates to 1¾ to 2¾ tablespoon equivalents of Virgin Coconut Oil.

Black Bean Soup

Ingredients

- 1 pound dried black beans
- 2 tablespoons Virgin Coconut Oil
- ½ teaspoon pepper
- 2 cloves garlic, minced
- 1 medium onion
- 1 teaspoon oregano
- 1 bay leaf

1. Cover beans with water, 2" above top of beans. Soak overnight.

2. Bring to boil, then add remaining ingredients and simmer 2 hours or until beans are tender.

3. You can then puree half and add back to the soup. Remove bay leaf before pureeing.

Servings: 6

Notes: Contains 1 teaspoon Virgin Coconut Oil per serving.

Nutritional Data

Calories (kcal): 307
% Calories from Fat: 16.2%
% Calories from Carbohydrates: 62.7%
% Calories from Protein: 21.1%

Per Serving Nutritional Information

Total Fat (g): 6g 9%
Saturated Fat (g): 4g 21%
Monounsaturated Fat (g): trace 2%
Polyunsaturated Fat (g): 1g 3%
Total Carbohydrate (g): 49g 16%
Dietary Fiber (g): 12g 48%
Protein (g): 17g 33%
Sodium (mg): 5mg 0%
Potassium (mg): 1161mg 33%
Calcium (mg): 103mg 10%
Iron (mg): 4mg 22%
Zinc (mg): 3mg 19%
Vitamin C (mg): 2mg 3%
Vitamin A (i.u.): 31IU 1%
Vitamin A (r.e.): 3 1/2RE 0%
Vitamin B6 (mg): .2mg 12%
Vitamin B12 (mcg): 0mcg 0%
Thiamin B1 (mg): .7mg 46%
Riboflavin B2 (mg): .1mg 9%
Folacin (mcg): 340mcg 85%
Niacin (mg): 2mg 8%

Percent Daily Values are based on a 2000 calorie diet.

Leftover Baked Potato Soup

Ingredients

- 3 tablespoons Virgin Coconut Oil
- 1½ cups Leeks, finely-diced
- 1½ tablespoons minced garlic
- 6 cups chicken stock, hot
- 4 large leftover baked potatoes, halved, pulp scooped out and put through a ricer
- 1½ cups buttermilk
- ½ cup sour cream
- ½ cup parmesan cheese, freshly-grated
- 2½ teaspoons sea salt
- 1 teaspoon fresh ground black pepper
- 2 tablespoons sherry vinegar
- ¼ cup chives, minced

1. In a large saucepot, over high heat, melt the butter and add the leeks and garlic. Cook over medium heat until they are translucent. Add the hot stock and whisk to combine.

2. In a separate bowl, whisk together the riced potatoes, buttermilk, sour cream, and grated Parmesan. Add this mixture to the soup stirring constantly. Season with salt and pepper. Remove from the heat and add the sherry vinegar.

3. Ladle into bowls and garnish with chives.

4. This recipe yields 4 servings.

Nutritional Data

Calories (kcal): 506
% Calories from Fat: 37.4%
% Calories from Carbohydrates: 50.5%
% Calories from Protein: 12.2%

Per Serving Nutritional Information

Total Fat (g): 21g 32%
Saturated Fat (g): 15g 76%
Monounsaturated Fat (g): 4g 19%
Polyunsaturated Fat (g): 1g 3%
Total Carbohydrate (g): 63g 21%
Dietary Fiber (g): 6g 22%
Protein (g): 15g 30%
Sodium (mg): 4717mg 197%
Potassium (mg): 1318mg 38%
Calcium (mg): 335mg 33%
Iron (mg): 6mg 32%
Zinc (mg): 2mg 10%
Vitamin C (mg): 38mg 64%
Vitamin A (i.u.): 491IU 10%
Vitamin A (r.e.): 113RE 11%
Vitamin B6 (mg): .8mg 42%
Vitamin B12 (mcg): .4mcg 7%
Thiamin B1 (mg): 1.8mg 117%
Riboflavin B2 (mg): .5mg 28%
Folacin (mcg): 61mcg 15%
Niacin (mg): 4mg 20%

Percent Daily Values are based on a 2000 calorie diet.

Servings: 4

Notes: Contains ¾ tablespoon Virgin Coconut Oil per serving.

Mediterranean Stew

Ingredients

- 1 10-ounce package frozen okra, or fresh, washed and quartered
- 1 medium butternut, or acorn squash
- 2 tablespoons Virgin Coconut Oil
- 1½ cups onions, chopped
- 1 clove garlic, minced
- ½ teaspoon ground cumin
- ½ teaspoon ground turmeric
- ¼ teaspoon ground cinnamon
- ¼ teaspoon ground red pepper
- ¼ teaspoon paprika
- 2 cups eggplant, cubed, unpeeled
- 2 cups zucchini, sliced
- 1 medium carrot, sliced
- 1 8-ounce can tomato sauce
- ½ cup vegetable broth
- 1 15-ounce can chickpeas, drained
- 1 medium tomato, chopped
- ⅓ cup raisins
- salt, to taste
- 6 cups couscous, hot, cooked
- parsley, minced, for garnish

1. Prepare okra by washing under cold running water. Cut into ¾ inch slices.

2. Prepare squash by removing skin with vegetable peeler. Trim stem. Cut squash lengthwise into halves. Discard seeds. Cut flesh into 1 inch pieces.

3. Heat oil in Dutch oven over high heat until hot. Add onions and garlic. Cook and stir 5 minutes or until tender. Stir in cumin, turmeric, cinnamon, red pepper and paprika. Cook and stir 2-3 minutes.

4. Add okra, squash, eggplant, zucchini, carrot, tomato sauce and broth. Bring to a boil over high heat. Reduce heat to low. Simmer, uncovered, 5 minutes.

Nutritional Data

Calories (kcal): 1174
% Calories from Fat: 16.8%
% Calories from Carbohydrates: 68.3%
% Calories from Protein: 14.9%

Per Serving Nutritional Information

Total Fat (g): 22g 34%
Saturated Fat (g): 5g 25%
Monounsaturated Fat (g): 4g 16%
Polyunsaturated Fat (g): 11g 51%
Total Carbohydrate (g): 203g 68%
Dietary Fiber (g): 27g 107%
Protein (g): 44g 89%
Sodium (mg): 411mg 17%
Potassium (mg): 1648mg 47%
Calcium (mg): 202mg 20%
Iron (mg): 9mg 48%
Zinc (mg): 5mg 35%
Vitamin C (mg): 25mg 41%
Vitamin A (i.u.): 4743IU 95%
Vitamin A (r.e.): 474RE 47%
Vitamin B6 (mg): .9mg 47%
Vitamin B12 (mcg): 0mcg 0%
Thiamin B1 (mg): .9mg 57%
Riboflavin B2 (mg): .4mg 26%
Folacin (mcg): 545mcg 136%
Niacin (mg): 9mg 45%

* Percent Daily Values are based on a 2000 calorie diet.

5. Add chick peas, tomato and raisins. Simmer, covered, 30 minutes. Season to taste with salt.

6. Serve over couscous. Garnish, if desired.

Servings: 6

Notes: Contains 1 teaspoon Virgin Coconut Oil per serving.

Minestrone Soup

Ingredients

- ½ cup Virgin Coconut Oil
- 1 clove garlic, minced
- 2 cups onions, chopped
- 1 cup celery, chopped
- 1 small can tomato paste
- 2 quarts beef broth
- 1 quart water
- 1 cup cabbage, shredded
- 2 whole carrots, sliced
- 1 teaspoon salt
- ¼ teaspoon black pepper
- ⅛ teaspoon ground sage
- 1 whole zucchini, sliced
- 1 package frozen green beans
- 1 can red kidney beans
- 1 cup macaroni

1. In a large soup pot, sauté garlic, onion and celery until soft.

2. Stir in tomato paste, broth, water, cabbage, carrots, salt, pepper and sage. Mix well, bring to a boil.

3. Lower heat. Cover and simmer slowly 1 hour.

4. Add remaining ingredients. Cook 10-12 minutes until macaroni is tender.

5. Serve hot

Servings: 8

Serving Ideas: Sprinkle with parmesan cheese immediately before serving.

Nutritional Data

Calories (kcal): 1108
% Calories from Fat: 37.7%
% Calories from Carbohydrates: 38.3%
% Calories from Protein: 24.0%

Per Serving Nutritional Information

Total Fat (g): 46g 70%
Saturated Fat (g): 26g 129%
Monounsaturated Fat (g): 10g 45%
Polyunsaturated Fat (g): 2g 7%
Total Carbohydrate (g): 104g 35%
Dietary Fiber (g): 5g 20%
Protein (g): 65g 131%
Sodium (mg): 41089mg 1712%
Potassium (mg): 1639mg 47%
Calcium (mg): 196mg 20%
Iron (mg): 6mg 33%
Zinc (mg): 3mg 17%
Vitamin C (mg): 10mg 17%
Vitamin A (i.u.): 5616IU 112%
Vitamin A (r.e.): 567 1/2RE 57%
Vitamin B6 (mg): .3mg 14%
Vitamin B12 (mcg): 4.7mcg 78%
Thiamin B1 (mg): .4mg 30%
Riboflavin B2 (mg): .5mg 28%
Folacin (mcg): 116mcg 29%
Niacin (mg): 16mg 78%

* Percent Daily Values are based on a 2000 calorie diet.

Notes: Contains 1 tablespoon of Virgin Coconut Oil per serving.

Pinto Bean Soup

Ingredients

- 1 pound dried pinto beans
- 2 tablespoons Virgin Coconut Oil
- ½ teaspoon pepper
- 2 cloves garlic, minced
- 1 medium onion, chopped
- 1 teaspoon oregano
- 1 bay leaf

1. Cover beans with water, 2" above top of beans. Soak overnight.

2. Bring to boil. Then add remaining ingredients and simmer 2 hours or until beans are tender.

3. You can then puree half and add back to the soup. Remove bay leaf before pureeing.

Servings: 6

Notes: Contains 1 teaspoon Virgin Coconut Oil per serving.

Nutritional Data

Calories (kcal): 306
% Calories from Fat: 15.6%
% Calories from Carbohydrates: 63.9%
% Calories from Protein: 20.5%

Per Serving Nutritional Information

Total Fat (g): 5g 8%
Saturated Fat (g): 4g 21%
Monounsaturated Fat (g): trace 2%
Polyunsaturated Fat (g): trace 2%
Total Carbohydrate (g): 50g 17%
Dietary Fiber (g): 19g 76%
Protein (g): 16g 32%
Sodium (mg): 8mg 0%
Potassium (mg): 1044mg 30%
Calcium (mg): 102mg 10%
Iron (mg): 5mg 26%
Zinc (mg): 2mg 13%
Vitamin C (mg): 7mg 12%
Vitamin A (i.u.): 22IU 0%
Vitamin A (r.e.): 2RE 0%
Vitamin B6 (mg): .4mg 18%
Vitamin B12 (mcg): 0mcg 0%
Thiamin B1 (mg): .4mg 28%
Riboflavin B2 (mg): .2mg 11%
Folacin (mcg): 387mcg 97%
Niacin (mg): 1mg 6%

Percent Daily Values are based on a 2000 calorie diet.

Squash Soup

Ingredients

- 6 cups butternut squash, seeded 2" wide chunks = (about 2 large squashes)
- 1 tablespoon Virgin Coconut Oil, for brushing
- 1 tablespoon sea salt, plus
- 1 teaspoon sea salt
- 1½ teaspoons freshly-ground white pepper
- 3 cups chicken stock, fresh, or vegetable stock
- 4 tablespoons honey
- 1 teaspoon minced ginger
- 4 ounces Coconut Cream Concentrate
- ¼ teaspoon nutmeg

1. Preheat the oven to 400 degrees.

2. Brush the flesh of the squash with a little Virgin Coconut Oil and season with 1 tablespoon salt and 1 teaspoon of the freshly ground white pepper. On a sheet pan lay the squash flesh-side up. Roast for about 30 to 35 minutes or until the flesh is nice and soft.

3. Scoop the flesh from the skin into a pot and add the stock, honey, and ginger. Bring to a simmer and puree using a stick blender. Stir in the Coconut Cream Concentrate and return to a low simmer. Season with salt, pepper, and nutmeg.

4. This recipe yields 4 servings.

Servings: 4

Nutritional Data

Calories (kcal): 396
% Calories from Fat: 70.7%
% Calories from Carbohydrates: 26.7%
% Calories from Protein: 2.6%

Per Serving Nutritional Information

Total Fat (g): 58g 90%
Saturated Fat (g): 52g 258%
Monounsaturated Fat (g): 8g 38%
Polyunsaturated Fat (g): trace 1%
Total Carbohydrate (g): 49g 16%
Dietary Fiber (g): 6g 26%
Protein (g): 5g 10%
Sodium (mg): 1900mg 79%
Potassium (mg): 819mg 23%
Calcium (mg): 106mg 11%
Iron (mg): 5mg 26%
Zinc (mg): trace 3%
Vitamin C (mg): 45mg 74%
Vitamin A (i.u.): 16428IU 329%
Vitamin A (r.e.): 1643RE 164%
Vitamin B6 (mg): .3mg 17%
Vitamin B12 (mcg): 0mcg 0%
Thiamin B1 (mg): 1.0mg 64%
Riboflavin B2 (mg): .1mg 7%
Folacin (mcg): 58mcg 15%
Niacin (mg): 3mg 13%

Percent Daily Values are based on a 2000 calorie diet.

Notes: Contains 1 ounce (2 tablespoons) of Coconut Cream Concentrate per serving, equivalent to 1⅓ tablespoons of Virgin Coconut Oil per serving.

Turkey Soup

Ingredients

- 2 quarts vegetable stock
- 1 turkey carcass
- 1 10-ounce box frozen mixed vegetables
- ½ cup rice
- 2 cups cooked turkey, cubed
- 1 cup Coconut Cream Concentrate
- 1 teaspoon seafood seasoning
- 2 teaspoons dried thyme
- salt, to taste
- fresh ground black pepper, to taste

1. Combine the vegetable stock and the turkey carcass in a large soup pot over low heat and bring to a simmer. Cover and simmer for 1 hour.

2. Add the remaining ingredients to the stock. Cover and simmer for an additional 20 minutes.

3. Remove the bones before serving.

Servings: 6

Notes: Contains 2⅔ tablespoons of Coconut Cream Concentrate per serving, equivalent to 1⅞ tablespoons of Virgin Coconut Oil.

Nutritional Data

Calories (kcal): 633
% Calories from Fat: 66.9%
% Calories from Carbohydrates: 23.2%
% Calories from Protein: 9.9%

Per Serving Nutritional Information

Total Fat (g): 81g 124%
Saturated Fat (g): 67g 334%
Monounsaturated Fat (g): 10g 45%
Polyunsaturated Fat (g): 3g 13%
Total Carbohydrate (g): 63g 21%
Dietary Fiber (g): 10g 40%
Protein (g): 27g 53%
Sodium (mg): 2249mg 94%
Potassium (mg): 776mg 22%
Calcium (mg): 83mg 8%
Iron (mg): 8mg 44%
Zinc (mg): 4mg 26%
Vitamin C (mg): 8mg 13%
Vitamin A (i.u.): 8016IU 160%
Vitamin A (r.e.): 802 1/2RE 80%
Vitamin B6 (mg): .4mg 22%
Vitamin B12 (mcg): .2mcg 3%
Thiamin B1 (mg): .3mg 21%
Riboflavin B2 (mg): .3mg 15%
Folacin (mcg): 47mcg 12%
Niacin (mg): 6mg 32%

Percent Daily Values are based on a 2000 calorie diet.

Velouté Base for Non-dairy Cream Soups

Ingredients

- 4 cups chicken stock, fresh
- 2 cups Coconut Cream Concentrate

Combine chicken stock and Coconut Cream Concentrate in saucepan and bring to a boil.

Servings: 4
Yield: 4 cups

Notes: Contains ½ cup (4 ounces) of Coconut Cream Concentrate per serving, equivalent to approximately 2.8 ounces of Virgin Coconut Oil.

Nutritional Data

Calories (kcal): 771
% Calories from Fat: 93.4%
% Calories from Carbohydrates: 5.0%
% Calories from Protein: 1.6%

Per Serving Nutritional Information

Total Fat (g): 218g 336%
Saturated Fat (g): 194g 972%
Monounsaturated Fat (g): 27g 122%
Polyunsaturated Fat (g): 0g 0%
Total Carbohydrate (g): 26g 9%
Dietary Fiber (g): 10g 41%
Protein (g): 8g 16%
Sodium (mg): 41mg 2%
Potassium (mg): 85mg 2%
Calcium (mg): 1mg 0%
Iron (mg): 10mg 54%
Zinc (mg): 0mg 0%
Vitamin C (mg): 0mg 0%
Vitamin A (i.u.): 0IU 0%
Vitamin A (r.e.): 0RE 0%
Vitamin B6 (mg): 0mg 0%
Vitamin B12 (mcg): 0mcg 0%
Thiamin B1 (mg): 1.0mg 67%
Riboflavin B2 (mg): .1mg 6%
Folacin (mcg): 2mcg 1%
Niacin (mg): 0mg 0%

Percent Daily Values are based on a 2000 calorie diet.

Velouté of Broccoli Soup

Ingredients

- 1 cup chopped broccoli, fresh
- 4 cups chicken stock, fresh
- 2 cups Coconut Cream Concentrate
- ½ teaspoon sea salt
- ¼ teaspoon fresh ground black pepper

1. Combine chicken stock and Coconut Cream Concentrate in saucepan and bring to a boil.

2. Add broccoli and simmer for 4-6 minutes until broccoli is crisp tender.

3. Adjust seasonings and serve.

Servings: 4
Yield: 4 Cups

Notes: Contains ½ cup (4 ounces) of Coconut Cream Concentrate per serving, equivalent to approximately 2.8 ounces of Virgin Coconut Oil.

Nutritional Data

Calories (kcal): 777
% Calories from Fat: 93.1%
% Calories from Carbohydrates: 5.2%
% Calories from Protein: 1.7%

Per Serving Nutritional Information

Total Fat (g): 218g 336%
Saturated Fat (g): 194g 972%
Monounsaturated Fat (g): 27g 122%
Polyunsaturated Fat (g): trace 0%
Total Carbohydrate (g): 28g 9%
Dietary Fiber (g): 11g 44%
Protein (g): 9g 18%
Sodium (mg): 282mg 12%
Potassium (mg): 158mg 5%
Calcium (mg): 12mg 1%
Iron (mg): 10mg 55%
Zinc (mg): trace 1%
Vitamin C (mg): 21mg 34%
Vitamin A (i.u.): 339IU 7%
Vitamin A (r.e.): 34RE 3%
Vitamin B6 (mg): trace 2%
Vitamin B12 (mcg): 0mcg 0%
Thiamin B1 (mg): 1.0mg 68%
Riboflavin B2 (mg): .1mg 7%
Folacin (mcg): 18mcg 4%
Niacin (mg): trace 1%

Percent Daily Values are based on a 2000 calorie diet.

Coconut Diet Vegetable Dishes

Artichoke Mashed Idaho® Potatoes

Ingredients

- 4 large russet potatoes, peeled and quartered
- 1 can artichoke hearts (non-marinated)
- 3 tablespoons Virgin Coconut Oil
- ¼ cup milk
- salt and pepper, to taste

1. Boil potatoes for 15 to 20 minutes or until potatoes are tender when pierced with a fork. Drain.

2. In a large mixing bowl, purée artichoke hearts using a hand blender or mixer with half the Virgin Coconut Oil and milk. Add potatoes and remaining Virgin Coconut Oil and milk, and blend or mix until smooth.

3. Add salt and pepper to taste.

Servings: 6

Notes: Contains 3 tablespoons (1½ ounces) Virgin Coconut Oil, equivalent to 1/2 tablespoons (¼ ounce) Virgin Coconut Oil per serving.

Nutritional Data

Calories (kcal): 111
% Calories from Fat: 55.8%
% Calories from Carbohydrates: 37.9%
% Calories from Protein: 6.4%

Per Serving Nutritional Information

Total Fat (g): 7g 11%
Saturated Fat (g): 6g 31%
Monounsaturated Fat (g): trace 2%
Polyunsaturated Fat (g): trace 1%
Total Carbohydrate (g): 11g 4%
Dietary Fiber (g): 2g 6%
Protein (g): 2g 4%
Sodium (mg): 21mg 1%
Potassium (mg): 336mg 10%
Calcium (mg): 22mg 2%
Iron (mg): 1mg 3%
Zinc (mg): trace 2%
Vitamin C (mg): 11mg 19%
Vitamin A (i.u.): 38IU 1%
Vitamin A (r.e.): 6 1/2RE 1%
Vitamin B6 (mg): .1mg 7%
Vitamin B12 (mcg): trace 1%
Thiamin B1 (mg): .1mg 3%
Riboflavin B2 (mg): trace 2%
Folacin (mcg): 14mcg 4%
Niacin (mg): 1mg 4%

Percent Daily Values are based on a 2000 calorie diet.

Artichokes Caponata: Caponata di Carciofi

Ingredients

- 8 artichokes
- 3 tablespoons fresh lemon juice
- 7 tablespoons Virgin Coconut Oil
- ½ cup onion, cut into medium dice
- ¼ cup carrot, peeled and chopped into rough ¼-inch dice
- 12 green olives, optional, pitted, preferably Sicilian variety
- 1 tablespoon capers, salt-packed , rinsed and dried
- 2 whole chilis
- ½ teaspoon sea salt
- ½ teaspoon fresh ground black pepper
- 2 tablespoons tomato paste
- 3 anchovy fillets, salt-packed , soaked in milk, rinsed, patted dry, chopped
- 4 roma tomatoes, peeled and seeded
- 4 tablespoons red wine vinegar
- 4 tablespoons granulated sugar

1. Using a bread knife, carefully slice off the tips of the artichokes, remove all of the tough outer leaves, and using a paring knife peel the base. Cut each artichoke into quarters and remove the choke, as well as any prickly tips that may have formed on the inner leaves. Place in water with lemon juice. Drain. Cut each of these quarters into halves, to make wedges.

2. In a medium saucepan, heat 4 tablespoons Virgin Coconut Oil. Add onions, carrots, olives, capers, chilis, and drained artichokes. Season with salt and pepper. Toss to caramelize.

3. Add more Virgin Coconut Oil season, add tomato paste and let ingredients bubble rapidly. Add anchovies.

Nutritional Data

Calories (kcal): 224
% Calories from Fat: 47.9%
% Calories from Carbohydrates: 42.7%
% Calories from Protein: 9.3%

Per Serving Nutritional Information

Total Fat (g): 13g 20%
Saturated Fat (g): 10g 52%
Monounsaturated Fat (g): 1g 6%
Polyunsaturated Fat (g): trace 2%
Total Carbohydrate (g): 26g 9%
Dietary Fiber (g): 8g 33%
Protein (g): 6g 11%
Sodium (mg): 477mg 20%
Potassium (mg): 722mg 21%
Calcium (mg): 90mg 9%
Iron (mg): 3mg 14%
Zinc (mg): 1mg 6%
Vitamin C (mg): 53mg 88%
Vitamin A (i.u.): 2047IU 41%
Vitamin A (r.e.): 206RE 21%
Vitamin B6 (mg): .2mg 12%
Vitamin B12 (mcg): trace 0%
Thiamin B1 (mg): .1mg 9%
Riboflavin B2 (mg): .1mg 7%
Folacin (mcg): 98mcg 24%
Niacin (mg): 2mg 12%

* Percent Daily Values are based on a 2000 calorie diet.

---

4. During the last 5 minutes add tomatoes. Add red wine vinegar and sugar, and reduce 1 minute.

5. Serve hot or at room temperature with a salad

Servings: 8

Notes: Contains 7 tablespoons (3½ ounces) Virgin Coconut Oil equivalent to ⅞ tablespoons Virgin Coconut Oil per serving.

Broccoli With Lemon-Caper Sauce

Ingredients

Blanched Broccoli
- 1½ pounds fresh broccoli, rinsed
- 1 tablespoon salt
- 4 quarts water, more, if possible
- 1 tablespoon Virgin Coconut Oil

Lemon Caper Sauce
- ⅔ cup dry white wine, may substitute chicken stock
- 2 tablespoons fresh lemon juice
- 2 teaspoons capers, drained
- 1 tablespoon Virgin Coconut Oil, chilled

1. Wash and trim broccoli. Break into flowerettes.

2. Bring water to boil in large saucepan. Add salt.

3. Add broccoli flowerettes and blanch for 3-4 minutes or until crisp-tender. Immediately remove and plunge into ice bath to stop cooking. Drain thoroughly.

4. In medium to large sauté pan, over medium-high heat, add Virgin Coconut Oil and blanched broccoli, and sauté for 1-2 minutes.

5. Add wine and lemon juice. Bring to a boil, stirring to dissolve any browned bits attached to skillet. Cook and stir 1 to 2 minutes or until slightly thickened. Remove from heat. Stir in capers and chilled Virgin Coconut Oil.

6. Serve immediately.

Nutritional Data

Calories (kcal): 171
% Calories from Fat: 67.3%
% Calories from Carbohydrates: 21.7%
% Calories from Protein: 11.0%

Per Serving Nutritional Information

Total Fat (g): 14g 22%
Saturated Fat (g): 12g 59%
Monounsaturated Fat (g): 1g 4%
Polyunsaturated Fat (g): 1g 2%
Total Carbohydrate (g): 10g 3%
Dietary Fiber (g): 5g 22%
Protein (g): 5g 11%
Sodium (mg): 1941mg 81%
Potassium (mg): 579mg 17%
Calcium (mg): 118mg 12%
Iron (mg): 2mg 10%
Zinc (mg): 1mg 7%
Vitamin C (mg): 161mg 269%
Vitamin A (i.u.): 2630IU 53%
Vitamin A (r.e.): 262 1/2RE 26%
Vitamin B6 (mg): .3mg 13%
Vitamin B12 (mcg): 0mcg 0%
Thiamin B1 (mg): .1mg 7%
Riboflavin B2 (mg): .2mg 12%
Folacin (mcg): 123mcg 31%
Niacin (mg): 1mg 6%

* Percent Daily Values are based on a 2000 calorie diet.

Servings: 4

Notes: Contains 1 ounce (2 tablespoons) Virgin Coconut Oil, equivalent to ¼ ounce per serving.

Broccoli With Lime-Cumin Sauce

Ingredients

Blanched Broccoli
- 1½ pounds fresh broccoli, rinsed
- 1 tablespoon salt
- 4 quarts water, more, if possible
- 1 tablespoon Virgin Coconut Oil

Lime-Cumin Sauce
- 1 teaspoon lime zest
- 1 tablespoon fresh lime juice
- ½ teaspoon ground cumin
- ½ teaspoon salt
- 1 dash Tabasco sauce, to taste
- 3 tablespoons Virgin Coconut Oil
- ¼ cup minced red onion

1. Wash and trim broccoli. Break into flowerettes.

2. Bring water to boil in large saucepan. Add salt.

3. Add broccoli flowerettes and blanch for 3-4 minutes or until crisp-tender. Immediately remove and plunge into ice bath to stop cooking. Drain thoroughly.

4. Whisk first four ingredients of Lime-Cumin sauce (pepper sauce to taste) in small bowl. Whisk in Virgin Coconut Oil until dressing is smooth; stir in onion.

5. In medium to large sauté pan over medium-high heat, add Virgin Coconut Oil and blanched broccoli and sauté for 1-2 minutes.

6. Remove to platter or bowl and toss with Lime-Cumin Sauce. Serve immediately.

Nutritional Data

Calories (kcal): 171
% Calories from Fat: 67.3%
% Calories from Carbohydrates: 21.7%
% Calories from Protein: 11.0%

Per Serving Nutritional Information

Total Fat (g): 14g 22%
Saturated Fat (g): 12g 59%
Monounsaturated Fat (g): 1g 4%
Polyunsaturated Fat (g): 1g 2%
Total Carbohydrate (g): 10g 3%
Dietary Fiber (g): 5g 22%
Protein (g): 5g 11%
Sodium (mg): 1941mg 81%
Potassium (mg): 579mg 17%
Calcium (mg): 118mg 12%
Iron (mg): 2mg 10%
Zinc (mg): 1mg 7%
Vitamin C (mg): 161mg 269%
Vitamin A (i.u.): 2630IU 53%
Vitamin A (r.e.): 262 1/2RE 26%
Vitamin B6 (mg): .3mg 13%
Vitamin B12 (mcg): 0mcg 0%
Thiamin B1 (mg): .1mg 7%
Riboflavin B2 (mg): .2mg 12%
Folacin (mcg): 123mcg 31%
Niacin (mg): 1mg 6%

* Percent Daily Values are based on a 2000 calorie diet.

Servings: 4

Notes: Contains 2 ounces (4 tablespoons) Virgin Coconut Oil, equivalent to 1 tablespoon Virgin Coconut Oil per serving.

Broccoli With Orange-Ginger Sauce

Ingredients

Blanched Broccoli
- 1 ½ pounds fresh broccoli, rinsed
- 1 tablespoon salt
- 4 quarts water, more, if possible
- 1 tablespoon Virgin Coconut Oil

Orange Ginger Sauce
- 1 tablespoon Virgin Coconut Oil
- 1 tablespoon soy sauce (traditionally fermented - type)
- 1 tablespoon honey
- 1 tablespoon orange zest
- 3 tablespoons fresh orange juice
- 1 medium garlic clove, peeled and chopped
- 1 piece fresh ginger root (about 1 inch) peeled and chopped
- ¼ teaspoon salt

1. Wash and trim broccoli. Break into flowerettes.

2. Bring water to boil in large saucepan. Add salt.

3. Add broccoli flowerettes and blanch for 3-4 minutes or until crisp-tender. Immediately remove and plunge into ice bath to stop cooking. Drain thoroughly.

4. Process all ingredients for Orange Ginger Sauce in workbowl of food processor or blender, scraping down sides as needed, until dressing is smooth.

5. In medium to large sauté pan over medium-high heat, add Virgin Coconut Oil and blanched broccoli, and sauté for 1-2 minutes.

6. Toss sautéed broccoli with Orange Ginger Sauce.

7. Serve immediately.

Nutritional Data

Calories (kcal): 137
% Calories from Fat: 43.3%
% Calories from Carbohydrates: 42.3%
% Calories from Protein: 14.4%

Per Serving Nutritional Information

Total Fat (g): 7g 11%
Saturated Fat (g): 6g 30%
Monounsaturated Fat (g): trace 2%
Polyunsaturated Fat (g): trace 2%
Total Carbohydrate (g): 16g 5%
Dietary Fiber (g): 5g 21%
Protein (g): 6g 11%
Sodium (mg): 2065mg 86%
Potassium (mg): 619mg 18%
Calcium (mg): 119mg 12%
Iron (mg): 2mg 10%
Zinc (mg): 1mg 7%
Vitamin C (mg): 167mg 278%
Vitamin A (i.u.): 2655IU 53%
Vitamin A (r.e.): 265RE 27%
Vitamin B6 (mg): .3mg 14%
Vitamin B12 (mcg): 0mcg 0%
Thiamin B1 (mg): .1mg 7%
Riboflavin B2 (mg): .2mg 12%
Folacin (mcg): 129mcg 32%
Niacin (mg): 1mg 7%

* Percent Daily Values are based on a 2000 calorie diet.

Servings: 4

Notes: Contains 1 ounce (2 tablespoons) Virgin Coconut Oil, equivalent to ¼ ounce per serving.

Broccoli With Spanish Green Herb Sauce

Ingredients

- *Blanched Broccoli*
- 1 ½ pounds fresh broccoli, rinsed
- 1 tablespoon salt
- 4 quarts water, more, if possible
- 1 tablespoon Virgin Coconut Oil

Spanish Green Herb Sauce

- 2 medium garlic cloves, peeled
- ½ cup tightly-packed fresh cilantro leaves
- ½ cup tightly-packed fresh parsley
- 3 tablespoons Virgin Coconut Oil
- 1 tablespoon fresh lemon juice
- ½ teaspoon salt

1. Wash and trim broccoli. Break into flowerettes.

2. Bring water to boil in large saucepan. Add salt.

3. Add broccoli flowerettes and blanch for 3-4 minutes or until crisp-tender. Immediately remove and plunge into ice bath to stop cooking. Drain thoroughly.

4. Process Spanish Green Herb Sauce ingredients in workbowl of food processor or blender, scraping down sides of bowl as needed, until sauce is smooth.

5. In medium to large sauté pan over medium-high heat, add Virgin Coconut Oil and blanched broccoli, and sauté for 1-2 minutes.

6. Toss with Spanish Green Herb Sauce to coat. Serve immediately.

Nutritional Data

Calories (kcal): 185
% Calories from Fat: 60.7%
% Calories from Carbohydrates: 28.7%
% Calories from Protein: 10.6%

Per Serving Nutritional Information

Total Fat (g): 14g 22%
Saturated Fat (g): 12g 59%
Monounsaturated Fat (g): 1g 4%
Polyunsaturated Fat (g): 1g 2%
Total Carbohydrate (g): 15g 5%
Dietary Fiber (g): 6g 23%
Protein (g): 6g 11%
Sodium (mg): 1945mg 81%
Potassium (mg): 677mg 19%
Calcium (mg): 130mg 13%
Iron (mg): 2mg 12%
Zinc (mg): 1mg 7%
Vitamin C (mg): 197mg 329%
Vitamin A (i.u.): 3036IU 61%
Vitamin A (r.e.): 303RE 30%
Vitamin B6 (mg): .3mg 15%
Vitamin B12 (mcg): 0mcg 0%
Thiamin B1 (mg): .1mg 8%
Riboflavin B2 (mg): .2mg 12%
Folacin (mcg): 140mcg 35%
Niacin (mg): 1mg 6%

Percent Daily Values are based on a 2000 calorie diet.

Servings: 4

Notes: Contains 2 ounces (4 tablespoons) Virgin Coconut Oil, equivalent to 1 tablespoon Virgin Coconut Oil per serving.

Broccoli With Spicy Balsamic Sauce

Ingredients

Blanched Broccoli
- 1½ pounds fresh broccoli, rinsed
- 1 tablespoon salt
- 4 quarts water, more, if possible
- 1 tablespoon Virgin Coconut Oil

Spicy Balsamic Sauce
- 2 teaspoons balsamic vinegar
- 2 teaspoons red wine vinegar
- 1 medium garlic clove, minced
- ½ teaspoon red pepper flakes, or to taste
- ¼ teaspoon salt
- ¼ cup Virgin Coconut Oil

1. Wash and trim broccoli. Break into flowerettes.

2. Bring water to boil in large saucepan. Add salt.

3. Add broccoli flowerettes and blanch for 3-4 minutes or until crisp-tender. Immediately remove and plunge into ice bath to stop cooking. Drain thoroughly.

4. Whisk first five ingredients for Spicy Balsamic Sauce in small bowl. Whisk in Virgin Coconut Oil until dressing is smooth.

5. In medium to large sauté pan over medium-high heat, add Virgin Coconut Oil and blanched broccoli, and sauté for 1-2 minutes.

6. Toss with Spicy Balsamic Sauce. Serve immediately.

Nutritional Data

Calories (kcal): 196
% Calories from Fat: 73.1%
% Calories from Carbohydrates: 17.5%
% Calories from Protein: 9.4%

Per Serving Nutritional Information

Total Fat (g): 18g 27%
Saturated Fat (g): 15g 74%
Monounsaturated Fat (g): 1g 5%
Polyunsaturated Fat (g): 1g 3%
Total Carbohydrate (g): 9g 3%
Dietary Fiber (g): 5g 21%
Protein (g): 5g 10%
Sodium (mg): 1807mg 75%
Potassium (mg): 562mg 16%
Calcium (mg): 114mg 11%
Iron (mg): 2mg 9%
Zinc (mg): 1mg 6%
Vitamin C (mg): 159mg 265%
Vitamin A (i.u.): 2638IU 53%
Vitamin A (r.e.): 263 1/2RE 26%
Vitamin B6 (mg): .3mg 13%
Vitamin B12 (mcg): 0mcg 0%
Thiamin B1 (mg): .1mg 6%
Riboflavin B2 (mg): .2mg 11%
Folacin (mcg): 121mcg 30%
Niacin (mg): 1mg 5%

* Percent Daily Values are based on a 2000 calorie diet.

Servings: 4

Notes: Contains 5 tablespoons Virgin Coconut Oil, equivalent to 1¼ tablespoons per serving.

Carrot Ginger Vichyssoise

Ingredients

- 8 medium carrots, chopped in large pieces
- 1 leek (white part only), sliced & washed well
- 2 medium potatoes, peeled, chopped in large pieces
- 1 clove garlic, sliced
- 1 ginger root slice, 1", sliced thin
- 2 tablespoons Virgin Coconut Oil
- 2 bay leaves
- 8 cups chicken stock
- 1 teaspoon sea salt
- ½ teaspoon fresh ground black pepper
- ½ cup cream
- ½ cup Coconut Cream Concentrate

1. Warm the Virgin Coconut Oil in a soup pot and slowly cook the garlic and ginger until soft. Add the leeks. Raise the heat and cook until the leeks begin to wilt. Add the carrots, potatoes, bay leaves, chicken stock, 1 teaspoon salt, and ½ teaspoon pepper, and bring to a boil. Reduce heat and cook slowly until all the vegetables are soft.

2. Carefully puree the soup in a blender at low speed until very smooth. Return to the pot and add the cream and Coconut Cream Concentrate, and adjust the salt and pepper. Place into a storage container and cool to room temperature before refrigerating.

3. Adjust the seasoning and consistency if needed before serving. Serve in chilled soup bowls and garnish with snipped chives.

Nutritional Data

Calories (kcal): 244
% Calories from Fat: 73.7%
% Calories from Carbohydrates: 18.8%
% Calories from Protein: 7.5%

Per Serving Nutritional Information

Total Fat (g): 34g 52%
Saturated Fat (g): 29g 144%
Monounsaturated Fat (g): 4g 19%
Polyunsaturated Fat (g): trace 2%
Total Carbohydrate (g): 19g 6%
Dietary Fiber (g): 4g 17%
Protein (g): 8g 16%
Sodium (mg): 1070mg 45%
Potassium (mg): 649mg 19%
Calcium (mg): 57mg 6%
Iron (mg): 2mg 14%
Zinc (mg): 1mg 4%
Vitamin C (mg): 14mg 24%
Vitamin A (i.u.): 20331IU 407%
Vitamin A (r.e.): 2045 1/2RE 205%
Vitamin B6 (mg): .2mg 12%
Vitamin B12 (mcg): .3mcg 5%
Thiamin B1 (mg): .1mg 6%
Riboflavin B2 (mg): .1mg 8%
Folacin (mcg): 26mcg 7%
Niacin (mg): 4mg 22%

Percent Daily Values are based on a 2000 calorie diet.

Servings: 8

Notes: Contains 2 tablespoons of Virgin Coconut Oil and 4½ tablespoon equivalents from Coconut Cream Concentrate for a total Virgin Coconut Oil equivalent of 6½ tablespoons (3¼ ounces) of Virgin Coconut Oil or ¾ to 1 tablespoon per serving.

Creamed Corn

Ingredients

- 2 cups chicken stock, fresh
- 1 cup Coconut Cream Concentrate
- 10 ounces frozen corn kernels, or fresh
- ¼ teaspoon sea salt, or to taste
- ⅛ teaspoon fresh ground black pepper, or to taste

1. Combine chicken stock and Coconut Cream Concentrate in medium saucepan. Bring to boil over medium-high heat.

2. Add corn kernels. Stir and return to boil. Then reduce heat to simmer. Cook 3-5 minutes or follow package directions.

Servings: 4

Notes: Contains the equivalent of 5.6 ounces Virgin Coconut Oil equivalent to 1.4 ounces (2.8 tablespoons) per serving.

Nutritional Data

Calories (kcal): 448
% Calories from Fat: 87.8%
% Calories from Carbohydrates: 10.0%
% Calories from Protein: 2.2%

Per Serving Nutritional Information

Total Fat (g): 110g 169%
Saturated Fat (g): 97g 486%
Monounsaturated Fat (g): 14g 61%
Polyunsaturated Fat (g): trace 1%
Total Carbohydrate (g): 28g 9%
Dietary Fiber (g): 7g 28%
Protein (g): 6g 12%
Sodium (mg): 140mg 6%
Potassium (mg): 192mg 5%
Calcium (mg): 4mg 0%
Iron (mg): 5mg 29%
Zinc (mg): trace 2%
Vitamin C (mg): 5mg 8%
Vitamin A (i.u.): trace 0%
Vitamin A (r.e.): 0RE 0%
Vitamin B6 (mg): .1mg 6%
Vitamin B12 (mcg): 0mcg 0%
Thiamin B1 (mg): .6mg 37%
Riboflavin B2 (mg): .1mg 6%
Folacin (mcg): 26mcg 7%
Niacin (mg): 1mg 6%

Percent Daily Values are based on a 2000 calorie diet.

Creamed Mixed Vegetables

Ingredients

- 2 cups chicken stock, fresh
- 1 cup Coconut Cream Concentrate
- 10 ounces frozen mixed vegetables, or fresh, parboiled to crisp-tender
- ¼ teaspoon sea salt, or to taste
- ⅛ teaspoon fresh ground black pepper, or to taste

1. Combine chicken stock and Coconut Cream Concentrate in medium saucepan. Bring to boil over medium-high heat.

2. Add mixed vegetables, stir, return to boil, then reduce heat to simmer. Cook 3-5 minutes.

Servings: 4

Notes: Contains the equivalent of 5.6 ounces Virgin Coconut Oil equivalent to 1.4 ounces (2.8 tablespoons) per serving.

Nutritional Data

Calories (kcal): 431
% Calories from Fat: 89.4%
% Calories from Carbohydrates: 8.3%
% Calories from Protein: 2.3%

Per Serving Nutritional Information

Total Fat (g): 110g 169%
Saturated Fat (g): 97g 486%
Monounsaturated Fat (g): 14g 61%
Polyunsaturated Fat (g): trace 1%
Total Carbohydrate (g): 23g 8%
Dietary Fiber (g): 8g 32%
Protein (g): 6g 13%
Sodium (mg): 171mg 7%
Potassium (mg): 194mg 6%
Calcium (mg): 19mg 2%
Iron (mg): 6mg 31%
Zinc (mg): trace 2%
Vitamin C (mg): 2mg 4%
Vitamin A (i.u.): 3599IU 72%
Vitamin A (r.e.): 360RE 36%
Vitamin B6 (mg): .1mg 3%
Vitamin B12 (mcg): 0mcg 0%
Thiamin B1 (mg): .6mg 39%
Riboflavin B2 (mg): .1mg 6%
Folacin (mcg): 22mcg 5%
Niacin (mg): 1mg 4%

Percent Daily Values are based on a 2000 calorie diet.

Creamed New Potatoes

Ingredients

- 1 pound new potatoes, preferably small boilers
- 2 cups chicken stock, fresh
- 1 cup Coconut Cream Concentrate
- ¼ teaspoon sea salt, or to taste
- ⅛ teaspoon fresh ground black pepper, or to taste

1. Wash potatoes. If larger than 1" in diameter, halve or quarter.

2. Boil potatoes in salted water until just fork-tender. Drain and set aside.

3. Combine chicken stock and Coconut Cream Concentrate in medium saucepan. Bring to boil over medium-high heat.

4. Add cooked potatoes. Stir and return to boil. Then reduce heat to simmer. Cook 3-5 minutes or hot throughout.

Servings: 4

Notes: Contains the equivalent of 5.6 ounces Virgin Coconut Oil equivalent to 1.4 ounces (2.8 tablespoons) per serving.

Nutritional Data

Calories (kcal): 475
% Calories from Fat: 86.0%
% Calories from Carbohydrates: 11.8%
% Calories from Protein: 2.3%

Per Serving Nutritional Information

Total Fat (g): 109g 168%
Saturated Fat (g): 97g 486%
Monounsaturated Fat (g): 14g 61%
Polyunsaturated Fat (g): trace 0%
Total Carbohydrate (g): 34g 11%
Dietary Fiber (g): 7g 28%
Protein (g): 6g 13%
Sodium (mg): 145mg 6%
Potassium (mg): 660mg 19%
Calcium (mg): 9mg 1%
Iron (mg): 6mg 32%
Zinc (mg): trace 3%
Vitamin C (mg): 22mg 37%
Vitamin A (i.u.): trace 0%
Vitamin A (r.e.): 0RE 0%
Vitamin B6 (mg): .3mg 14%
Vitamin B12 (mcg): 0mcg 0%
Thiamin B1 (mg): .6mg 40%
Riboflavin B2 (mg): .1mg 5%
Folacin (mcg): 16mcg 4%
Niacin (mg): 2mg 8%

* Percent Daily Values are based on a 2000 calorie diet.

Creamed Peas & Onions

Ingredients

- 2 cups chicken stock, fresh
- 1 cup Coconut Cream Concentrate
- 10 ounces frozen peas and onions
- ¼ teaspoon sea salt, or to taste
- ⅛ teaspoon fresh ground black pepper, or to taste

1. Combine chicken stock and Coconut Cream Concentrate in medium saucepan. Bring to boil over medium-high heat.

2. Add peas and onions. Stir and return to boil. Then reduce heat to simmer. Cook 3-5 minutes or follow package directions.

Servings: 4

Notes: Contains the equivalent of 5.6 ounces Virgin Coconut Oil equivalent to 1.4 ounces (2.8 tablespoons) per serving.

Nutritional Data

Calories (kcal): 435
% Calories from Fat: 89.2%
% Calories from Carbohydrates: 8.3%
% Calories from Protein: 2.5%

Per Serving Nutritional Information

Total Fat (g): 109g 168%
Saturated Fat (g): 97g 486%
Monounsaturated Fat (g): 14g 61%
Polyunsaturated Fat (g): trace 0%
Total Carbohydrate (g): 23g 8%
Dietary Fiber (g): 8g 31%
Protein (g): 7g 14%
Sodium (mg): 181mg 8%
Potassium (mg): 187mg 5%
Calcium (mg): 17mg 2%
Iron (mg): 6mg 33%
Zinc (mg): trace 2%
Vitamin C (mg): 10mg 17%
Vitamin A (i.u.): 386IU 8%
Vitamin A (r.e.): 38 1/2RE 4%
Vitamin B6 (mg): .1mg 5%
Vitamin B12 (mcg): 0mcg 0%
Thiamin B1 (mg): .7mg 47%
Riboflavin B2 (mg): .1mg 7%
Folacin (mcg): 33mcg 8%
Niacin (mg): 1mg 6%

Percent Daily Values are based on a 2000 calorie diet.

Creamed Peas and Carrots

Ingredients

- 2 cups chicken stock, fresh
- 1 cup Coconut Cream Concentrate
- 10 ounces frozen peas and carrots
- ¼ teaspoon sea salt, or to taste
- ⅛ teaspoon fresh ground black pepper, or to taste

1. Combine chicken stock and Coconut Cream Concentrate in medium saucepan. Bring to boil over medium-high heat.

2. Add peas and carrots. Stir and return to boil. Then reduce heat to simmer. Cook 3-5 minutes or follow package directions.

Servings: 4

Notes: Contains the equivalent of 5.6 ounces Virgin Coconut Oil equivalent to 1.4 ounces (2.8 tablespoons) per serving.

Nutritional Data

Calories (kcal): 423
% Calories from Fat: 89.9%
% Calories from Carbohydrates: 7.7%
% Calories from Protein: 2.4%

Per Serving Nutritional Information

Total Fat (g): 110g 169%
Saturated Fat (g): 97g 486%
Monounsaturated Fat (g): 14g 61%
Polyunsaturated Fat (g): trace 1%
Total Carbohydrate (g): 21g 7%
Dietary Fiber (g): 8g 31%
Protein (g): 7g 13%
Sodium (mg): 194mg 8%
Potassium (mg): 181mg 5%
Calcium (mg): 20mg 2%
Iron (mg): 6mg 31%
Zinc (mg): trace 2%
Vitamin C (mg): 8mg 13%
Vitamin A (i.u.): 6731IU 135%
Vitamin A (r.e.): 673 1/2RE 67%
Vitamin B6 (mg): .1mg 4%
Vitamin B12 (mcg): 0mcg 0%
Thiamin B1 (mg): .6mg 42%
Riboflavin B2 (mg): .1mg 6%
Folacin (mcg): 26mcg 7%
Niacin (mg): 1mg 5%

* Percent Daily Values are based on a 2000 calorie diet.

Creamed Spinach

Ingredients

- 1 cup heavy cream
- ¼ cup Coconut Cream Concentrate
- 1 10-ounce package frozen spinach
- ¼ teaspoon fresh ground nutmeg, or to taste
- ½ teaspoon sea salt, or to taste
- ¼ teaspoon fresh ground black pepper, or to taste
- ¼ cup grated Parmesan cheese, or to taste

1. Preheat oven to 350°F (175°C)

2. Combine heavy cream and Coconut Cream Concentrate in small saucepan. Heat to boiling over medium heat.

3. Defrost spinach and squeeze dry. Season with fresh ground nutmeg, salt, and pepper.

4. Place spinach in greased casserole and add boiling cream mixture. Stir to combine.

5. Grate Parmesan cheese over the top. Cover and place in pre-heated oven for 20 minutes.

Servings: 4

Notes: Contains the equivalent of 1.4 ounces of Virgin Coconut Oil from Coconut Cream Concentrate, equivalent to ¾ tablespoon per serving.

Nutritional Data

Calories (kcal): 340
% Calories from Fat: 88.9%
% Calories from Carbohydrates: 6.3%
% Calories from Protein: 4.9%

Per Serving Nutritional Information

Total Fat (g): 51g 79%
Saturated Fat (g): 39g 195%
Monounsaturated Fat (g): 10g 44%
Polyunsaturated Fat (g): 1g 4%
Total Carbohydrate (g): 8g 3%
Dietary Fiber (g): 3g 14%
Protein (g): 6g 13%
Sodium (mg): 408mg 17%
Potassium (mg): 281mg 8%
Calcium (mg): 187mg 19%
Iron (mg): 3mg 15%
Zinc (mg): 1mg 4%
Vitamin C (mg): 18mg 29%
Vitamin A (i.u.): 6409IU 128%
Vitamin A (r.e.): 811RE 81%
Vitamin B6 (mg): .1mg 6%
Vitamin B12 (mcg): .2mcg 3%
Thiamin B1 (mg): .1mg 5%
Riboflavin B2 (mg): .2mg 11%
Folacin (mcg): 87mcg 22%
Niacin (mg): trace 2%

Percent Daily Values are based on a 2000 calorie diet.

Green Beans With Lemon Caper Sauce

Ingredients

Blanched Green Beans
- 1½ pounds green beans, rinsed
- 1 tablespoon salt
- 4 quarts water, more, if possible
- 1 tablespoon Virgin Coconut Oil

Lemon Caper Sauce
- ⅔ cup dry white wine, may substitute chicken stock
- 2 tablespoons fresh lemon juice
- 2 teaspoons capers, drained
- 1 teaspoon Virgin Coconut Oil, chilled

1. Wash and string green beans.

2. Bring water to boil in large saucepan. Add salt.

3. Add green beans and blanch for 3-4 minutes or until crisp-tender. Immediately remove and plunge into ice bath to stop cooking. Drain thoroughly.

4. In medium to large sauté pan over medium-high heat, add Virgin Coconut Oil and blanched green beans and sauté for 1-2 minutes.

5. Add wine and lemon juice. Bring to a boil, stirring to dissolve any browned bits attached to skillet. Cook and stir 1 to 2 minutes or until slightly thickened. Remove from heat. Stir in capers and chilled Virgin Coconut Oil.

6. Toss with sautéed green beans. Serve immediately.

Nutritional Data

Calories (kcal): 143
% Calories from Fat: 30.0%
% Calories from Carbohydrates: 60.9%
% Calories from Protein: 9.1%

Per Serving Nutritional Information

Total Fat (g): 5g 7%
Saturated Fat (g): 4g 20%
Monounsaturated Fat (g): trace 1%
Polyunsaturated Fat (g): trace 1%
Total Carbohydrate (g): 22g 7%
Dietary Fiber (g): 6g 22%
Protein (g): 3g 6%
Sodium (mg): 1652mg 69%
Potassium (mg): 496mg 14%
Calcium (mg): 97mg 10%
Iron (mg): 2mg 10%
Zinc (mg): 1mg 5%
Vitamin C (mg): 81mg 134%
Vitamin A (i.u.): 1025IU 21%
Vitamin A (r.e.): 103RE 10%
Vitamin B6 (mg): .2mg 8%
Vitamin B12 (mcg): 0mcg 0%
Thiamin B1 (mg): .1mg 10%
Riboflavin B2 (mg): .1mg 9%
Folacin (mcg): 70mcg 18%
Niacin (mg): 1mg 6%

* Percent Daily Values are based on a 2000 calorie diet.

Servings: 4

Notes: 1⅓ tablespoons (0.665 ounces) Virgin Coconut Oil, equivalent to 1 teaspoon per serving.

Green Beans With Lime-Cumin Sauce

Ingredients

Blanched Green Beans
- 1 ½ pounds green beans, rinsed
- 1 tablespoon salt
- 4 quarts water, more, if possible
- 1 tablespoon Virgin Coconut Oil

Lime-cumin Sauce
- 1 teaspoon lime zest
- 1 tablespoon fresh lime juice
- ½ teaspoon ground cumin
- ½ teaspoon salt
- 1 dash Tabasco sauce, to taste
- 3 tablespoons Virgin Coconut Oil
- ¼ cup minced red onion

1. Wash and string green beans

2. Bring water to boil in large saucepan. Add salt.

3. Add green beans and blanch for 3-4 minutes or until crisp-tender. Immediately remove and plunge into ice bath to stop cooking. Drain thoroughly.

4. Whisk first four ingredients of Lime-Cumin Sauce (pepper sauce to taste) in small bowl. Whisk in Virgin Coconut Oil until dressing is smooth. Stir in onion.

5. In medium to large sauté pan over medium-high heat, add Virgin Coconut Oil and blanched green beans, and sauté for 1-2 minutes.

6. Remove to platter or bowl and toss with Lime-Cumin Sauce. Serve immediately.

Nutritional Data

Calories (kcal): 170
% Calories from Fat: 67.5%
% Calories from Carbohydrates: 26.2%
% Calories from Protein: 6.3%

Per Serving Nutritional Information

Total Fat (g): 14g 21%
Saturated Fat (g): 12g 59%
Monounsaturated Fat (g): 1g 4%
Polyunsaturated Fat (g): trace 2%
Total Carbohydrate (g): 12g 4%
Dietary Fiber (g): 5g 21%
Protein (g): 3g 6%
Sodium (mg): 1904mg 79%
Potassium (mg): 339mg 10%
Calcium (mg): 92mg 9%
Iron (mg): 2mg 10%
Zinc (mg): 1mg 4%
Vitamin C (mg): 27mg 45%
Vitamin A (i.u.): 1006IU 20%
Vitamin A (r.e.): 101RE 10%
Vitamin B6 (mg): .1mg 6%
Vitamin B12 (mcg): 0mcg 0%
Thiamin B1 (mg): .1mg 8%
Riboflavin B2 (mg): .1mg 8%
Folacin (mcg): 57mcg 14%
Niacin (mg): 1mg 6%

* Percent Daily Values are based on a 2000 calorie diet.

Servings: 4

Notes: Contains 2 ounces (4 tablespoons) Virgin Coconut Oil, equivalent to 1 tablespoon Virgin Coconut Oil per serving.

Green Beans With Orange-Ginger Sauce

Ingredients

Blanched Green Beans
- 1½ pounds green beans, rinsed
- 1 tablespoon salt
- 4 quarts water, more, if possible
- 1 tablespoon Virgin Coconut Oil

Orange Ginger Sauce
- 1 tablespoon Virgin Coconut Oil
- 1 tablespoon soy sauce
- 1 tablespoon honey
- 1 tablespoon orange zest
- 3 tablespoons fresh orange juice
- 1 medium garlic clove, peeled and chopped
- 1 piece fresh ginger root (about 1 inch) peeled and chopped
- ¼ teaspoon salt

1. Wash and string green beans.

2. Bring water to boil in large saucepan. Add salt.

3. Add green beans and blanch for 3-4 minutes or until crisp-tender. Immediately remove and plunge into ice bath to stop cooking. Drain thoroughly.

4. Process all ingredients for Orange Ginger Sauce in workbowl of food processor or blender, scraping down sides as needed, until dressing is smooth.

5. In medium to large sauté pan over medium-high heat, add Virgin Coconut Oil and blanched green beans, and sauté for 1-2 minutes.

6. Toss sautéed green beans with Orange Ginger Sauce.

7. Serve immediately.

Nutritional Data

Calories (kcal): 136
% Calories from Fat: 42.6%
% Calories from Carbohydrates: 48.8%
% Calories from Protein: 8.7%

Per Serving Nutritional Information

Total Fat (g): 7g 11%
Saturated Fat (g): 6g 30%
Monounsaturated Fat (g): trace 2%
Polyunsaturated Fat (g): trace 1%
Total Carbohydrate (g): 18g 6%
Dietary Fiber (g): 5g 21%
Protein (g): 3g 6%
Sodium (mg): 2028mg 84%
Potassium (mg): 378mg 11%
Calcium (mg): 93mg 9%
Iron (mg): 2mg 10%
Zinc (mg): 1mg 5%
Vitamin C (mg): 33mg 55%
Vitamin A (i.u.): 1030IU 21%
Vitamin A (r.e.): 103 1/2RE 10%
Vitamin B6 (mg): .1mg 7%
Vitamin B12 (mcg): 0mcg 0%
Thiamin B1 (mg): .1mg 8%
Riboflavin B2 (mg): .1mg 9%
Folacin (mcg): 63mcg 16%
Niacin (mg): 1mg 7%

* Percent Daily Values are based on a 2000 calorie diet.

Servings: 4

Notes: Contains 1 ounce (2 tablespoons) Virgin Coconut Oil, equivalent to ¼ ounce per serving.

Green Beans With Spanish Green Herb Sauce

Ingredients

Blanched Green Beans
- 1½ pounds green beans, rinsed
- 1 tablespoon salt
- 4 quarts water, more, if possible
- 1 tablespoon Virgin Coconut Oil

Spanish Green Herb Sauce
- 2 medium garlic cloves, peeled
- ½ cup tightly-packed fresh cilantro leaves
- ½ cup tightly-packed fresh parsley
- 3 tablespoons Virgin Coconut Oil
- 1 tablespoon fresh lemon juice
- ½ teaspoon salt

1. Wash and string green beans.

2. Bring water to boil in large saucepan. Add salt.

3. Add green beans and blanch for 3-4 minutes or until crisp-tender. Immediately remove and plunge into ice bath to stop cooking. Drain thoroughly.

4. Process Spanish Green Herb Sauce ingredients in workbowl of food processor or blender, scraping down sides of bowl as needed, until sauce is smooth.

5. In medium to large sauté pan over medium-high heat, add Virgin Coconut Oil and blanched green beans, and sauté for 1-2 minutes.

6. Toss with Spanish Green Herb Sauce to coat. Serve immediately.

Nutritional Data

Calories (kcal): 184
% Calories from Fat: 60.7%
% Calories from Carbohydrates: 32.9%
% Calories from Protein: 6.4%

Per Serving Nutritional Information

Total Fat (g): 14g 21%
Saturated Fat (g): 12g 59%
Monounsaturated Fat (g): 1g 4%
Polyunsaturated Fat (g): trace 2%
Total Carbohydrate (g): 17g 6%
Dietary Fiber (g): 6g 22%
Protein (g): 3g 7%
Sodium (mg): 1908mg 79%
Potassium (mg): 437mg 12%
Calcium (mg): 104mg 10%
Iron (mg): 2mg 12%
Zinc (mg): 1mg 5%
Vitamin C (mg): 63mg 105%
Vitamin A (i.u.): 1411IU 28%
Vitamin A (r.e.): 141 1/2RE 14%
Vitamin B6 (mg): .2mg 8%
Vitamin B12 (mcg): 0mcg 0%
Thiamin B1 (mg): .1mg 9%
Riboflavin B2 (mg): .1mg 9%
Folacin (mcg): 74mcg 19%
Niacin (mg): 1mg 6%

* Percent Daily Values are based on a 2000 calorie diet.

Servings: 4

Notes: Contains 2 ounces (4 tablespoons) Virgin Coconut Oil, equivalent to 1 tablespoon Virgin Coconut Oil per serving.

Green Beans With Spicy Balsamic Sauce

Ingredients

Blanched Green Beans
- 1 ½ pounds green beans, rinsed
- 1 tablespoon salt
- 4 quarts water, more, if possible
- 1 tablespoon Virgin Coconut Oil

Spicy Balsamic Sauce
- 2 teaspoons balsamic vinegar
- 2 teaspoons red wine vinegar
- 1 medium garlic clove, minced
- ½ teaspoon red pepper flakes, or to taste
- ¼ teaspoon salt
- ¼ cup Virgin Coconut Oil

1. Wash and string Green Beans.

2. Bring water to boil in large saucepan. Add salt.

3. Add green beans and blanch for 3-4 minutes or until crisp-tender. Immediately remove and plunge into ice bath to stop cooking. Drain thoroughly.

4. Whisk first five ingredients for Spicy Balsamic Sauce in small bowl. Whisk in Virgin Coconut Oil until dressing is smooth.

5. In medium to large sauté pan over medium-high heat, add Virgin Coconut Oil and blanched green beans, and sauté for 1-2 minutes.

6. Toss with Spicy Balsamic Sauce. Serve immediately.

Nutritional Data

Calories (kcal): 195
% Calories from Fat: 73.4%
% Calories from Carbohydrates: 21.3%
% Calories from Protein: 5.3%

Per Serving Nutritional Information

Total Fat (g): 17g 26%
Saturated Fat (g): 15g 74%
Monounsaturated Fat (g): 1g 4%
Polyunsaturated Fat (g): trace 2%
Total Carbohydrate (g): 11g 4%
Dietary Fiber (g): 5g 20%
Protein (g): 3g 6%
Sodium (mg): 1770mg 74%
Potassium (mg): 322mg 9%
Calcium (mg): 87mg 9%
Iron (mg): 2mg 9%
Zinc (mg): 1mg 4%
Vitamin C (mg): 25mg 42%
Vitamin A (i.u.): 1014IU 20%
Vitamin A (r.e.): 101 1/2RE 10%
Vitamin B6 (mg): .1mg 6%
Vitamin B12 (mcg): 0mcg 0%
Thiamin B1 (mg): .1mg 7%
Riboflavin B2 (mg): .1mg 8%
Folacin (mcg): 55mcg 14%
Niacin (mg): 1mg 6%

* Percent Daily Values are based on a 2000 calorie diet.

Servings: 4

Notes: Contains 5 tablespoons Virgin Coconut Oil, equivalent to 1¼ tablespoons per serving.

Roasted Eggplant

Ingredients

- 1 12-ounce eggplant, halved
- 2 tablespoons Virgin Coconut Oil, or more if needed
- 1 teaspoon sea salt
- ½ teaspoon fresh ground black pepper

1. Pre-heat oven to 350°F (177°C)

2. Brush eggplant halves with Virgin Coconut Oil. Place on greased or foil lined baking sheet, cut side down.

3. Roast for 30-45 minutes until soft.

4. Cut into serving pieces.

Servings: 4

Notes: Contains at least 2 tablespoons Virgin Coconut Oil, equivalent to ½ tablespoon Virgin Coconut Oil per serving.

Nutritional Data

Calories (kcal): 77
% Calories from Fat: 75.4%
% Calories from Carbohydrates: 21.0%
% Calories from Protein: 3.5%

Per Serving Nutritional Information

Total Fat (g): 7g 11%
Saturated Fat (g): 6g 30%
Monounsaturated Fat (g): trace 2%
Polyunsaturated Fat (g): trace 1%
Total Carbohydrate (g): 4g 1%
Dietary Fiber (g): 2g 7%
Protein (g): 1g 1%
Sodium (mg): 472mg 20%
Potassium (mg): 153mg 4%
Calcium (mg): 6mg 1%
Iron (mg): trace 1%
Zinc (mg): trace 1%
Vitamin C (mg): 1mg 2%
Vitamin A (i.u.): 58IU 1%
Vitamin A (r.e.): 5 1/2RE 1%
Vitamin B6 (mg): .1mg 3%
Vitamin B12 (mcg): 0mcg 0%
Thiamin B1 (mg): trace 2%
Riboflavin B2 (mg): trace 1%
Folacin (mcg): 13mcg 3%
Niacin (mg): trace 2%

* Percent Daily Values are based on a 2000 calorie diet.

Sautéed Zucchini With Lime-Cumin Sauce

Ingredients

- 1½ pounds zucchini
- 1 tablespoon Virgin Coconut Oil

Lime-Cumin Sauce
- 1 teaspoon lime zest
- 1 tablespoon fresh lime juice
- ½ teaspoon ground cumin
- ½ teaspoon salt
- 1 dash Tabasco sauce, to taste
- 3 tablespoons Virgin Coconut Oil
- ¼ cup minced red onion

1. Wash and slice zucchini into ¼" thick coins or ovals.

2. Whisk first four ingredients of Lime-Cumin Sauce (pepper sauce to taste) in small bowl. Whisk in Virgin Coconut Oil until dressing is smooth. Stir in onion.

3. In medium to large sauté pan over medium-high heat, add Virgin Coconut Oil and zucchini, and sauté for 1-2 minutes.

4. Remove to platter or bowl and toss with Lime-Cumin Sauce. Serve immediately.

Servings: 4

Notes: Contains 2 ounces (4 tablespoons) Virgin Coconut Oil equivalent to 1 tablespoon Virgin Coconut Oil per serving.

Nutritional Data

Calories (kcal): 146
% Calories from Fat: 79.3%
% Calories from Carbohydrates: 15.5%
% Calories from Protein: 5.2%

Per Serving Nutritional Information

Total Fat (g): 14g 21%
Saturated Fat (g): 12g 59%
Monounsaturated Fat (g): 1g 4%
Polyunsaturated Fat (g): trace 2%
Total Carbohydrate (g): 6g 2%
Dietary Fiber (g): 2g 9%
Protein (g): 2g 4%
Sodium (mg): 273mg 11%
Potassium (mg): 427mg 12%
Calcium (mg): 31mg 3%
Iron (mg): 1mg 5%
Zinc (mg): trace 2%
Vitamin C (mg): 17mg 29%
Vitamin A (i.u.): 555IU 11%
Vitamin A (r.e.): 55 1/2RE 6%
Vitamin B6 (mg): .2mg 8%
Vitamin B12 (mcg): 0mcg 0%
Thiamin B1 (mg): .1mg 8%
Riboflavin B2 (mg): trace 3%
Folacin (mcg): 38mcg 10%
Niacin (mg): 1mg 3%

* Percent Daily Values are based on a 2000 calorie diet.

Coconut Diet Main Dishes

40 Cloves And A Chicken

Ingredients

- ¼ lb. broiler/fryer chicken, cut into 8 pieces
- ½ cup Virgin Coconut Oil, plus
- 2 tablespoons Virgin Coconut Oil
- 10 sprigs fresh thyme
- 40 cloves garlic, peeled
- ½ teaspoon salt, to taste
- ¼ teaspoon fresh ground black pepper, to taste

1. Preheat oven to 350 degrees.

2. Season chicken with salt and pepper.

3. Toss with 2 tablespoons Virgin Coconut Oil and brown on both sides in a wide oven-safe fry pan or oven-safe skillet over high heat.

4. Remove from heat. If skillet is oven-safe, add remaining Virgin Coconut Oil, thyme, garlic. Otherwise, transfer chicken to oven-safe baking dish before adding remaining Virgin Coconut Oil, thyme, garlic. Deglaze skillet and add to baking dish.

5. Cover and bake for 1½ hours

6. Remove chicken from the oven. Let rest for 5 to 10 minutes. Carve, and serve.

Servings: 6

Notes: Contains 5 ounces of Virgin Coconut Oil or 5/6 ounce per serving.

Nutritional Data

Calories (kcal): 672
% Calories from Fat: 72.1%
% Calories from Carbohydrates: 4.3%
% Calories from Protein: 23.6%

Per Serving Nutritional Information

Total Fat (g): 54g 83%
Saturated Fat (g): 28g 142%
Monounsaturated Fat (g): 14g 63%
Polyunsaturated Fat (g): 7g 32%
Total Carbohydrate (g): 7g 2%
Dietary Fiber (g): 1g 2%
Protein (g): 40g 79%
Sodium (mg): 327mg 14%
Potassium (mg): 484mg 14%
Calcium (mg): 66mg 7%
Iron (mg): 3mg 18%
Zinc (mg): 3mg 22%
Vitamin C (mg): 14mg 23%
Vitamin A (i.u.): 1674IU 33%
Vitamin A (r.e.): 486½ RE 49%
Vitamin B6 (mg): .9mg 45%
Vitamin B12 (mcg): 2.3mcg 39%
Thiamin B1 (mg): .1mg 8%
Riboflavin B2 (mg): .4mg 23%
Folacin (mcg): 64mcg 16%
Niacin (mg): 14mg 70%

* Percent Daily Values are based on a 2000 calorie diet.

Beef Curry With Vegetables

Ingredients

- 6 tablespoons Virgin Coconut Oil
- 1 cup fresh mushrooms, sliced
- ½ cup onion, chopped
- 1 clove garlic, minced
- ¼ can rice flour
- 1 teaspoon sea salt (or to taste)
- 2 tablespoons sugar (or to taste)
- 4 teaspoons curry powder
- 1 teaspoon fresh ginger root, grated
- 2 cups beef broth
- 1½ pounds cooked beef brisket, or rump
- 1 cup carrots, cooked
- 1 cup sour cream.

1. In a large skillet, melt the Virgin Coconut Oil. Add the mushrooms, onion, and garlic. Sauté until the onions are clear.

2. Combine the rice flour, salt, sugar, curry powder, and grated gingerroot. Add the sautéed vegetables. Slowly add the beef broth, stirring constantly.

3. Bring to a boil and simmer until thickened.

4. Add the meat and carrots, and cook on low heat until they are heated through.

5. Add the sour cream and stir until blended and warm.

6. Serve with brown rice.

Nutritional Data

Calories (kcal): 466
% Calories from Fat: 49.4%
% Calories from Carbohydrates: 30.1%
% Calories from Protein: 20.5%

Per Serving Nutritional Information

Total Fat (g): 26g 40%
Saturated Fat (g): 19g 94%
Monounsaturated Fat (g): 3g 14%
Polyunsaturated Fat (g): 1g 3%
Total Carbohydrate (g): 36g 12%
Dietary Fiber (g): 4g 15%
Protein (g): 24g 49%
Sodium (mg): 1523mg 63%
Potassium (mg): 331mg 9%
Calcium (mg): 75mg 8%
Iron (mg): 10mg 57%
Zinc (mg): 1mg 4%
Vitamin C (mg): 5mg 8%
Vitamin A (i.u.): 7072IU 141%
Vitamin A (r.e.): 771 1/2RE 77%
Vitamin B6 (mg): .1mg 6%
Vitamin B12 (mcg): .1mcg 2%
Thiamin B1 (mg): .1mg 5%
Riboflavin B2 (mg): .1mg 9%
Folacin (mcg): 17mcg 4%
Niacin (mg): 1mg 7%

Percent Daily Values are based on a 2000 calorie diet.

Servings: 6

Notes: Contains 3 ounces Virgin Coconut Oil equivalent to 1 tablespoon (½ ounce) Virgin Coconut Oil per serving.

Beef Stroganoff

Ingredients

- 2 tablespoons Virgin Coconut Oil
- 12 ounces beef tenderloin (fillet), thinly sliced
- 1 pound mushrooms (about 6 cups), quartered
- ½ cup chopped onions
- ½ teaspoon dried dill weed
- ½ teaspoon salt
- ¼ teaspoon ground black pepper
- ¼ cup dry white wine
- ½ cup sour cream

1. In a large non-stick skillet, melt 2 tablespoons Virgin Coconut Oil over high heat.

2. Add beef, half at a time. Cook until browned on both sides, turning once, about 4 minutes. Remove from skillet. Repeat with remaining beef.

3. Add mushrooms, onions, dill, salt and pepper; cook, stirring constantly, for 5 minutes.

4. Add wine and return beef to skillet.

5. Cook until heated through, about 3 minutes.

6. Remove from heat. Stir in sour cream until blended.

Note: Substituting Coconut Cream Concentrate for ½ of the sour cream (¼ cup), will increase the Virgin Coconut Oil content by approximately 1.4 ounces for the recipe or approximately 1 teaspoon per serving.

Nutritional Data

Calories (kcal): 269
% Calories from Fat: 49.3%
% Calories from Carbohydrates: 16.4%
% Calories from Protein: 34.2%

Per Serving Nutritional Information

Total Fat (g): 14g 22%
Saturated Fat (g): 9g 45%
Monounsaturated Fat (g): 3g 13%
Polyunsaturated Fat (g): 1g 2%
Total Carbohydrate (g): 11g 4%
Dietary Fiber (g): 2g 7%
Protein (g): 22g 45%
Sodium (mg): 347mg 14%
Potassium (mg): 806mg 23%
Calcium (mg): 54mg 5%
Iron (mg): 4mg 22%
Zinc (mg): 4mg 30%
Vitamin C (mg): 5mg 9%
Vitamin A (i.u.): 8IU 0%
Vitamin A (r.e.): 1RE 0%
Vitamin B6 (mg): .4mg 19%
Vitamin B12 (mcg): 1.7mcg 28%
Thiamin B1 (mg): .2mg 11%
Riboflavin B2 (mg): .8mg 45%
Folacin (mcg): 32mcg 8%
Niacin (mg): 7mg 36%

Percent Daily Values are based on a 2000 calorie diet.

Servings: 4

Notes: Contains 1 ounce Virgin Coconut Oil equivalent to ½ tablespoon (¼ ounce) Virgin Coconut Oil per serving.

Beef Tips in Madeira Sauce

Ingredients

- 4 Virgin Coconut Oil
- 2 pounds beef tenderloin, cut into chunks
- salt and pepper, to taste

Madeira Sauce
- 2 shallots, minced
- 1 pound sliced mushrooms
- 2 cups Madeira
- 2 cups demi glace
- 2 tablespoons Virgin Coconut Oil, chilled and cut into tablespoon cubes

1. Season the beef with salt and pepper.

2. Sauté in the Virgin Coconut Oil to desired temperature and reserve.

3. Add shallots and mushrooms to pan and sauté briefly.

4. Deglaze pan with Madeira and reduce until almost dry.

5. Add demi-glace and bring to a simmer.

6. Finish sauce with chilled Virgin Coconut Oil and salt and pepper to taste.

7. Return beef to pan just to heat through.

8. Serve with rice pilaf or buttered egg noodles.

Nutritional Data

Calories (kcal): 517
% Calories from Fat: 76.3%
% Calories from Carbohydrates: 3.6%
% Calories from Protein: 20.1%

Per Serving Nutritional Information

Total Fat (g): 37g 56%
Saturated Fat (g): 19g 97%
Monounsaturated Fat (g): 12g 52%
Polyunsaturated Fat (g): 1g 6%
Total Carbohydrate (g): 4g 1%
Dietary Fiber (g): 1g 3%
Protein (g): 22g 43%
Sodium (mg): 350mg 15%
Potassium (mg): 612mg 17%
Calcium (mg): 16mg 2%
Iron (mg): 4mg 20%
Zinc (mg): 4mg 26%
Vitamin C (mg): 2mg 4%
Vitamin A (i.u.): 313IU 6%
Vitamin A (r.e.): 31 1/2RE 3%
Vitamin B6 (mg): .5mg 24%
Vitamin B12 (mcg): 2.9mcg 48%
Thiamin B1 (mg): .2mg 12%
Riboflavin B2 (mg): .5mg 28%
Folacin (mcg): 20mcg 5%
Niacin (mg): 6mg 29%

* Percent Daily Values are based on a 2000 calorie diet.

Servings: 8

Notes: Contains 3 ounces Virgin Coconut Oil equivalent to ¾ tablespoons Virgin Coconut Oil per serving.

Braised Beef Tips

Ingredients

- 2 pounds beef sirloin
- 2 tablespoons Virgin Coconut Oil
- 1 medium yellow onion, chopped
- 2 cloves garlic, minced
- 8 ounces fresh mushrooms, halved or quartered
- salt and pepper, to taste
- 2 each bay leaves
- 1 tablespoon Worcestershire sauce
- 3 cups beef broth

1. Trim fat and cube sirloin into ¾" cubes. Brown in Virgin Coconut Oil in pressure cooker base.

2. Add onion, garlic cloves, mushrooms, salt and pepper, bay leaves, and Worcestershire sauce. Add beef broth.

3. Bring to pressure and cook about 10 minutes. Remove from heat and let sit about 5 minutes. Release pressure.

4. Thicken with organic corn starch, arrowroot, or roux.

Serving Ideas: Serve over rice, farfalle (bow-tie pasta), or barley pilaf.

Servings: 6

Nutritional Data

Calories (kcal): 400
% Calories from Fat: 59.8%
% Calories from Carbohydrates: 5.9%
% Calories from Protein: 34.3%

Per Serving Nutritional Information

Total Fat (g): 26g 40%
Saturated Fat (g): 13g 63%
Monounsaturated Fat (g): 9g 43%
Polyunsaturated Fat (g): 1g 4%
Total Carbohydrate (g): 6g 2%
Dietary Fiber (g): 1g 3%
Protein (g): 34g 68%
Sodium (mg): 742mg 31%
Potassium (mg): 794mg 23%
Calcium (mg): 29mg 3%
Iron (mg): 5mg 26%
Zinc (mg): 6mg 39%
Vitamin C (mg): 8mg 14%
Vitamin A (i.u.): 5IU 0%
Vitamin A (r.e.): 1RE 0%
Vitamin B6 (mg): .6mg 31%
Vitamin B12 (mcg): 4.2mcg 69%
Thiamin B1 (mg): .2mg 13%
Riboflavin B2 (mg): .5mg 26%
Folacin (mcg): 24mcg 6%
Niacin (mg): 7mg 34%

* Percent Daily Values are based on a 2000 calorie diet.

Notes: Contains 1 ounce (2 tablespoons) Virgin Coconut Oil equivalent to 1/6 ounce (1 teaspoon) per serving.

Chicken Cacciatore

Ingredients

- 1¼ - 2½ pound whole chicken, to 3-Pound Cut Up
- ⅓ cup Virgin Coconut Oil
- ⅝ cup unbleached flour, preferably organic
- 2½ cups sliced onions, thinly sliced
- ⅝ cup green pepper, chopped
- 2½ cloves garlic, crushed
- 1¼ 15-ounce cans crushed tomatoes, drained
- 1¼ 16-ounce cans tomato sauce
- 7½ ounces sliced fresh mushrooms, drained
- 1¼ teaspoons salt
- ⅓ teaspoon oregano

1. Wash chicken and pat dry.

2. Heat Virgin Coconut Oil in large skillet until almost smoking.

3. Coat chicken pieces with flour.

4. Cook chicken in Virgin Coconut Oil over medium heat 15 to 20 minutes or until light brown. Remove chicken. Set aside.

5. Add onion rings, green pepper, and garlic to skillet. Cook and stir over medium heat until onion and pepper are tender.

6. Stir in remaining ingredients.

7. Add chicken to sauce. Cover tightly. Simmer 30 to 40 minutes or until thickest pieces are fork-tender.

Nutritional Data

Calories (kcal): 692
% Calories from Fat: 55.6%
% Calories from Carbohydrates: 20.3%
% Calories from Protein: 24.1%

Per Serving Nutritional Information

Total Fat (g): 43g 67%
Saturated Fat (g): 20g 101%
Monounsaturated Fat (g): 13g 57%
Polyunsaturated Fat (g): 7g 31%
Total Carbohydrate (g): 36g 12%
Dietary Fiber (g): 6g 22%
Protein (g): 42g 85%
Sodium (mg): 1500mg 63%
Potassium (mg): 1410mg 40%
Calcium (mg): 97mg 10%
Iron (mg): 6mg 31%
Zinc (mg): 4mg 26%
Vitamin C (mg): 44mg 73%
Vitamin A (i.u.): 3487IU 70%
Vitamin A (r.e.): 648RE 65%
Vitamin B6 (mg): 1.1mg 57%
Vitamin B12 (mcg): 2.2mcg 36%
Thiamin B1 (mg): .3mg 21%
Riboflavin B2 (mg): .7mg 40%
Folacin (mcg): 107mcg 27%
Niacin (mg): 18mg 88%

Percent Daily Values are based on a 2000 calorie diet.

Servings: 5

Notes: Contains 2⅔ ounces (8 teaspoons) of Virgin Coconut Oil, equivalent to 1 teaspoon of Virgin Coconut Oil per serving.

Coconut Fish Fingers

Ingredients

- 1 pound fish fillets
- ½ cup dry sherry
- 1 teaspoon curry powder
- 1¼ cup organic whole wheat pastry flour
- 1½ teaspoons cornstarch
- ¼ teaspoon baking powder
- ½ cup milk
- ¾ cup Coconut Flakes
- ¾ cup coarse fresh bread crumbs
- Natural Palm Oil for deep frying
- 3 cups hot cooked brown rice
- ½ cup mango (or peach) chutney

1. Cut fish fillets into "fingers" by slicing diagonally across fillets in strips as wide as fillet is thick.

2. Combine sherry & curry powder. Marinate "fingers" in sherry mixture in refrigerator for 30-60 minutes.

3. Combine ½ cup flour, cornstarch , baking powder, & milk in small bowl. Stir until batter is thin & smooth.

4. Combine coconut & bread crumbs.

5. Coat "fingers" in remaining ¾ cup flour, shaking off excess, then in batter, then in coconut mixture. Let stand 20 minutes before cooking.

6. Heat 1 inch Natural Palm Oil to 350 degrees in heavy pan with 3-inch side rim. Fry "fingers" till golden. Drain on paper towels. Serve on rice with chutney.

Nutritional Data

Calories (kcal): 657
% Calories from Fat: 20.8%
% Calories from Carbohydrates: 59.0%
% Calories from Protein: 20.2%

Per Serving Nutritional Information

Total Fat (g): 14g 21%
Saturated Fat (g): 9g 46%
Monounsaturated Fat (g): 2g 11%
Polyunsaturated Fat (g): 1g 5%
Total Carbohydrate (g): 86g 29%
Dietary Fiber (g): 5g 21%
Protein (g): 30g 59%
Sodium (mg): 642mg 27%
Potassium (mg): 582mg 17%
Calcium (mg): 89mg 9%
Iron (mg): 1mg 5%
Zinc (mg): 1mg 9%
Vitamin C (mg): 1mg 2%
Vitamin A (i.u.): 100IU 2%
Vitamin A (r.e.): 29RE 3%
Vitamin B6 (mg): 1.4mg 72%
Vitamin B12 (mcg): 2.6mcg 44%
Thiamin B1 (mg): .5mg 32%
Riboflavin B2 (mg): .1mg 8%
Folacin (mcg): 95mcg 24%
Niacin (mg): 5mg 24%

Percent Daily Values are based on a 2000 calorie diet.

Servings: 4

Notes: Contains approximately 4 ounces equivalent Virgin Coconut Oil from Coconut Flakes, equivalency to 1 ounce per serving.

Halibut Piccata

Ingredients

- 1 pound halibut steaks, cut ¼ inch thick
- 2 tablespoons whole grain flour, finely ground
- ½ teaspoon salt
- ⅛ teaspoon paprika
- ⅛ teaspoon white pepper, ground
- 1 tablespoon Virgin Coconut Oil, divided

Lemon Caper Sauce
- ⅔ cup dry white wine, may substitute chicken stock
- 2 tablespoons fresh lemon juice
- 2 teaspoons capers, drained
- 1 teaspoon Virgin Coconut Oil

1. Combine flour, salt, paprika and white pepper in a flat pie plate or dish.

2. Lightly coat both sides of halibut steaks with flour mixture.

3. In large, nonstick skillet, heat half of the Virgin Coconut Oil over medium heat until hot. Place half of the halibut in skillet and cook 2 minutes on each side or until just cooked through. Remove halibut and keep warm. Repeat with remaining halibut and oil.

4. Add wine and lemon juice. Bring to a boil, stirring to dissolve any browned bits attached to skillet. Cook and stir 1 to 2 minutes or until slightly thickened. Remove from heat; stir in capers and Virgin Coconut Oil.

5. Return halibut to pan with sauce to warm. Serve Immediately.

Nutritional Data

Calories (kcal): 237
% Calories from Fat: 29.5%
% Calories from Carbohydrates: 25.7%
% Calories from Protein: 44.8%

Per Serving Nutritional Information

Total Fat (g): 7g 11%
Saturated Fat (g): 4g 22%
Monounsaturated Fat (g): 1g 5%
Polyunsaturated Fat (g): 1g 5%
Total Carbohydrate (g): 14g 5%
Dietary Fiber (g): 1g 5%
Protein (g): 25g 49%
Sodium (mg): 344mg 14%
Potassium (mg): 711mg 20%
Calcium (mg): 71mg 7%
Iron (mg): 1mg 8%
Zinc (mg): 1mg 5%
Vitamin C (mg): 59mg 98%
Vitamin A (i.u.): 244IU 5%
Vitamin A (r.e.): 60RE 6%
Vitamin B6 (mg): .5mg 23%
Vitamin B12 (mcg): 1.3mcg 22%
Thiamin B1 (mg): .1mg 8%
Riboflavin B2 (mg): .1mg 6%
Folacin (mcg): 26mcg 7%
Niacin (mg): 7mg 35%

* Percent Daily Values are based on a 2000 calorie diet.

Servings: 4

Notes: Contains approximately 2 tablespoons Virgin Coconut Oil equivalent to ½ tablespoon per serving.

Horseradish Crusted Salmon

Ingredients

Dilled cucumber slices
- 2 large cucumbers, English preferred, peeled, seeded, and sliced thin
- 2 teaspoons sea salt
- 1 tablespoon chives, fresh chopped
- 1 tablespoon fresh dill, minced
- 2 tablespoons crème fraîche, or sour cream
- 1 teaspoon lemon juice
- grain mustard sauce (listed in this book)

Horseradish crust
- ½ cup horseradish, fresh grated
- 2 egg whites
- ½ teaspoon sea salt

1. Prepare dilled cucumber slices in advance.

2. Peel, seed, and slice cucumbers very thin, using a mandoline, if available.

3. Combine the cucumbers and the salt together in a small bowl and allow to rest for 15 minutes. Squeeze out liquid and combine with the fresh herbs and crème fraîche. Refrigerate until needed.

4. Prepare grain mustard sauce in advance.

5. In heavy-bottomed stainless steel pan, reduce first six ingredients of Grain Mustard Sauce by about ⅔. Add cream and bring to heavy foam. Whisk Virgin Coconut Oil slowly. Season with salt and strain through a chinois or a fine mesh strainer, pressing firmly on shallots to extract maximum flavor.

6. Hold the sauce in a warm water bath.

7. In a small bowl mix together the grain mustard, horseradish, crème fraiche. Whisk sauce in to the prepared mixture. Return mustard in the warm water bath. Add the fresh herbs just before serving.

8. Herb Crusted Salmon, assembly: Cut the salmon fillet into ¾ inch widths. Roll the thick end into the center and ending with the belly flap, form a medallion. Secure the medallion with a bamboo skewer.

9. Place about one tablespoon of the horseradish mixture on top of the salmon and spread evenly around the top of the fish. Refrigerate until needed.

11. Brush a non-stick pan lightly with Virgin Coconut Oil. Over medium high heat sear the horseradish side first.

12. Cook gently until golden brown crust is formed, about 2 to 3 minutes.

13. Turn over and cook for 2 minutes.

Servings: 6

Notes: Contains 6 tablespoons Virgin Coconut Oil equivalent to 1 tablespoon per serving.

Nutritional Data

Calories (kcal): 366
% Calories from Fat: 61.1%
% Calories from Carbohydrates: 10.1%
% Calories from Protein: 28.8%

Per Serving Nutritional Information

Total Fat (g): 24g 37%
Saturated Fat (g): 16g 82%
Monounsaturated Fat (g): 4g 17%
Polyunsaturated Fat (g): 2g 9%
Total Carbohydrate (g): 9g 3%
Dietary Fiber (g): 1g 6%
Protein (g): 25g 51%
Sodium (mg): 1023mg 43%
Potassium (mg): 671mg 19%
Calcium (mg): 68mg 7%
Iron (mg): 2mg 9%
Zinc (mg): 1mg 9%
Vitamin C (mg): 13mg 22%
Vitamin A (i.u.): 897IU 18%
Vitamin A (r.e.): 158 1/2RE 16%
Vitamin B6 (mg): .3mg 15%
Vitamin B12 (mcg): 9.6mcg 161%
Thiamin B1 (mg): .3mg 18%
Riboflavin B2 (mg): .2mg 14%
Folacin (mcg): 24mcg 6%
Niacin (mg): 6mg 30%

Percent Daily Values are based on a 2000 calorie diet.

Jalapeno Orange Mustard Turkey

Ingredients

- 2 tablespoons Virgin Coconut Oil
- 2 tablespoons dijon mustard
- 3 tablespoons orange marmalade
- 2 tablespoons jalapeno pepper, seeded and minced
- 1 cup white wine, chicken stock or any combination of the two
- 2 teaspoons fresh lime juice
- 1 teaspoon sliced black olives
- 4 six-ounce turkey breast slices
- 2 tablespoons Coconut Cream Concentrate

1. Seed the jalapeno, being careful to keep away from eyes. Combine the mustard, marmalade, lime juice. Add a pinch of cayenne pepper if you want it hotter.

2. Heat Virgin Coconut Oil over medium/ high heat until hot; add turkey breast slices and sauté until golden color is acquired. Do not cook through. Remove from heat and keep warm.

3. Drain excess oil. Add jalapenos and sauté for 15-30 seconds; do not burn. Immediately deglaze pan with white wine or chicken stock and reduce by ⅓.

4. Add mustard mixture to pan, then add back the turkey breast slices and cook until chicken is done.

5. Remove turkey and reduce sauce further if necessary.

6. Add 2 tablespoons of Coconut Cream Concentrate at this point to finish sauce.

Nutritional Data

Calories (kcal): 378
% Calories from Fat: 50.4%
% Calories from Carbohydrates: 12.3%
% Calories from Protein: 37.3%

Per Serving Nutritional Information

Total Fat (g): 24g 36%
Saturated Fat (g): 19g 94%
Monounsaturated Fat (g): 3g 13%
Polyunsaturated Fat (g): 1g 3%
Cholesterol (mg): 70mg 23%
Total Carbohydrate (g): 13g 4%
Dietary Fiber (g): 2g 7%
Protein (g): 39g 78%
Sodium (mg): 2548mg 106%
Potassium (mg): 544mg 16%
Calcium (mg): 30mg 3%
Iron (mg): 2mg 9%
Zinc (mg): 2mg 13%
Vitamin C (mg): 3mg 4%
Vitamin A (i.u.): 16IU 0%
Vitamin A (r.e.): 1 1/2RE 0%
Vitamin B6 (mg): .6mg 29%
Vitamin B12 (mcg): 3.4mcg 57%
Thiamin B1 (mg): trace 1%
Riboflavin B2 (mg): .2mg 10%
Folacin (mcg): 14mcg 4%
Niacin (mg): 14mg 71%

Percent Daily Values are based on a 2000 calorie diet.

Servings: 4

Notes: Estimated to contain the equivalent of 2 tablespoons Virgin Coconut Oil, equivalent to ½ tablespoon per serving.

Lamb Steaks With Milk, Honey, and Cumin Marinade

Ingredients

- 4 teaspoons cumin seed, lightly toasted
- 6 tablespoons honey, warmed
- 1 cup milk, warmed
- 4 cloves garlic, minced
- 5 tablespoons Virgin Coconut Oil
- sea salt, to taste
- fresh ground black pepper
- 6 seven-ounce lamb steaks, cut from leg, 1¼" thick
- 1 tablespoon fresh lemon juice

1. In a mortar, grind the toasted cumin seeds to a coarse powder. Stir in the warmed honey and reserve one tablespoon of the mixture.

2. In a baking dish large enough to hold the lamb steaks in a single layer, combine the remaining honey mixture with the milk. Stir in the minced garlic, 3 tablespoons of Virgin Coconut Oil, 1 teaspoon of sea salt, and ¼ teaspoon fresh ground black pepper. Add the lamb steaks and turn to coat well. Cover and refrigerate overnight.

3. Preheat oven to 450°F (230°C). Heat a heavy-duty baking sheet in the oven.

4. Remove lamb from marinade. Season with salt and pepper.

5. In a large skillet, heat the remaining 2 tablespoons of Virgin Coconut Oil until almost smoking, about 325°F (160°C). Add the lamb and cook until browned on both sides.

6. Transfer to hot baking sheet and roast for 8 minutes (for medium rare). Transfer to warmed platter.

7. Stir lemon juice into the reserved tablespoon of honey mixture and lightly brush half of the mixture on the lamb steaks.

Nutritional Data

Calories (kcal): 691
% Calories from Fat: 70.5%
% Calories from Carbohydrates: 13.8%
% Calories from Protein: 15.7%

Per Serving Nutritional Information

Total Fat (g): 55g 84%
Saturated Fat (g): 29g 146%
Monounsaturated Fat (g): 18g 83%
Polyunsaturated Fat (g): 4g 16%
Cholesterol (mg): 122mg 41%
Total Carbohydrate (g): 24g 8%
Dietary Fiber (g): trace 2%
Protein (g): 27g 55%
Sodium (mg): 112mg 5%
Potassium (mg): 490mg 14%
Calcium (mg): 92mg 9%
Iron (mg): 4mg 20%
Zinc (mg): 4mg 28%
Vitamin C (mg): 20mg 33%
Vitamin A (i.u.): 76IU 2%
Vitamin A (r.e.): 18RE 2%
Vitamin B6 (mg): .3mg 13%
Vitamin B12 (mcg): 3.3mcg 56%
Thiamin B1 (mg): .2mg 13%
Riboflavin B2 (mg): .4mg 23%
Folacin (mcg): 35mcg 9%
Niacin (mg): 10mg 52%

* Percent Daily Values are based on a 2000 calorie diet.

8. Put the baking sheet on a burner on the range over moderately high heat until sizzling. Deglaze with ½ cup water, scraping up the browned bits from the bottom of th pan. Add any accumulated juices from the lamb and simmer for 2 minutes.

9. Remove from the heat and stir in remaining lemon-honey-cumin mixture. Adjust seasoning.

10. Pour sauce around lamb and serve.

Servings: 6

Notes: Estimated to contain 3 tablespoons Virgin Coconut Oil equivalent to ½ tablespoon per serving.

Shish Kofte

Ingredients

- 2½ slices firm organic white bread (crusts removed)
- ⅓ cup fresh parsley
- ⅜ cup fresh mint leaves
- ⅝ small onion (peeled - cut in half)
- ⅝ pound lamb, cut into 1-inch cubes and chilled
- 1¼ teaspoons sea salt (or to taste)
- ⅓ teaspoon fresh ground black pepper
- ⅓ teaspoon ground allspice
- 1 teaspoon ground cinnamon
- 1¼ large egg (lightly beaten)
- 1¼ medium green bell pepper (seeded & cut into 1-inch squares)
- 3¾ tablespoons Virgin Coconut Oil
- 10 cherry tomatoes (stems removed)

1. Soak wooden skewers in water for at least 30-60 minutes (to avoid burning on grill or under broiler).

2. In the food processor fitted with the metal blade, process the bread until finely chopped into crumbs. Set aside.

3. Process the parsley and mint in the food processor until finely chopped. With the motor running, drop the onion through the feed tube and process until finely chopped. Add half the lamb pieces and using about a dozen on/off pulses, process until finely chopped. Remove the mixture to a large mixing bowl.

4. Chop the remaining lamb in the food processor and remove to the mixing bowl. Add the bread crumbs, salt, pepper, spices and egg. Combine well with your hands.

5. Preheat the oven broiler. Prepare 4 skewers about 10-inches long. If you are using wooden skewers, soak them for about 30 minutes.

6. Divide the meat mixture into 8 equal balls and shape them into ovals. Starting with a pepper piece, thread 2 meat ovals and

Nutritional Data

Calories (kcal): 280
% Calories from Fat: 67.9%
% Calories from Carbohydrates: 16.9%
% Calories from Protein: 15.2%

Per Serving Information

Total Fat (g): 21g 33%
Saturated Fat (g): 13g 67%
Monounsaturated Fat (g): 5g 23%
Polyunsaturated Fat (g): 1g 6%
Total Carbohydrate (g): 12g 4%
Dietary Fiber (g): 2g 8%
Protein (g): 11g 22%
Sodium (mg): 585mg 24%
Potassium (mg): 337mg 10%
Calcium (mg): 53mg 5%
Iron (mg): 3mg 15%
Zinc (mg): 2mg 12%
Vitamin C (mg): 40mg 67%
Vitamin A (i.u.): 972IU 19%
Vitamin A (r.e.): 111RE 11%
Vitamin B6 (mg): .2mg 9%
Vitamin B12 (mcg): 1.1mcg 19%
Thiamin B1 (mg): .2mg 10%
Riboflavin B2 (mg): .2mg 12%
Folacin (mcg): 45mcg 11%
Niacin (mg): 4mg 18%

* Percent Daily Values are based on a 2000 calorie diet.

---

2 pepper pieces alternately on each of 4 skewers.

7. Baste the meat with Virgin Coconut Oil and cook about 4-inches from the heat about 5 minutes. Thread 2 tomatoes on the end of the skewer, and baste again with the Virgin Coconut Oil.

8. Broil on the other side about 5 minutes, or until the meat is just cooked through. You can use an instant-read thermometer as a probe.

Servings: 5

Notes: Estimated to contain approximately 2 tablespoons (1 ounce) Virgin Coconut Oil, equivalent to 0.2 ounces Virgin Coconut Oil per serving.

Note, you may substitute ground lamb for the lamb cubes.

Appendix 1

CANDIDA QUESTIONAIRE

History	Point Score
1. Have you taken tetracycline or other antibiotics for acne for one month or longer?	25
2. Have you at any time in your life taken other "Broad-spectrum" antibiotics for respiratory, urinary, or other infections for two months or longer, or in short courses four or more times in a one-year period?	20
3. Have you ever taken a broad-spectrum antibiotic (even a single course)?	6
4. Have you at anytime in your life been bothered by persistent prostatitis, vaginitis, or other problems affecting your reproductive organs?	25
5. Have you been pregnant....	
One time?	3
Two or more times?	5
6. Have you taken birth control pills....	
For six months to two years?	8
For more than two years?	15
7. Have you taken prednisone or other cortisone type drugs...	
For two weeks or less?	6
For more than two weeks?	15
8. Does exposure to perfumes, insecticides, fabric shop odors, and other chemicals provoke	
Mild symptoms?	5
Moderate to severe symptoms?	20

9.	Are your symptoms worse on damp, muggy days or moldy places?	20
10.	Have you had athlete's foot, ringworm, "jock itch," or other chronic infections of the skin or nails?	
	Mild to moderate?	10
	Severe or persistent?	20
11.	Do you crave sugar?	10
12.	Do you crave breads?	10
13.	Do you crave alcoholic beverages?	10
14.	Does tobacco smoke really bother you?	10

TOTAL SCORE FOR THIS SECTION _____

Major Symptoms	**Point Score**

For each of your symptoms, enter the appropriate figure in the point Score Column.

If symptom is occasional or mild	score 3 points
If symptom is frequent and/or moderately severe	score 6 points
If a symptom is severe and/or disabling	score 9 points

1.	Fatigue or lethargy	_____
2.	Feeling of being drained	_____
3.	Poor Memory	_____
4.	Feeling "spacey" or "unreal"	_____
5.	Depression	_____
6.	Numbness, burning, or tingling	_____
7.	Muscle aches	_____
8.	Muscle weakness or paralysis	_____
9.	Pain and/or swelling in joints	_____
10.	Abdominal pain	_____
11.	Constipation	_____
12.	Diarrhea	_____
13.	Bloating	_____
14.	Persistent vaginal itch	_____

15. Persistent vaginal burning _____
16. Prostatitis _____
17. Impotence _____
18. Loss of sexual desire _____
19. Endometriosis _____
20. Cramping and other menstrual irregularities _____
21. Premenstrual tension _____
22. Spots in front of eyes _____
23. Erratic vision _____

TOTAL SCORE FOR THIS SECTION_____

Other Symptoms

For each of your symptoms, enter the appropriate figure in the point Score Column.

If symptom is occasional or mild	score 3 points
If symptom is frequent and/or moderately severe	score 6 points
If a symptom is severe and/or disabling	score 9 points

1. Drowsiness _____
2. Irritability _____
3. Lack of coordination _____
4. Inability to concentrate _____
5. Frequent mood swings _____
6. Headache _____
7. Dizziness/loss of balance _____
8. Pressure above ears, feeling of head swelling and tingling _____
9. Itching _____
10. Other rashes _____
11. Heartburn _____
12. Indigestion _____
13. Belching and intestinal gas _____
14. Mucus in stools _____
15. Hemorrhoids _____
16. Dry mouth _____

17. Rash or blisters in mouth _____
18. Bad breath _____
19. Joint swelling or arthritis _____
20. Nasal congestion or discharge _____
21. Postnasal drip _____
22. Nasal itching _____
23. Sore or dry throat _____
24. Cough _____
25. Pain or tightness in chest _____
26. Wheezing or shortness of breath _____
27. Urinary urgency or frequency _____
28. Burning on urination _____
29. Failing Vision _____
30. Burning or tearing of eyes _____
31. Recurrent infections or fluid in ears _____
32. Ear pain or deafness _____

TOTAL SCORE FOR THIS SECTION _____

Total Score from section one _____

Total score from section two _____

Total score for section three _____

TOTAL ALL SECTIONS _____

	Women	Men
Yeast- connected health problems are almost certainly present	>180	>140
Yeast-connected health problems are probably present	120-180	90-140
Yeast-connected health problems are possibly present	60-119	40-89
Yeast-connected health problems are less likely to be present	<60	<40

Appendix 2

Peace with God

How I Found Peace with God

I was driving down a rural highway in north-central Wisconsin that autumn night in 1977, thoughts running wildly through my mind. "Why wasn't I dead?" I thought unbelievingly. I had fully intended to overdose on drugs and end my life just hours before. But after swallowing some one hundred assorted pills that I thought were pretty potent, I woke up surprised not only to find myself alive, but my head clear also. Didn't even catch a buzz!

As a senior in high school, I was hanging around with the wrong crowd, and heavily into the drug culture. My parents being divorced when I was young, I had tried living with both sets of parents and couldn't get along with either one. I didn't strike it off too well with girls either, so with one failed relationship after another, I had decided that death was preferable to life, thinking that somehow it would be a gateway to a better life.

But now I was confused, off balance. Overdosing on drugs seemed like the easiest, most painless, way of ending my life, and when I decided to finally go through with it, there was no turning back. The thought never occurred to me that I would not succeed. So there I was back in my car driving down a rural highway pondering what to do next. I remembered a junior high teacher once reading an article to our class about a guy who killed himself instantly by driving his car 55 mph into a telephone pole. That was it! It would be instantaneous—painless.

There was one problem, however. As I drove down this unfamiliar rural road somewhere north of Appleton (about 2 hours north of my home in Milwaukee), there were drainage ditches between the edge of the road and where the telephone poles were. I feared my car would never make it over the ditch.

Finally the road led through a small country town consisting of not much more than a bar and grocery store. But it was lit up with a few light poles on the gravel shoulder of the main highway. This was it. I backed the car up several hundred yards, and then floored it, racing towards one of the light poles. A glance at the speedometer read 85 mph just before impact. And then total darkness...... for maybe 10-15 seconds.

The sound of my car horn blaring woke me up.... again. Again I had failed. With nothing better to do, I decided to try and crawl out of the wreckage. The car was now upside down, but my driver-side window was missing, so I began to climb out. The people who were in the bar across the street rushed over and helped me the rest of the way out. One guy exclaimed to his buddies, "Wow! Check it out! He knocked down the light pole!" It was probably the most excitement that little town had seen in years. They called an ambulance and took me to a nearby hospital.

At the hospital they did some routine checks on me, but other than a few bruises, I had driven my car into a light pole 85 mph and walked away from it. The police were able to contact my father through my licenses plates. I was kept in the hospital overnight for observations, mostly out of concern for the drugs I had taken.

So I laid there in the hospital bed staring at the ceiling and wondering why I was alive. The thought had never occurred to me that I would not succeed in ending my life. Then it hit me. I did not have control over my own life. God did. It was not mine to take. This was not some tremendous revelation or anything like that, it was just something I had learned that day through practical experience. And it gave me comfort. I felt as if God was saying to me: "I have a purpose for your life. Just wait." From that night on I never again had the desire to take my own life.

The next day confirmed my suspicions that God had been in control the whole time. First the sheriff's report from the "accident" came in. I learned that my car had gone right through the light pole shearing it out of the ground, and then continued up the road, veered off into a drainage ditch, hit a culvert that went underneath a driveway which upended the car and flipped it over three times finally coming to rest upside down. Wow! And I walked away from that! But wait, it gets better….

My dad said to me, "Let's go to the crash site on the way home." Ok, I thought, why not? As we drive down the rural highway heading north out of Appleton, we come to the small town where I crashed the car. The name of the town: Freedom. We drove over to the place where the car finally came to rest: right in front of a big country church. As I looked at that church and reflected on God's control over my life, my Dad said to me: "Hey, look at the name of that bar across the street." I turned around and looked at it: The Crash Inn. My Dad chuckled, and I felt like I was in the twilight zone or something.

It was time to drive back to Milwaukee, but we decided to stop at the junk yard where they hauled my car. We asked the guy where the Torino was that they brought in this morning. The guy took us to the car. He looked at the car, looked at me, and then asked, "Were you driving that car??" I nodded in affirmation. The guy shook his head in disbelief. "You see that car over there?" he says, pointing to a large wrecked car, "It's not half as smashed up as yours, but the guy driving that car didn't make it."

We walked over to what used to be my car. Totally demolished. The engine was pushed off its block, and half of it was in the passenger side front seat. The car basically crumpled when it took out the light pole. The guy said he couldn't even tow it, because the wheels and axles were bent. He had to use a flat-bed truck and lift it up there with a crane. After hauling it to the junk yard, he had to return a second time to pick up all the pieces. But the driver's seat was still intact. It was almost as if a protective bubble had been placed around it. I left there feeling like my life was worth something to God, and that he had me on this earth for some reason.

Going back to school, my whole outlook on life changed. I now had hope, believing that God had some purpose for my life. I had been brought up in church, and had been taught the Bible and the creeds of my Protestant denomination, but my faith was very "creedal" also—it didn't have much of an impact on my day to day life. So I went back to my old friends and my partying way of life.

But my attitude in school changed. I was enrolled in a specialty program in my senior year of high school majoring in business and marketing. With my new found self confidence, I excelled in the program, especially in demonstrating sales abilities. I won some awards in some city and state wide competitions, and purposed to graduate from high school and make a lot of money in sales. After graduating from high school, I quickly got certified and began to sell accident and health insurance door-to-door. I was doing great, and even sold a policy my first day on the field. But there was something missing, and I often felt guilty having "conned" someone into buying a policy that they probably didn't need, and wasn't quite what they expected it to be.

So I got a job in a factory working a graveyard shift from 6:00 p.m. to 6:00 a.m. three days on and three days off. It was a good hourly rate, and a lot of my buddies from high school were working there. It was boring work, and we all "got high" to help us make it through the long shifts. But I always saw it as temporary work, until I found a good sales job that I really liked. It allowed me some financial freedom, and I was able to rent a condominium with another friend. I was also able to buy a nice sports car. Life was great in many ways. I could now party as much as I wanted. But I was still empty and unsatisfied with my life. I knew there had to be more, and I just thought that if I could get a good job with the potential to advance in a career, that I would be happy.

After about a year out of high school and having worked at the factory for several months, I decided to get back into sales. This time I got a job selling educational books. It seemed like a more "worthy" product to be selling. But something inside of me said that I would not be happy doing this either, if I didn't have God's blessing. So facing discouragement again, and having nowhere to go but forward, because I had already tried running away from my problems, and I had already tried exiting life and God wouldn't let me, I decided to try not getting high for a few days and just read the Bible, to try and understand what God's will was for my life.

This was July of 1979, and at that point I had been getting high on drugs every day for almost 4 years straight. As I read the Bible, and I don't even remember what exactly I was reading, I became acutely aware of my sins. I had always considered myself a Christian, and a good person. Even though I got high on drugs, I was no junkie. I rationalized my behavior as being no different than the casual social drinker of alcohol. It was just that one was legal and the other wasn't. But I thought the laws were wrong, not me.

But now two major sins in my life were staring me right in the face: one was my drug usage, and the other one was planning my life without considering what God wanted me to do with my life. Without even really understanding what the word "repentance" means, I saw myself in a different light, and knew that my sins were keeping me from knowing God's will. I immediately confessed my sins to God, and told him that I was not going to make any more decisions about my life until He told me what He wanted me to do.

What happened next is truly the miracle in my life, and words cannot come close to describing the inner transformation that occurred in me that summer day in 1979. First of all, a joy and peace flooded my being, such that I had never known could even exist in this life. It was the ultimate high, and it was from the Holy Spirit. It was so wonderful, that I took all my paraphernalia that I used to smoke pot and threw it into the dumpster outside our building. What I had found was so much better than drugs, that I never had a desire to get high on drugs again.

Secondly, the words in the Bible now came alive. It was as if God was speaking directly to me through them—and indeed He was. The facts I had studied for years as a kid growing up in church now became part of a vibrant relationship with the living God, and with the Savior of the world—Jesus Christ. Having never doubted the facts of Jesus' life, death, and resurrection, they now came alive with fresh meaning. I read the entire Bible in about two weeks: I just couldn't get enough of it. When I read verses like Romans 5:7-8 "Very rarely will anyone die for a righteous man, though for a good man someone might possibly dare to die. But God demonstrates His own love for us in this: while we were still sinners, Christ died for us," I would just fall down and weep over the incredible love God was showing me through Christ.

I now knew beyond a shadow of a doubt that God had saved me, not just from a suicide attempt, but He had truly saved me from my sins, and that I was now going to be with Him in eternity: "Never will I leave you; never will I forsake you." Hebrews 13:5

Since I had dedicated my life to God, I decided to go back to school and study for the ministry. I did study the Bible for a number of years, and served God in full-time ministry in various parts of the world. But I have also learned that one does not have to be in full-time Christian ministry to be serving God, you can serve God wherever you are. Today my business is helping people regain their health, and I seek to serve God in that task to the best of my ability. The Bible says, and science now confirms, that a "joyful heart is good medicine." The Bible has much to say about good health, and not all of it is physical. Our spiritual and emotional state has more to do with our health than our modern rationalistic society and medical system would care to admit. So if you are seeking better health, don't just look at your physical symptoms. Look to the Great Physician, and healer of your soul, and give your heart to Christ for true peace with God. Then you will discover true health and life! Everything else in this book, and any product we have to offer you, is worthless if you don't know God and understand His will for your life. The best part is that his offer of eternal life is free for you, because he already paid the price of your sins through the blood of his Son. We have nothing here to offer you that can beat that!

Peace!

Brian Shilhavy

How You can find Peace with God

First, acknowledge God as the one who created you and has exclusive rights to your life:

"This is what the Lord says; your redeemer who formed you in the womb: I am the Lord who has made all things, who alone stretched out the heavens, who spread out the earth by myself." Isaiah 44:24 *"I am the Lord, and there is no other; apart from me there is no God. I will strengthen you, though you have not acknowledged me, so that from the rising of the sun to the place of its setting men may know there is none besides me. I am the Lord, and there is no other. I form the light and create darkness, I bring prosperity and create disaster; I, the Lord, do all these things."* Isaiah 45:5-7 *"For You formed my inward parts; You wove me in my mother's womb. I will give thanks to You, for I am fearfully and wonderfully made; Wonderful are Your works, And my soul knows it very well. My frame was not hidden from You, When I was made in secret, And skillfully*

220

wrought in the depths of the earth; Your eyes have seen my unformed substance; And in Your book were all written The days that were ordained for me, When as yet there was not one of them." Psalms 139:13-16

Second, admit that there is sin in your life, and confess it before God:

"For all have sinned and fall short of the glory of God." Romans 3:23
"There is no one righteous, not even one." Romans 3:10
"If we confess our sins, he is faithful and just and will forgive us our sins, and cleanse us from all unrighteousness." I John 1:9

Third, believe that God sent Jesus Christ to be the sacrifice for your sins:

"For the wages of sin is death, but the gift of God is eternal life in Christ Jesus our Lord." Romans 6:23
"But God demonstrates his own love for us in this: while we were yet sinners, Christ died for us." Romans 5:8
"For God so loved the world, that he gave his only begotten son, that whoever believes in him might not die, but have everlasting life." John 3:16

Fourth, put your faith in God and receive the gift of eternal salvation:

"Yet to all who received him, to those who believed in his name, he gave the right to become children of God." John 1:12
"For it is by grace you have been saved, through faith; and this is not of yourselves, it is the gift of God- not by works, so that no one can boast." Ephesians 2:8-9

Recipe Index

222

About the Authors

Marianita Jader Shilhavy, CND (Certified Nutritionist/ Dietician in the Philippines)

Marianita earned her Bachelor of Science degree in nutrition in Manila. Understanding the nutrition of Filipino foods, Marianita worked for over eight years as a hospital dietician and nutritional counselor in the Philippines, using her knowledge of Asian foods to help people recover from illness.

Brian W. Shilhavy, BA, MA

Brian earned his Bachelor of Arts degree in Bible/Greek from Moody Bible Institute in Chicago, and his Master of Arts degree in linguistics from Northeastern Illinois University in Chicago. He is the Chief Executive Officer of Tropical Traditions, Inc.

Tropical Traditions, Inc.
PMB 219
823 S. Main St.
West Bend, WI 53095
USA
www.tropicaltraditions.com
1-866-311-COCO (2626)